LISTENING: READINGS

Volume 2

compiled by

Sam Duker

The Scarecrow Press, Inc.
Metuchen, N.J. 1971

Other Scarecrow Press Books by Sam Duker

Listening: Readings

Listening Bibliography, second edition

Individualized Reading: An Annotated Bibliography

Individualized Reading: Readings

ISBN 0-8108-0364-X

Library of Congress Catalog Card Number 65-22752

Dedicated to the late David Prall, teacher, philosopher, friend, and interested listener

Table of Contents

Preface

Compiling a book of readings would be impossible without the cooperation of many persons. Foremost among these are, of course, the authors and publishers of the material from which the excerpted portions are taken for this book. These persons have not only granted the necessary permissions but have done so in such a gracious and encouraging manner that my debt to them is vastly greater than usual.

The reception accorded my first book of readings on the subject of listening has encouraged me to supplement that 1966 publication, which the Scarecrow Press has assured me will continue to be available. I have selected articles on the basis of what I felt to be their intrinsic interest rather than on the basis of their date of publication. Most of the articles, it is true, were written since my first collection went to press, but that is more coincidental than intentional. The arrangement of the book is not the same as that used in my first effort because I felt that the nature of the articles rather than precedent should govern the chapter titles and sequence.

All my work on listening has been made possible by the cooperation of librarians in many libraries in New York and elsewhere, but in particular by the staff at Brooklyn College's library. For this help I am deeply grateful.

The following formal acknowledgments of permissions granted to reprint material excerpted from theses and journal articles are in no way wholly indicative of my deep sense of warm gratitude for these contributions.

The excerpts from Dr. Brimer's article, "Sex Differences in Listening Comprehension," which appeared in the Fall 1969 issue of the *Journal of Research and Development in Education*, are used with the kind permission of the *Journal* and of the author.

The three items by Dr. Charles T. Brown are taken

from an article which appeared in June 1965 issue of Speech Monographs under the title "Three Studies of the Listening of Children." The material is used with the kind permission of the author and of the Speech Association of America, publisher of Speech Monographs.

The article by Professor John Cohen is taken from "Mind Wandering" which appeared in the February 1956 issue of the British Journal of Psychology. It is used with the kind permission of Professor Cohen and of the British Psychological Society, publisher of the British Journal of Psychology.

The article by Stuart Condon is taken from his master's thesis, Management Communication, completed at the University of California at Santa Barbara. It is used with the kind permission of the author.

Excerpts from an article entitled "The Physiological Response to the Communication Modes: Reading, Listening, Writing, Speaking, and Evaluating," which appeared in the September 1970 issue of the Journal of Communication, are used with the kind permission of the three authors, Loren D. Crane, Richard J. Dieker, and Charles T. Brown, and of the International Communication Association, publishers of the Journal of Communication.

The material by Thomas G. Devine is taken from his Elementary English article, "Reading and Listening: New Research Findings," which appeared in the March 1968 issue. It is used with the kind permission of the author and of the National Council of Teachers of English, publishers of Elementary English.

The article by Thomas C. Dreiling is taken from his 1967 University of Oklahoma doctoral dissertation, An Experimental Study Toward the Development of a Non-Reading Version of the General Aptitude Test Battery. The excerpts are used with the kind permission of the author.

My article, "Listening and Reading," which appeared in the March 1965 issue of Elementary School Journal is used with the kind permission of the University of Chicago Press, publisher of the Elementary School Journal.

Material by Arlene Kessler Feltman is taken from her 1967 Ohio State University master's thesis, The Effect of Reinforcement on Listening Skills of Culturally Deprived

School Children. The excerpts are used with the kind permission of the author.

Excerpts from his 1967 Stanford University doctoral dissertation, Aural and Visual Instruction with Slow Learners, are used with the kind permission of the author, James J. Fenwick.

With the kind permission of Herbert Friedman excerpts are used from his article, "Compressed Speech Correlates of Listening Ability," which appeared in the September 1968 issue of the Journal of Communication. The International Communication Association, publisher of the Journal, also kindly granted permission to use this material.

The material by Charles L. Fry is taken from his 1961 University of Rochester doctoral dissertation, The Effects of Training in Communication and Role Perception on the Communication Abilities of Children. The excerpts are used with the kind permission of the author.

Professor Milton W. Horowitz and Perceptual and Motor Skills have graciously granted permission for the inclusion in this volume of excerpts from an article, "Listening and Reading, Speaking and Writing: An Experimental Investigation of Differential Acquisition and Reproduction of Memory" which appeared in Perceptual and Motor Skills in February, 1967.

Excerpts from her Bradley University master's thesis entitled A Survey of Listening Programs of a Hundred major Industries are used with kind permission of the author, Janice D. Johnson.

Material from Dr. Ralph E. Kellogg's 1967 University of California at Los Angeles doctoral thesis, A Study of the Effect of a First Grade Listening Instructional Program Upon Achievement in Listening and Reading, is used in this volume with the kind permission of the author.

Excerpts from Charles M. Kelly's article, "Listening: Complex of Activities--and a Unitary Skill?", which appeared in the November 1967 issue of Speech Monographs, are used with the kind permission of the author and the Speech Association of America, publisher of Speech Monographs.

The article by Edward B. Kenny is excerpted from his 1967 Cornell University doctoral dissertation,

Exploratory Study of the Orality of Language of College Instructors. This material is used with the kind permission of the author.

Excerpts from an article, "Communication Skills or Pink Pills?" which appeared in the May 1966 issue of Training in Business and Industry, are used with the kind permission of Dugan Laird and Joseph R. Hayes, the authors, and of Gellert Publishing Corporation, publishers of Training in Business and Industry.

Dr. William B. Legge kindly granted permission for the inclusion in this book of excerpts from Comparisons of Listening Abilities of Intermediate Grade Pupils Categorized According to Intelligence, Achievement, and Sex, his doctoral dissertation completed at the University of Southern Illinois in 1966.

The selection by Sara W. Lundsteen was excerpted from her article in the Fall 1967 issue of the Journal of Research and Development in Education which was entitled: "Critical Listening and Thinking: A Recommended Goal for Future Research." These excerpts are used with the kind permission of the Journal and of the author.

The material from the Los Angeles School District's curriculum publication, Speech 1 and 2, Instructional Guide, is used with the kind permission of that school district.

Excerpts from Dr. Melvin Mart's Columbia University thesis entitled The Relationship Between Achievement and Verbal Communication of Secondary School Children are used with the kind permission of the author.

The article by Paul McKee is used with the kind permission of the author and of the publisher, Houghton Mifflin Company.

Excerpts from The English Language Arts Program, a curriculum publication of the Malcolm Rice Laboratory School of the University of Northern Iowa, are used with the kind permission of Dr. Howard Vander Beek, Chairman of the committee which prepared the publication, and of Dr. Guy Wagner, Chairman of the University of Northern Iowa's University Publications Committee.

The article by Air Force Lieutenant Colonel Kenneth W. Patterson is taken from his graduate thesis written at the Air Command and Staff College at Maxwell Air Force Base in 1965. It is used with the kind permission of Air Command and Staff College.

The material from Elizabeth Pflaumer's 1968 Ohio State University master's thesis, A Definition of Listening, is used with the kind permission of the author.

Boyd A. Purdom wrote his doctoral dissertation, An Analysis of Listening Development Using the Midwest Program on Airborne Television Instruction at George Peabody College for Teachers in 1968. Dr. Purdom has kindly permitted the use of excerpts from that thesis in this volume.

The excerpts from an article by J. Buckminster Ranney and Mary Virginia Moore, "An Auditory Language Quantum," which appeared in the May 1968 issue of the Journal of Learning Disabilities, are used with the kind permission of Dr. Ranney and of the Journal.

Professor Harry Singer has kindly granted permission for the use of extensive excerpts from his Summer 1965 article in Educational and Psychological Measurement: "Validity of the Durrell-Sullivan Reading Capacity Test." Permission has also been granted by Educational and Psychological Measurement.

The material in this book by Dr. A. Van Wingerden is taken from his 1965 Washington State University doctoral thesis, A Study of Direct, Planned Listening Instruction in the Intermediate Grades in Four Counties in the State of Washington. It is used with the kind permission of the author.

Professor Guy Wagner of the University of Northern Iowa and Bobbs Merrill Company, Inc., publishers of Education, have kindly given permission to use excerpts from Dr. Wagner's column "What Schools are Doing" which appeared in the November 1967 issue of Education.

The extensive excerpts from Dr. Belle Ruth Witkin's article, "Auditory Perception--Implications for Language Developments," which appeared in the Fall 1969 issue of the Journal of Research and Development in Education, are used with the kind permission of the author and of the Journal.

Dr. C. David Wood has kindly granted permission to

include in this book excerpts from his 1965 Indiana University doctoral thesis, Comprehension of Compressed Speech by Elementary School Children.

George M. Zimmerman and the Music Educators Journal have kindly permitted the inclusion in this book of excerpts from an article, "Listen!" which appeared in April 1957.

Introduction

The State of Listening in 1970

The past two decades have been marked by an increased emphasis on the importance of communication. The manifestations of this emphasis have been widely varied. The technological developments exemplified by the communication satellites, now accepted by most of us as another ordinary facet of life, have occurred at a rate that has exceeded the wildest dreams of even a Jules Verne-type prophet in 1950. In the long run, however, the technological improvements, remarkable as they are, may not constitute the most important development in communication during this period. Since 1950 there can be observed an accelerated emphasis on interhuman communication, whether inter-personal, inter-group, or a combination of these. Reams have been written on the unparalleled importance of communication to the individual, to marriage, to family life, to community life, to national life, and to international affairs. Recently I even saw a book expounding the importance of devising means of communicating with extraterrestrial creatures, who, the author was certain, would soon be landing on the earth. It is easy to scoff at such an idea or at any other situation which seems highly unlikely to us but in another 20 years it is not impossible or inconceivable that such communication might be taking place. Many developments which were considered even more unlikely in 1950 have occurred since that time.

In all these technological developments and in all the theorizing about communication, one fact seems to remain constant: communication cannot be a one-way process. A communication satellite in orbit around the moon sending messages like mad every minute would not be part of a communication process, for no one would hear these messages. In a classroom where children have learned to shut out the teacher's voice, there may be no communication, even if a teacher scolds, pleads, lectures, and shouts. When management speaks to employees on a loudspeaker system or sends out a strictly company-oriented house letter, there is no communication when the employee tunes out the announcement and throws the house organ into the waste basket. Such efforts at one-way communication are part of the American scene every hour of the day.

With a few exceptions, such as are involved in tasting, smelling, feeling, extrasensory perception and the like, the prime prerequisite of communication is that there must be someone who either reads or listens to the message that is sent. Here I use reading in a broad sense: any comprehending treatment of visual symbols, verbal or non-verbal. Listening can also be defined broadly to include all comprehending treatment of any aural stimulus, either verbal or non-verbal.

It is not surprising, then, in an age of communication, that there should be great concern about the ability of people to read and to listen with adequate comprehension as well as with discrimination.

As in the past, the major emphasis still tends to be on reading, the lesser used of the two receptive modes of communication. If anyone doubts the above statement, note that an estimated 740 million people in the world are unable to read. In addition, the availability of reading matter in developing nations is very small compared to the availability of the aural messages of radio, for instance. Even in developed countries like our own there is a high incidence of functional illiteracy--people who do not read even if perhaps, technically speaking, they can read. Here also, as in under-developed countries, there are large sectors of the population which are not reached by the printed press, by libraries, or by other sources of written material. On the other hand, again as in less developed countries, few people in the United States are out of reach of the radio and other aural communication devices.

It would be a grievous error to assume that listening is more prevalent than reading only among the illiterate. The fact is that a relatively small portion of the population in the United States reads books, magazines, or, for that matter, the daily or weekly press. The results of every possible variety of survey reveal that the hours spent by literate people in listening to television and radio are far beyond what most of us would judge likely.

The United States federal government has made the

ability to read a universal goal for the 1970's. Interestingly enough at a time of crisis, however, the President typically appears on television and elects to speak to the people rather than to issue a written document.

If in fact it is true that the art of listening is a stepchild compared to reading, insofar as school curricula, recognition, research, and written materials are concerned, then it is certainly not a Cinderella type of stepchild but one that is well fed, growing, and cherished.

The fact is that listening is now being directly taught on a wide front. Only a few years ago it was difficult to find curriculum bulletins that made any specific mention of listening. Most books on teaching the language arts in elementary schools which were published prior to 1965 gave only lip service to the concept of teaching listening, if they mentioned it at all. Today all this has been changed. It would be hard to find recently published curriculum bulletins or textbooks concerned with the teaching of language arts which do not give adequate treatment to the subject of listening. In fact, a number of curriculum bulletins are devoted solely to this subject. Not only do books about language arts include full chapters and other references to listening, but authors of books on methods of teaching reading are including material on listening as well, showing their recognition of the close relationship between these skills. Surveys have been made of the teaching of listening in the elementary school curriculum. Successive surveys show this subject's being taught in an increasing number of classrooms and the time devoted to this topic increasing markedly.

In the secondary school there still appears to be a lack of emphasis on listening compared to the elementary school. In the high school, speech textbooks and speech courses of study tend to mention listening in a casual and minimal manner. One notices, for example, that professional education journals directed to the secondary school teacher include very little material on listening, while journals directed to the elementary school teacher and to college teachers tend to devote much more of their space to the topic.

At the college level the situation is not quite so clear as in the pre-collegiate schools. There is a considerable number of courses on the specific subject of listening taught at the college level. More often than not they are taught as part of the speech curriculum but there are also instances of such courses being offered by education and sociology departments. It is difficult to pinpoint the extent to which courses listed in college bulletins are regularly taught because such lists of courses frequently include those that are seldom, if ever, in fact offered. Most college speech departments, however, do include a substantial degree of emphasis on listening as part of one or more speech courses.

The steadily increasing number of graduate theses concerned with various aspects of listening, both at the master's and doctoral levels, indicates that this subject is regarded as worthy of scholarly investigation.

In executive training in business and industry there has been an increasing concern about the inclusion of listening training in the plans for employee improvement. I recently had occasion to write an article reviewing courses especially designed for business and industrial use. There has been a growing recognition of the dollars and cents loss caused by poor listening in business situations.

The literature on listening has been increasing at an accelerating pace, as revealed by the relative number of items in my 1964 and 1968 bibliographies. Based on present information it seems likely that the number of items in the 1972 edition will be double that in the 1968 issue. This literature consists not only of theses and periodical articles but also of a number of books devoted solely to listening.

The Fall 1969 issue of the Journal of Development and Research in Education was devoted entirely to listening and its relationship to critical thinking. Three articles from this issue, edited by Sara Lundsteen, are included in this volume. The September 1968 issue of the Journal of Communication was devoted entirely to the subject of compressed speech. One article from this issue, ably edited by David Orr, is also included in this collection.

A good deal could be said concerning the changing quality of current writing and research on listening. It appears to me, at least, that the general tone of the material in the new collection differs considerably in emphasis from the material in my first book of readings, published only four years ago. If this judgment is correct, the outlook is promising concerning future literature in the field of listening. I regard the material selected as quite representative of the better writing on this subject during recent years.

Chapter 1

The Nature of "Listening"

The authors of the five items in this chapter are much more concerned about various aspects of the listening act than they are with giving and rationalizing precise definitions of "listening." This is an excellent illustration of the progress that is being made in the field in terms of new emphases in the interests of investigators.

The first article is taken from a well-designed and thoughtful doctoral dissertation written at Cornell University by Edward B. Kenny. The material included here is taken from the introductory portion of his thesis, followed by an analysis of the degree to which college lectures show evidence that the lecturers are aware of factors which will aid or hamper effective listening on the part of the students to whom these lectures are directed. The thorough study of the issues discussed in this article will amply repay the student of listening for the time and effort expended. As is true of most doctoral dissertations written at major institutions in recent years, microfilm and photocopy reproductions of this thesis are available from University Microfilms of Ann Arbor, Michigan.

My bibliographies and a book of selections like this one are only possible as a result of wide reading and study of all items having to do with listening. Among these items are from thirty to fifty master's theses each year. Very often one despairs and wonders if it is really necessary to read all these theses. The majority are indeed disappointing, and some cause one to speculate on what the author and his sponsor might have had in mind. But occasionally one finds a real gem which makes all the reading worthwhile. The thesis written by Elizabeth Pflaumer at Ohio State University, under the sponsorship of Professor Robert Monaghan, who himself has made major contributions to knowledge about listening, is an example of such a gem. Miss Pflaumer has explored a variety of qualities of a number of types of listening in a more thoughtful and thorough manner than any of her predecessors in the literature on listening. The importance of this work lies not in the combinations of characteristics in certain types of listeners but in the nature of the listening characteristics isolated, described, and discussed. While Miss Pflaumer has allowed me to use a substantial portion of her thesis, some of the flavor of the original is necessarily lost by the excerpting process. The entire thesis is available on interlibrary loan and its perusal is earnestly recommended to those who wish to read further in this perceptive analysis of listening characteristics.

The third portion of this chapter is by Dr. John Cohen and his associates. Dr. Cohen is connected with the Psychology Department of Manchester University in England. He is an author of note and his books are recommended as fascinating as well as highly informative reading. The selection itself is a concise description of a small experiment designed to gain information about that aspect of listening known as "attention." Several major periodical indexes still list all listening items under "attention." One could wish that editors of those indexes had read the Cohen material and thus learned that while attention is indeed an important aspect of listening, it is only one aspect, not the entire act.

The next article is also by an English professor. Mr. Brimer is associated with the School of Education of the University of Bristol where he is Head of the Research Unit. His article appeared in one of the outstanding new journals in the educational area, The Journal of Research and Development in Education, in a special issue devoted to the subject of listening and critical thinking and ably edited by Sara Lundsteen. I am privileged to include in this book, in addition to the Brimer article, two other articles which also appeared in this issue. Brimer's article analyzes the differences he found in the listening performance of boys and girls. A comment on this article by Dr. John B. Carroll immediately follows the article in the Fall 1969 issue of the Journal. While there is much richness in the three articles included here, the entire issue is highly recommended to all those interested in probing further into the relationship between listening and critical thinking.

The last selection in this chapter is by Dr. G. Buckminster Ranney and Mary Virginia Moore. Dr. Ranney was until recently Head of the Speech Clinic at Auburn University in Alabama. He is presently associated with the National Institutes of Health in Bethesda, Maryland. His article is concerned with the measurement of hearing and listening abilities of very young children. The student of listening must of necessity have added to his understanding of the process after reading this material.

The Process of Listening

Edward B. Kenny

The listener as a mature translator, the student in college, is, for the most part, exposed to linguistic stimuli, or verbal language. These stimuli may be found in printed matter and in speech. The recipient of a message found on a printed page must undergo a different kind of structuring process in perceiving meaning than does the listener of oral discourse. Part of this differing process may be accounted for by the greater degree of inference that besets the decoder of an oral explanation. We will discuss first the kinds of interference that the listener contends with and, secondly, the needs of the listener as a result of the oral-aural character of the classroom situation.

Kinds of interference

There are many kinds of interference between the listener and speaker. In general these are:

(1) Noise. This is a term used to cover the multiple disruptive factors that are external to both the speaker and the listener and that interfere with the translation of the message by the receiver that is intended by the sender. Lewis and Nichols[1] catalogue a number of these noise factors. Among them are environmental noises, such as shouting in a nearby classroom; band practice on the playing field outside the classroom window; movements and whisperings of fellow students in the same room; or a pretty girl in the next seat.

Noise may also consist of internal interference, or those distracting elements that may be found within the context of the sender-message-receiver system. Among these are: voice, articulation and gestural peculiarities of the sender; low level of vocabulary of the listener; level of physical vigor of the speaker; motivation on the part of both speaker and listener; poor attention span of the listener. At another level, we can enumerate such internal interference factors as: personality traits of the speaker and listener that are distracting; anxiety levels of both speaker and listener produced by tensions springing from a multitude of causes that "threaten," and thus obscure accurate transmission and reception.

(2) Conditioning of Mass Media. The influence of mass media such as printing, viewed here as a special medium, may have far-reaching effects on the listener that we have not been aware of. Innis[2] has brought to our attention the effects of the various kinds of writing implements as a conditioning influence or "bias" in communication. He has related these influences to the economic and political development of western civilization. McLuhan[3] also enlarges our understanding of the printed page as a determinant of social patterns affecting learning. According to him, a listener in a "print culture" experiences a greater variety of difficulties than does a listener in a predominantly "oral culture."

Chaytor in commenting on the effects of a "print culture" writes:

> The speaker or writer can now hardly conceive of language except in printed or written forms; the reflex actions by which the process of reading or writing is performed have become so 'instructive' and are performed with such facile rapidity that the change from the auditory to the visual is concealed from the reader or writer and makes analysis of it a matter of great difficulty. It may be that acoustic and kinesthetic images are inseparable and that 'image' as such is an abstraction made for analysis, but which is nonexistent considered in itself and as pure. But whatever account the individual may render of his own mental processes, and most of us are far from competent in this respect, the fact remains that his idea of language is irrevocably modified by his experience of printed matter.[4]

Riesman[5] has written about one of the effects of a print culture that is related to our discussion of interference. He suggests that the act of reading is an isolating experience for the reader, in which he can temporarily cut himself off from the business of interpersonal reaction. If this practice becomes habituated in a given population of listeners, one can see how it can become a source of interference when they are exposed to oral communication of content that usually comes in the form of print. The numerous cases of students having difficulty taking lecture notes come to mind.

The exposure to printed media can be viewed as an interference factor if we regard the authority that printed matter has for many as compared with the spoken word. On this matter James writes:

> Sound and sight, speech and print, eye and ear, have nothing in common. The human brain has done nothing that compares in complexity with this fusion of ideas involved in linking up the two forms of language. But the result of the fusion is that once it is achieved in our early years, we are forever after unable to think clearly, independently and surely about any one aspect of the matter .... The invention of printing broadcast the printed language and gave to print a degree of authority that it has never lost.[6]

McLuhan in a later work[7] interprets the conditioning aspects of radio and, particularly, television, in terms of the different expectancies that listeners and viewers will attain after long exposure to these forms of mass media. In a sense, he is commenting on the "authority" that television has come to have when he says "the medium is the message."

Hoggart's[8] study of the effects of mass literacy in England among the working classes dispels somewhat the previously mentioned positions regarding the interference aspects of printed media. Although his study was confined to members of the working class society in England, it probably has some implications for Americans. His position is that a strong oral tradition has remained untouched in many ways. The part of his study that one finds relevant here is that the teacher, who is probably more a product of a print culture than his students, finds himself in some difficulty when using language patterns that show this conditioning influence of print. The inference to be drawn from this is that, in America, teachers who are assigned to teach the underprivileged face the problem of "interference" in the conditioning or lack of conditioning effects of a print culture.

We have discussed two aspects of interference that

impinge upon the listener and work against the accurate reception of encoded messages. The point of this discussion was to show that, since this interference exists, all the resources of language should be explored by the speaker as teacher in trying to attain clarity in exposition.

Arnold has synopsized the findings of many studies in the field of rhetoric and communication as they relate to listener needs. He enumerates these needs as follows:

> (1) Time to review, 'catch up,' reflect and take rest. A reader sets his own pace. He can review, reflect, or reread. A listener is at the mercy of the speaker's pace .... This is one reason why all effective oral communication exhibits more redundancy ....
>
> (2) Constant refreshment of interest. The span of human attention is brief. Readers come to written communication when they are ready for it .... Listeners have no such freedom .... Hence it becomes the responsibility of the composer of oral discourse to try to predict where his hearers' interest may waver .... Not logic, but the listener's psychology dictates what and where the composer's special insertions shall be.
>
> (3) Obvious distinctions between most important and less important ideas.
>
> (4) Listeners seek 'something for me' in what (they) hear, and insist that speech must teach us quickly or not at all. (They) demand that new knowledge be made enjoyable as well as intelligible, (and) insist that whoever brings the message identify himself with our special interests...[9]

Oral Style and the Needs of Listeners

Since these, in brief, are the needs of listeners and since the listener is confronted with some or all of the interference factors mentioned above, what are the peculiar resources of language found in the characteristics of oral style that aim to meet these needs?

Other studies which have examined the differences between oral and written style are worthy of notation.

DeVito's[10] study, which compared samples of written communication and oral discourse by the same speech professors on the same topic, dealt with selected elements thought to be determinants of ease of comprehension. He found that the written samples differed significantly from the oral in four ways. The written sample had: (1) more difficult words, (2) greater verbal density, (3) greater density of ideas, (4) more sentences that were grammatically simple. A study made by Gibson and others[11] investigated the differences and similarities between spoken and written style. They concluded that spoken style was more readable, more interesting, and contained a simpler vocabulary than the written style. Empirical research dealing with oral and written style generally supports the hypothesis that there are significant differences between the two modes of expression.

The characteristics of oral style have as their aim the reduction of the interference that is part of the oral communication process between human beings. Wiener has characterized the oral transfer of information as "a joint game between the talker and the listener against the forces of confusion."[12] At the heart of learning theories and the needs of listeners lies this problem of trying to overcome these "forces of confusion."

Many of the observations found in the literature on the subject of listening have as their focal point, and rightly so, the psychological aspects of listening and call for efforts on the listener's part to be aware of (1) the listening problem, and (2) ways and means that he may use to reduce the interference that is concurrent with listening. This is not to say that studies have not been made of the effects of oral style on intelligibility. Flesch,[13] although his studies deal with the improvement of writing for greater readability, is also pertinent to this discussion. One is left with the impression, however, that the linquistic resources of the speaker, as prescribed in traditional and contemporary rhetorical theory, have not been connected, in any useful way, with studies in listening.

A case can be made, therefore, that the needs of listeners can be accommodated by the special features of oral style characteristics. The psychological aspects of the speaker-listener situation require that adjustments be made by both speaker and listener. It is a common observation that ordinary conversational communication between talkers seems to incorporate these adjustments. We seem to grasp intuitively the need for these adjustments. Common talk is replete with repetition, indigenous language, informality of syntax, simplicity and informality of vocabulary, figurative language (note the recurrence of slang metaphors that become habitual with some talkers), questions, and paraphrased or direct quotations. The listener expects these characteristics to be part of the linguistic expression of his partner in conversation.

For some inexplicable reason, however, the formalized speaking situation seems to be construed as basically different from the conversational situation. Just because in the more formalized speaking-listening situation we have one speaker and many listeners, and the discourse of the former is usually uninterrupted, it does not follow that the psychological character of the situation is appreciably changed. Yet the needs of the <u>many</u> listeners appear to be forgotten by the <u>one</u> speaker. Perhaps it is the uninterrupted character of discourse of the speaker that may account for his sudden neglect. We can only speculate as to what may account for this new attitude on the speaker's part. In any event, the "good" speaker struggles against this change in attitude, and remembers how he acted in a linguistic way when he was "conversing" and not "speaking." The characteristics of oral style, then, may be viewed as the product of this remembering.

In order to meet effectively the needs of listeners, oral discourse must be characterized by the features we have enumerated.

To summarize the answers to the three questions dealt with in this section: we have suggested that the characteristics of oral style have as their principal aims (1) to meet the "identification" and "translation" needs of learners and (2) to meet the needs of learners as listeners.

Notes

Abbreviated references, such as No. 1 below, refer to the entry number in Sam Duker's <u>Listening Bibliography</u> 2nd Ed. (Scarecrow, 1968) where the full citation may be found.

1. Lewis and Nichols, 728.

2. Harold A. Innis. <u>The Bias of Communication.</u> Toronto:

University of Toronto Press, 1952, p. 3-32.

3. Marshall McLuhan. The Gutenberg Galaxy. Toronto: University of Toronto Press, 1962.

4. H. J. Chaytor. "Reading and Writing." In Explorations in Communications (Edited by Edmund Carpenter and Marshall McLuhan). Boston: Beacon Press, 1960, p. 118-19.

5. David Riesman. The Lonely Crowd. New Haven: Yale Univ. Press, 1950, p. 110-17.

6. A. Lloyd James. Our Spoken Language. London: Thomas Nelson and Sons, 1938, p. 29.

7. Marshall McLuhan. Understanding Media: The Extensions of Man. New York: McGraw-Hill, 1964, p. 297-337.

8. Richard Hoggart. The Uses of Literacy. London: Chatto and Windus, 1957, p. 27-31.

9. Carroll C. Arnold. "Reader or Listener? Oral Composition." Today's Speech 13(1):6, February 1965.

10. Joseph A. DeVito. "Comprehension Factors in Oral and Written Discourse of Skilled Communicators." Speech Monographs 32:124-28, 1965.

11. James W. Gibson and others. "A Quantitative Examination of Differences and Similarities in Written and Spoken Messages." Speech Monographs 33:444-51, 1966.

12. Norbert Wiener. The Human Use of Human Beings--Cybernetics and Society. Boston: Houghton Mifflin, 1950, p. 26.

13. Rudolph Flesch. How to Make Sense. New York: Harper, 1954, Chapter 6. See also his Art of Plain Talk. New York: Harper, 1941, Chapter 7.

A Definition of Listening

Elizabeth Mae Pflaumer

Basically the writer wanted to find out how people listen. Just what do they do when they go to listen? A wide variety of persons were interviewed informally to elicit items or factors related to and involved with listening. These items were then used to construct a Q Sort which was given to 23 people.

After describing themselves through the listening sorts under four sets of instructions (actual self, ideal self, others actually, others ideally) the respondents were given the standardized Brown-Carlsen Listening Comprehension Test.

The Q data were submitted to The Ohio State University Scatran Computer for factor analysis according to Pearson Product Moment Correlation and Kaiser's Varimax.

The results revealed four effective-ineffective listening types, with the highest correlated factors conceived to be the ideal listening system. The results from the Brown-Carlsen test indicated very little correlation or predictive value compared to the results of the Q sort.

It would seem that these personalities or patterns of listening would have predictive value in representativeness of society. These definitions would allow more close scrutiny in devising means and methods of listening instruction. By diagnosing the listening type the program of education can be tailored to the personal needs of the individual, thereby increasing total effectiveness of the listening program.

Results of the Q sorts showed four effective and ineffective personality types of listeners. These may be conceptualized briefly according to social desirability.

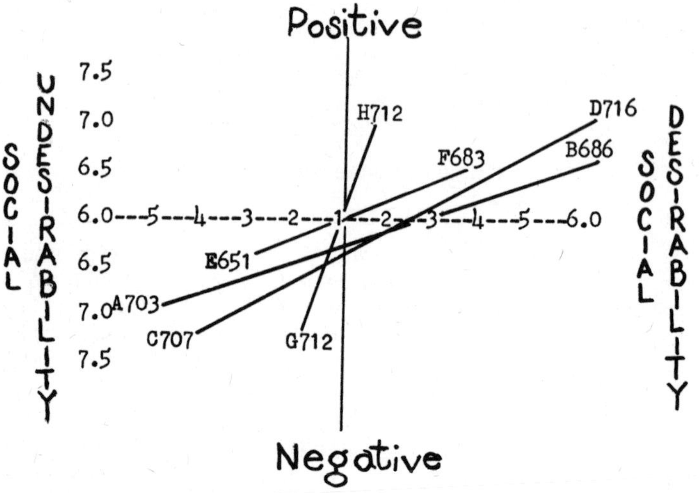

These indeed might also be plotted throughout space in third dimensionality in that they are not to be compared with each other but with preference patterns of individual personalities. This means that they can be said to be in relation to the Kellian constructs of various personality types. Each person can then be placed along the continuum between ends of the four personalities, AB, CD, EF, GH.

There seems to be a dual listening system at work within the best listeners, as coveted ideals. One system is internalized in that it is developed within the individual and is a personal code and introspective--almost semi- or subconscious--listening system.

The other system is externalized in that it is outer-directed consciously and critically and analytically evaluative. We listen emotionally and intellectually. One cannot say "active" and "passive," since both systems are active and indeed success may depend upon control of the two listening systems. It might also seem feasible that intelligence is related to the second system as far as comprehension is measurable (I.Q., STEP, Brown-Carlsen, etc.). However, intelligence is <u>not</u> referable to the first mentioned system. It is an internalized subsystem, active, but not always measurable and indeed a great deal of the listener's success may depend upon his ability to decode and interpret this system's reporting realistically. Then comes the process of integration which must surely depend upon a certain balance between the two inputs.

In considering the various types of composite "people" for each of the four sorts it became apparent to this writer that the sorters were better able to describe themselves and society as depicted by the 'real' people they described as "others" than they were to describe either their own ideal or others' ideals. In other words, they can know pretty much how they think they are but have very little idea of where their strengths and weaknesses lie. Indeed they have only a vague concept of how to become a better listener. They have no goal toward which to aspire. Possibly necessity is the "mother" of invention and they could adjust were a need to arise but it is also possible that they would not see the need or worse have no way of achieving it in time.

Listening

Since the central nervous system controls the pathways off all sense modalities (optical, audial, tactile, olfactory, and tasting), and since in a living organism all senses are normally functioning interactively, we must synthesize in order to decode, evaluate and interpret reception.

In normal operation these can be said to facilitate, rather than inhibit, communication; since without these receptor devices communication would certainly be inhibited, these modalities enhance input sensitivity. These modalities do not necessarily act except as receptors and hence are involved in the integral receptive end of the communication event. This is at any given moment of stimulation rather than as a dimension isolated. In order to have listened or done any part of the above, that which was heard must have been used.

Thus in working toward a definition of listening for the purpose of this study the writer has generally conceptualized listening as the process of using and synthesizing combinations of perceptive sense modalities (interacting) to facilitate communication.

It is this process of using and synthesizing that is under speculation in this research rather than the physical mechanisms facilitating the process. It is for this reason that attitudes and desires, degrees of involvement, abstract and organizational ability, reality, alertness and logicality versus emotional passivity, perceptivity and introspectiveness, standards of toleration and satisfaction are considered integrally in the process of listening.

With this general definition of the process of listening one can now look at much of listening research available and see that very little attention has been given to more than an assumption of the word's meaning. Rather, many studies are concerned with isolating components of listening, principles of listening, kinds of listening, "good" or "bad" listening, and methods of improving and measuring listening.

One can see only a hazy implied area of consensus on just what is listening.

It is this writer's premise that the "City of Listening" may have more than one suburb or type of listening within it, depending upon the given needs and situation at a particular time. There seems to be an intercommunication system which is used more frequently by some listeners than by others.

Suburbanite A may try to listen to suburbanite B without ever leaving his home--does he meet with success or maximum effectiveness?

All suburbs share points of commonality, but where are the boundaries? In this age of specialization, are the benefits worth the cost?

What factors and categories distinguish types of listeners? How do listeners become acquainted with intercommunication? Are there inherited tendencies or is their system developed and adapted? Are there those listeners whose needs are completely met without extended effort? What kinds of people are they? Is their system of education in need of readaptation to better serve the needs of its students? Does intelligence and education vary with kinds of listeners?

How do suburbanites A and B communicate with each other and with C? Do they necessarily have to mutually compromise or adjust? Or can they more conveniently balance and counterbalance each other's adaptations?

What is their private direct subsystem of communication? How are time and distance, speed, and availability and qualifications involved? What impressions and attitudes sensorily facilitate this subsystem of listening? How is aid given to the handicapped or is there anything done? How is feedback improved or inhibited? Are there choices in processes of listening? What is the influence of sport and competition in listening? Is listening demonstrable and enforceable? What conditions of climate or atmosphere are conducive to good or effective listening? What reinforcement is there?

It seems that from this analogy alone there is an infinite number of questions that for the most part are unanswered. A model of listening could be conceptualized in the figure below.

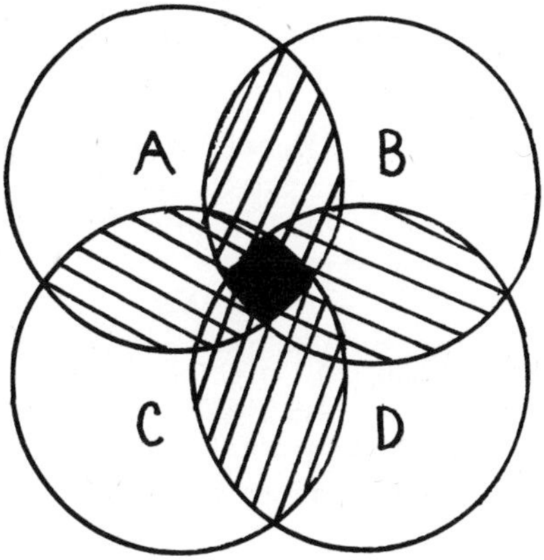

The darkened area connected to A, B, C and D is the point of commonality to all four "suburbs." The areas slashed indicate points highly salient to any three areas simultaneously. The dotted areas are commonalities shared by only two areas. The areas of the circles which are not connected represent the characteristics which make each type, or suburb, different.

Depending upon the need, it would be possible to find different destinations at each of the four shades of areas.

This model is readily adaptable to the varying "types" of speeches. The areas of exploration which lie within the concept of listening research are also highly vivified by this diagram. Also applicable are the types, purposes, principles and components of listening as proposed by R. G. Nichols, Stevens, Brown, Petrie, Duker, etc.

If we focus on the persons listening we may also posit that there are differing personalities clustered within the model. "A" can start with himself or his "surburb" and move to his goal or a destination shared commonly by fellow citizens B, C, and D in communication. If he reaches his "goal"--the darkened area on the model map--it can be posited that he moved through a different space from the path traveled by any of the listeners B, C, or D. It is possible that A's system in listening has worked as well for A as B's did for B. A's system may be working more efficiently for A than B's system would for A. This may be why A uses this system. It is also possible that A had not used systems B, C, or D and thus has no evidence that he could not operate just as efficiently or even more so elsewhere. It is also possible that A being A could not operate under any of the other systems efficiently even though his system is known not to be the most satisfactory by maximum standards. It may even be possible that there is system X with which A is totally unacquainted but in which A could more efficiently operate though he would first have to discard his present system A.

It would seem logically probable that educators could hope to develop a system of listening instruction through which A could maximize his efficiency and efforts within the realm of his systems. Before this can be done, obviously his system must be isolated and identified in all its uniqueness and components.

It is said that people follow the principle of least effort and Leon Festinger discusses tension reduction in conflict and decision making in his theory of cognitive dissonance.

Given then that these preferences were accurately identified and interpreted, they could be incorporated into a new program of instruction with a reasonable prediction of favorable increased listening effectiveness through the new system.

In other words, if we can identify the kinds of listeners (A, B, C, etc.) and build the instruction along their particular constructs, then the chances are quite good that the efficiency of these listeners would increase. This individualized specialization of instruction should then increase proportionately the overall effectiveness of A, B, C, and D.

It can also be posited that between a person's actual conduct and his ideal may be a difference providing information for improvement, actualization and maximum effectiveness in a program of listening instruction. Thus one should be concerned with this difference in developing a new program based on an ideal rather than actual present or past listening performance.

The potentiality of this individualization forms the rationale for this study in search of a meaningful definition of listening.

Computation of the Q sort data indicates two types of people as listeners in each of the four sorted categories.

Personality A-(Self-Actual)

Positive

"Gets" the message without worrying about ideas, organization, arguments or other isolated facts, and the like.
Integrates what he hears with what he already knows.
Listens with feeling and intuition.
Is curious.
Listens to the essence of things.
Looks for ideas, organization, arguments.

Negative

Seldom can feel and think and also be turned inward in listening.
Likes to argue.
Strives to be primarily an organ for the passive reception of sound.
Listens to details rather than overall essence generally.
Regards new data as fresh, not something to be crowded into compartments with his past experiences and old data.
Avoids personal involvement in listening, preferring to remain detached.

In the following the data have been expanded. Each of the listener types has been interpreted as a personality type. This is not necessarily a scientific interpretation but is a creative expansion of the data as seen by this writer.

TYPE A is unimaginative and unassuming. He prefers to remain detached. He does not worry with personal involvement or the lack of it. He is a methodical person, somewhat lackadaisical. He probably listens peripherally, almost unintentionally. He is curious but unambitious. He has no intentions of becoming great in the world, but is rather quiet and plodding. He probably is pretty smooth in getting about as much as he wants out of something, which is probably not very much. As long as things are organized and easy for him, he's content in his own little world. He does not like to argue or have to apply himself with any effort or energy. He is uninspiring and is content doing as little as possible to just get by. His eyes are only half open and he is only about a third awake. Probably not too smart, and certainly he is not very ambitious. He just does not care. Reluctant, sluggish.

Personality B--(Self-Actual)

Positive

Likes to argue.
Is curious.
Is content to accept the speaker's style, and let him talk in his own way.
Looks for possible distortions, misinterpretations of information and facts.
Recognizes his own favorite ideas.
Is unwilling to blindly follow the listening crowd.
Wants to know what the speaker is talking about in a down-to-earth sense.
Seeks to clarify vagueness and ambiguity.
Becomes an active though silent, co-partner in the speech situation.
Compares data with his past experiences.
Looks for ideas, organization, arguments.
Keeps in mind while listening that some degree of total awareness and finer details will be blotted out or missed in the final picture.
Integrates what he hears with what he already knows.

Negative

Avoids personal involvement in listening, preferring to remain detached.
Strives to be primarily an organ for the passive reception of sound.
Isolates sounds.
Listens to details rather than overall essence generally.

Is satisfied with the message others receive.
Keeps his personal feelings and reactions to himself.
Regards new data as fresh, not something to be crowded into compartments with his past experiences and old data.
Abandons or puts aside all prejudices when entering the listening situation.
Avoids influence of visual cues in listening.
Listens only to what the speaker says literally.
Is tolerant of abstractions.
Is intolerant of abstractions.
Is satisfied without undue demands for further proof or evidence.
Is seldom introspective in listening.
Seldom or rarely plans what he is going to say in rejoining, instead devotes full attention to better listening.
Avoids personal influence in listening to a message.

TYPE B is discriminating, alive and alert. He is stepping high and getting ahead in a smiling optimistic way. Energetic, bustling, and ambitious, he is sharp-witted and looks for total involvement both emotionally and intellectually. He is aware and maintains presence of mind greatly. This person is bright, alert, and spritely. He "gets in there" and fast, and holds on valiantly. He is tight, fastened to the speaker, and does not let go so he does not miss much. He is probably able to interpret pretty objectively and accurately what is going on around him and also knows what to do about it. He is a thinker, leader, getting ahead, active, knowing. He is confident and stands on his own two feet, sure and responsible. He probably experiences very little doubt and very little failure. He is success personified. Healthy, he is a busy man in there pitching, friendly and outgoing, helpful and willing. You can go to him for help and receive it.

Personality C--(Self Ideal)

Positive

Listens for new ideas everywhere.
Keeps an open mind.
Is mentally alert. Outlines, objects, approves, adds illustrations of his own.
Listens to the speaker's ideas.
Listens with his total self.

Is curious.
Tries hard to listen constantly.
Is unwilling to blindly follow the listening crowd.
Maintains total awareness in receiving fine details in the total picture.

Negative

Keeps his personal feelings and reactions to himself.
Disregards symbols of authority.
Exercises his standards of opinions and prejudices in all listening situations.
Seldom catches what other people do not say.
Strives to be primarily an organ for the passive reception of sound.
Accepts words at their face value with their usual connotations.
Is content to receive the message.
Is seldom introspective in listening.
Avoids personal involvement in listening, preferring to remain detached.
Is intolerant of abstractions.
Usually hears about the same things heard by most others.
Is very sensitive in interpersonal relations. (Is accustomed to sets of words which at times may convey no meaningful information.)
Avoids influence of visual cues in listening.

TYPE C is not so sure, confident, or easy going and breezy. Therefore he is not so successful as B probably is. He may be trying too hard. He is like a do-gooder who tries to be good by only, but always, going to church on Sunday. This is the only thing he thinks he ought to do. He is too rigid to be discriminating and free to adapt. He strives to obey the rules whether they are good or not. This guy is too much of a dreamer to exist in the real world. He is in his own little world of unreality. He is the type who would go swimming by standing on the shore, never getting wet or plunging into the water, because it might be cold and wet and because it might never have occurred to him that he never was actually in the water. He is unimaginative, unalive and unthinking. He is a living ghost, bloodless. Once in a while he looks on quizzically and wonders what is going on anyway and why.

Personality D--(Self Ideal)

Positive

Avoids vagueness and ambiguity.
Always attempts to get the speaker's intended interpretation.
Keeps an open mind.
Is responsible for what he hears but knows it may not be the same heard by others.
Listens with his total self.
Focuses his mind on the listening.
Is conscious of what is going on.
Is open minded, knows no two people listen the same.
Is popular with people. (Accustomed to sets of words which have special appeal to feeling.)
Uses visual cues such as lip reading and facial expression to listen.
Seldom or rarely plans what he is going to say in rejoining, instead devotes full attention to better listening.
Can empathize easily. Utilizes his special senses, attitudes, beliefs.
Realizes that the speaker's intent is not always correctly interpreted.

Negative

Avoids personal involvement in listening, preferring to remain detached.
Strives to be primarily an organ for the passive reception of sound.
Invents his own implications of what is said by the speaker.
Has a "Show me" attitude.
Will let conflicting affections hinder the intake of the intended message. These are basic to his criteria in judgment.
Prefers to "read into" the unsaid.
Avoids the passive reception of sound.
Keeps his personal feelings and reactions to himself.
Exercises his standards of opinions and prejudices in all listening situations.
Looks for possible distortions, misinterpretations of information and facts.

TYPE D is the ultimate good guy. He is practical,

real and down to earth. He is with it, conscious, mature, pleasant, and accepting; he is gentle but never takes his eyes off what he is doing. He is probably very popular but not superficial or shallow. He goes his own way but not because he is trying to be different but because it is probably the right way. He is not stirring up any great dust because he is busy out plowing. He is getting somewhere and not making any great noise about doing it either. He is the salt of the earth, constructive. He is sensitive and serious but with some sense of humor and understanding.

Personality E--(Others Actual)

Positive

Keeps an open mind.
Looks for possible distortions, misinterpretations of information and facts.
Listens to the essence of things.
Listens to the speaker's ideas.
Is mentally alert. Outlines, objects, approves, adds illustrations.
Avoids personal involvement in listening, preferring to remain detached.
Always attempts to get the speaker's intended interpretation.
Avoids distortions, misinterpretations of information or facts.
Is conscious of what is going on.
Maintains total awareness in receiving fine details in the total picture.
Realistically appraises what the speaker does and does not say.
Looks for ideas, organization, arguments.
Makes use of extra time by constructing his response.
Wants data, photographs, and demonstrations.
Is unwilling to blindly follow the listening crowd.
Integrates what he hears with what he already knows.
Avoids transferring his values, attitudes and relationships from himself to others.
Wants to know what the speaker is talking about in a down-to-earth sense.

Negative

Strives to be primarily an organ for the passive reception of sound.

Is satisfied with the message others receive.
Will let conflicting affections hinder the intake of the intended message. These are basic to his criteria in judgment.
Is satisfied without undue demands for further proof or evidence.
Is seldom preoccupied while listening. Avoids preformulations and daily activities, etc. (other external or internal pressures) in listening.
Isolates sounds.
Avoids conflicting affections which may hinder intake of the intended message.
Listens to details rather than overall essence generally.
Avoids an aggressive, demanding attitude in listening.
Avoids influence of visual cues in listening.
Seldom can feel and think and also be turned inward in listening.

TYPE E is tough-minded and sharp. Ever present, factual, not a dreamer, he is a thinker, with reason and logic. He is a knowledgeable individualist. Rather stoic, harsh and judgemental. He might attempt to get the speaker's intentions but does not always succeed. Sometimes he can not be trusted too far. He does not try too hard. He is a hard-nosed business man and can not easily be fooled but is also sometimes obstinate and thus insensitive. He will give the speaker a fair chance or try but then does not wait overlong in patience with inability. He puts it on the line in no-nonsense terms. Don't mess around with him as he is somewhat like a machine and nonemotional.

Personality F--(Others Actual)

Positive

Integrates what he hears with what he already knows.
Wants to know what the speaker is talking about in a down-to-earth sense.
Listens with feeling and intuition.
Is conscious of what is going on.
"Gets" the message without worrying about ideas, organization, arguments or other isolated facts and the like.
Focuses his mind on the listening.
Listens to the speaker's ideas.
Is content to accept the speaker's style, and let him

talk in his own way.
Listens to the essence of things.
Looks for ideas, organization, arguments.
Usually hears about the same things heard by most others.
Is content to receive the message.
Has the capacity and desire to critically examine, understand and attempt to transform some of his values, attitudes, and relationships from himself to others.

Negative

Makes use of extra time and constructing his response.
Likes to argue.
Isolates sounds.
Wants data, photographs, and demonstrations.
Prefers to "read into" the unsaid.
Is introspective.
Disregards symbols of authority.
Regards new data as fresh, not something to be crowded into compartments with his past experiences and old data.
Avoids the passive reception of sound.
Plans what he is going to say as a rejoinder.
Insists that generalizations are indefensible.
Invents his own implications of what is said by the speaker.
Avoids influence of visual cues in listening.
Seeks to clarify vagueness and ambiguity.
Is good at reading other people's minds. (Has developed the social habit of guidance by utterances of sounds and words aloud).
Is suspicious of words and distrusts connotations.
Avoids conflicting affections which may hinder intake of the intended message.

TYPE F is fatherly, sensitive, kindly and patient. He is easy going, not harsh or aggressive. He is gentle and always has plenty of time to listen (really listen) to you and understand in a thoughtful way. He is trusting and gives of himself in a totally unselfish way. He is totally open and quiet (a compliment); undemanding, courteous, attentive, a deeply conscious feeling person. He is well liked and good. He is not always the best qualified to help in a concrete competitive way though he would like to if he could.

He tries but sometimes it is just beyond him.

Personality G--(Others Ideal)

Positive

Is curious.
Integrates what he hears with what he already knows.
Is open minded, knows no two people listen the same.
Makes use of extra time by constructing his response.
Wants to know what the speaker is talking about in a down-to-earth sense.
Looks for ideas, organization, arguments.
Is mentally alert. Outlines, objects, approves, adds illustrations of his own.
Politely waits his turn to speak.
Plans what he is going to say as a rejoinder.
Can catch what other people do not say.

Negative

Is satisfied without undue demands for further proof or evidence.
Usually hears about the same things heard by most others.
Is seldom introspective in listening.
Is content to receive the message.
Accepts words at their face value with their usual connotations.
Will let conflicting affections hinder the intake of the intended message. These are basic to his criteria in judgment.
Avoids an aggressive, demanding attitude in listening.
Seldom catches what other people do not say.
Sometimes allows pressures or conflicts to enter into the listening situation.
Is not always able to communicate well. (Is accustomed to sets of words which at times may have little real meaning personally.)

TYPE G is double the thinking of personality F (Others Actual) but not as flattering. He is good but not outstanding in any way. He is very human and not perfect. He is not nearly as satisfying as F as he sometimes gets pressured by time and issues. Sometimes he only half listens and misses the point. But he tries and does a better than average job.

Personality H--(Others Ideal)

Positive

Listens to the essence of things.
Realistically appraises what the speaker does and does not say.
Is content to accept the speaker's style, and let him talk in his own way.
Listens with feeling and intuition.
Listens to the speaker's ideas.

Negative

Exercises his standards of opinions and prejudices in all listening situations.
Invents his own implications of what is said by the speaker.
Strives to be primarily an organ for the passive reception of sound.
Avoids influence of visual cues in listening.
Is good at reading other people's minds. (Has developed the social habit of guidance by utterances of sounds and words alone.)

TYPE H is a stranger and rather impersonal but he is fair and just and tries. He is somewhat unambitious but fairly sensitive. He is extremely good at adapting to the speaker totally but he doesn't add any of himself to the situation. Merely he becomes a mold around the message. This is sometimes frustrating to the speaker since he wants some detached objectivity. He sometimes misses finer points and implications.

A Composite Ideal Personality

These characteristics can be viewed as habits of listening to achieve and retain, or as goals toward which to strive in developing a program of listening instruction.

Positive Listening Characteristics

Keeps an open mind.
Is curious.
Listens for new ideas everywhere.
Integrates what he hears with what he already knows.
Listens with his total self.

Perceives self.
Becomes personally involved with what he hears.
Is unwilling to blindly follow the listening crowd.
Is conscious of what is going on.
Listens to the essence of things.
Looks for ideas, organization, and arguments.
Is open minded. Knows no two people listen the same.
Is mentally alert. Outlines, objects, approves, adds illustrations of his own.
Has the capacity and desire to critically examine, understand and attempt to transform some of his values, attitudes and relationships within himself to others.
Listens to the speaker's ideas.
Is introspective.
Focuses his mind on the listening.
Listens with feeling and intuition.
Politely waits his turn to speak.
Realizes that the speaker's intent is not always correctly interpreted.
Notes the effect of that which he hears has upon him and also notes the effect that this knowing how he is being affected affects him.
Wants to know what the speaker is talking about in a down-to-earth sense.
Categorizes facts.
Seeks to utilize all five senses to help himself listen.
Realistically appraises what the speaker does and does not say.
Plans what he is going to say as a rejoinder.
Maintains total awareness in receiving fine details in the total picture.
Seeks to clarify vagueness and ambiguity.
Can empathize easily.
Looks for possible distortions, misinterpretations of information and facts.
Is suspicious of words and distrusts connotations.

Negative Listening Characteristics

Avoids personal involvement in listening, preferring to remain detached.
Strives to be primarily an organ for the passive reception of sound.
Is seldom introspective in listening.
Isolates sounds.

Sometimes allows pressures or conflicts to enter into the listening situations.
Is satisfied without undue demands of further proof or evidence.
Is satisfied with the message others receive.
Listens to details rather than overall essence generally.
Seldom can feel and think and also be turned inward in listening.
Is content to receive the message.
Is good at reading other people's minds.
Avoids transferring his values, attitudes and relationships from himself to others.
Seldom catches what other people do not say.
Will let conflicting affections hinder the intake of the intended message. These are basic to his criteria in judgment.
Finds real personal meaning in sets of words even though they may not convey information.
Is tolerant of abstractions.
Listens only to what the speaker says literally.
Usually hears about the same things heard by most others.
Keeps his personal feelings and reactions to himself.
Prefers to "read into" the unsaid.
Disregards symbols of authority.
Avoids influence of visual cues in listening.
"Gets" the message without worrying about ideas, organization, arguments or other isolated facts and the like.
Insists that generalizations are indefensible.
Is tolerant of abstractions.
Accepts words at their face value with their usual connotations.
Is suspicious of words and distrusts connotations.
Invents his own implications of what is said by the speaker.
Avoids imposing his attitudes and beliefs onto the situation.

Any overlapping items must be viewed as so many shades of gray in the judgment of the individual listener who must cognitively exercise the extent and direction of acceptableness to which he will affiliate the particular item.

The ideal listener primarily keeps an open, curious mind. He listens for new ideas everywhere, integrating what he hears with what he already knows. He is also self-perceptive and thus listens to others with his total being or self. Thus he becomes personally involved with what he hears. Being this aware he is not willing to blindly follow the listening crowd. He maintains conscious perspectives in what is going on instead. He looks for ideas, organization and arguments but always listens to the essence of things. Knowing that no two people listen the same, he stays mentally alert by outlining, objecting, approving, adding illustrations of his own. He is introspective but he has the capacity and desire to critically examine, understand and attempt to transform some of his values, attitudes, and relationships within himself and with others. He focuses his mind on the listening and listens to the speaker's ideas, but he also listens with feeling and intuition.

Mind Wandering

John Cohen, C.E.M. Hansel and J.D. Sylvester

The experiments here briefly described were primarily an attempt to devise and evaluate methods for investigating certain basic characteristics of attention. The two questions we asked may be put as follows: (i) How often does the mind wander? (ii) Does the frequency or duration of the mind wandering vary in any systematic way? The experiments were intended as preparatory to a search for the factors determining the presumed variations.

Three methods were employed:

(a) Each member of a class listening to a lecture, or of a group listening to gramophone music, was provided with a bell-push and instructed to press it whenever he became aware that his attention had returned to the lecturer or the music. The bell-pushes were so arranged that when any one was pressed, a corresponding torch-bulb lit up an adjoining room and was recorded either on a continuously moving film or by observers. By this means up to fifty subjects could be studied at the same time.

(b) Observers watched a class of normal children through a one-way screen. They noted when a child seemed not to be attending to the teacher, the criteria of inattention being, for example, looking out of the window, talking to another child, fidgeting, falling asleep and so on.

(c) Observers watched a small class of deaf children through a one-way screen. Attention to the teacher required lip-reading on the part of the child, and the observers noted when each child was not looking at the teacher.

Methods (b) and (c) were indirect and enabled us to estimate how long each child's attention wandered on any occasion. Method (a) was direct, though it yielded only the frequency of wandering.

We found that in the lecture classes the subjects, on the average, pressed the bell-push about four times during a 40 min. period. The frequency was a little higher in the music group. In both cases individual differences were relatively enormous. Of the 165 subjects in the lecture classes, 14% did not press the bell-push at all, about 9% pressed it once, and four subjects pressed it twenty times or more. The mode was about three or four in the different lectures. Much the same results were obtained with the group listening to music.

Table 1.

Mean frequency with which bell-push was pressed during lectures, in 5 min. intervals from commencement (N = 165)

Minutes	5	10	15	20	25	30	35	40
Mean	0.27	0.52	0.56	0.61	0.62	0.64	0.55	0.43
S.D.	0.62	0.81	0.86	0.94	0.88	1.11	1.07	0.83

As may be seen from Table 1 the mean frequency with which the bell-push was pressed during the lectures, in intervals of 5 min., ranged from 0.27 to 0.64, the corresponding standard deviations ranging from 0.62 to 1.11. In the case of the music groups the mean frequency of pressing ranged from 0.18 to 0.87, with standard deviations ranging from 0.46 to 1.47 (see Table 2). Apart from the infrequency of pressing during the initial 5 min., no significant variation in frequency of pressing with time was observed.

Table 2.

Mean frequency with which bell-push was pressed by members of music group, in 5 min. intervals from commencement (N = 33)

Minutes	5	10	15	20	25	30	35	40	45
Mean	0.18	0.67	0.76	0.82	0.58	0.82	0.87	0.65	0.80
S.D.	0.46	0.94	1.02	1.47	0.82	1.19	0.90	0.87	1.07

Subjects' reports revealed the considerable difficulties many of them had in carrying out the instructions. Pressing the bell-push was found to be distracting and itself to divert the attention. It was often hard to decide when the attention seemed to have returned. Any particular wandering might feel like a definite lapse or daydream or, at the other extreme, like a slight oscillation or mere flicker of attention. When the mind wanders it may be to ponder more deeply the lecturer's theme without being a lapse in any sense or it may be due to a 'pull' from some other direction which has nothing at all to do with the topic of the lecture.

In the experiments with twenty-nine normal children, judging by the criteria we employed, a child's attention seemed to return, on the average, about once a minute. The means for 5 min. intervals ranged from 4.95 to 5.73, with standard deviations ranging from 2.45 to 3.33. The duration of the wanderings on this basis ranged from a momentary flicker too short to be timed to about 3.75 min., with a mean of 13.74 sec. The details are set out in Table 3. Rather similar results were obtained from the observations of the deaf children by method (c), see Table 4. The mean duration of their inattention was about 4.8 sec.

Table 3.

Mean frequency with which the attention of normal children seemed to return, in 5 min. intervals (*N* = 29)

Minutes	5	10	15	20	25	30
Mean	5.42	5.21	5.68	4.95	5.38	5.73
S.D.	2.92	2.67	3.33	3.47	2.45	3.13

Table 4.

Mean frequency with which the attention of deaf children seemed to return, in 5 min. intervals (*N* = 4)

Minutes	0-5	5-10	10-15	15-20	20-25	25-30	30-35
Mean	4.75	6.25	5.25	7.25	4.0	5.0	4.5
S.D.	1.61	2.15	6.93	4.03	2.35	1.87	2.68

Further use of direct and indirect methods on the same subjects, with the experimental material and conditions held constant, may enable us to validate these methods. If the two types of method yield similar results, then the simpler and more expeditious direct method of bell-pushing might usefully be employed in investigating the two questions formulated above and allied problems.

Sex Differences in Listening Comprehension

M. A. Brimer

Following an experimental trial with the Peabody Picture Vocabulary Test with English children in which the investigators reported that, "the PPVT is potentially a useful instrument for use with English children," the present author was invited to reconstruct the test for use with English children between the ages of 5.0 and 11.11. Two tests resulted, English Picture Vocabulary Tests 1 and 2, covering respectively the age ranges 5.0 to 8.11 and 7.0 to 11.11.

The tests were separately standardized on samples of English children representing children in maintained schools in England. Schools were drawn to represent proportionately by type, locality, and size the national distribution of maintained schools in England and Wales.

The participating schools were asked to test all children on roll aged 7.0 to 11.11, 5.0 to 7.11, or 8.0 to 8.11 according to which sample the schools were representing. Separate representation of the 8.0 to 8.11 age range was necessary for Test 1 because of the presence of children of such age in other than infant and junior with infant schools. All testing was completed within a period of one month. Table 1 displays the number of children taking each test by sex and age.

All administrations of Test 1 were individual. In the case of Test 2, provision had been made for the test to be administered individually to children who might not be able to follow the group instruction. The provision was found to be unnecessary; in the one school where individual testing was carried out, it was undertaken because of the head teacher's interest in the working of the tests. Even children who had been ascertained educationally sub-normal and who

Table 1

Numbers of Children by Age and by Sex in Test 1 Standardization

	5:0 - 5:11	6:0 - 6:11	7:0 - 7:11	8:0 - 8:11	Total
Boys	442	487	430	321	1680
Girls	425	460	390	285	1560
Total	867	947	820	606	3240

Numbers of Children by Age and by Sex in Test 2 Standardization

	7:0-7:11	8:0-8:11	9:0-9:11	10:0-10:11	11:0-11:11	Total
Boys	251	584	639	616	537	2627
Girls	254	605	546	537	515	2457
Total	505	1189	1185	1153	1052	5084

Table 2

Test 1 - Means and Standard Deviations of Raw Score By Age and By Sex

	5:0 - 5:11	6:0 - 6:11	7:0 - 7:11	8:0 - 8:11	Total
$\overline{X}$ Boys	13.82	19.35	23.83	27.78	20.65
$\overline{X}$ Girls	13.33	17.95	22.62	26.35	19.39
Total	13.58	18.67	23.26	27.11	20.05
σ Boys	6.22	6.33	6.11	5.06	7.89
σ Girls	5.49	6.32	6.63	5.91	7.74
Total	5.88	6.32	6.32	5.52	7.84

Table 3

Test 2 - Means and Standard Deviations of Raw Score by Age and by Sex

	7:0-7:11	8:0-8:11	9:0-9:11	10:0-10:11	11:0-11:11	Total
$\overline{X}$ Boys	13.68	17.60	22.36	26.80	29.20	22.91
$\overline{X}$ Girls	12.50	15.98	19.34	23.60	26.88	20.32
Total	13.08	16.78	20.96	25.30	28.06	21.66
σ Boys	5.67	7.48	7.96	7.84	6.91	9.02
σ Girls	5.29	6.65	8.00	8.05	8.29	8.90
Total	5.51	7.11	8.14	8.09	7.70	9.05

belonged to the youngest age group in the sample followed the group instructions for Test 2 without procedural error and without apparent difficulty. The means and standard deviations of raw score by age and by sex are given in Tables 2 and 3.

All the differences between means are in favor of boys and only that at the five year old level for Test 1 fails to reach the 5% level of confidence. There are some significant differences between standard deviations for the sexes but these are not consistent and appear to be a function of the variability of scores relative to the mean.

The consistent direction of difference in favor of boys appears to be an unusual feature of the test and generally appears to be in conflict with the familiar linguistic superiority of girls. However, close scrutiny of the literature on orally administered vocabulary tests confirms that male superiority is characteristically found. Dunsdon and Fraser-Roberts[1] in their study of four orally-administered vocabulary tests, reported differences in favor of boys at every age level from five to fourteen. They do not seem to regard the oral administration as being the critical feature associated with the difference. Templin[2] in her study of language skills, reports, "The higher scores of the boys in the six - eight-year-old range are particularly apparent in the vocabulary of recognition. At these ages it is the boys who occasionally receive higher scores on verbalization and on the more difficult articulation measures. Nevertheless, with the exception of the recognition vocabulary scores, girls obtain the greater proportion of higher scores in each area." The recognition vocabulary scores to which Templin refers were derived from the orally-administered Seashore-Eckerson English Recognition Vocabulary Test. Similar evidence of male superiority on listening vocabulary and listening comprehension measures have been found for adolescent and young adult groups (Dow,[3] Hampleman,[4] and Hollow[5]).

That such findings do not merely represent artifacts of test construction, biased sampling or sex-biased modes of response is attested by a number of other studies. Male superiority in oral vocabularyttest performance in the presence of female "language" superiority has been reported of five-year-old children.[6] That the male superiority is not restricted to single word presentation is born out by a study of listening and reading comprehension reported by King.[7] King's experiment involved a changeover trial of oral reading paragraph comprehension, and his findings were that "boys tend to obtain higher mean scores on the oral test, and girls the visual test." Caffrey[8] (1955) demonstrated that the male superiority among his high school student groups was attributable to neither chronological age, mental age nor sex bias in item content.

Some difficulty of interpretation arises through the failure of investigators to attend closely enough to the mode of testing involving both the way in which the stimulus is presented and the way in which the response is elicited. Thus, Spearritt[9] created a listening vocabulary test from a word knowledge reading test by requiring a child to select from five printed words that which most nearly fitted the meaning of the orally presented test word. The five alternatives were read out by the test administrator but the choice was made from the printed word. This was particularly unfortunate in a study which involved a factorial analysis of listening comprehension since the test functionally failed to differentiate between listening effectiveness, as such, and reading vocabulary. Nevertheless, Spearritt's study is one of the most significant in that it not only succeeded in demonstrating the existence of a separate and distinctive listening comprehension factor but also showed that the factor loadings on the tests for boys and girls were markedly different. It is of particular interest that the listening vocabulary test had its highest loading on the listening comprehension factor for girls but did not achieve a significant loading for boys. This is the result one would expect if the item difficulty were for boys dependent upon reading skill and for girls dependent upon listening skill.

The identification of a consistent male superiority in listening vocabulary in the context of female expressive language superiority and of superior female reading vocabulary raises interesting questions of the origin of such differences and their implications for individual differences with each sex. The failure to explain the phenomenon through biased sampling, topic bias, interest bias, or response bias invites a search for an alternative hypothesis and developmental rather than organic explanations suggest themselves. McCarthy,[10] in summarizing the research literature, demonstrates a higher rate of language acquisition by girls than by boys. This earlier linguistic development is consistent with the more advanced physical development of girls at every age level. It would seem that the most likely explanation of the male superiority in listening comprehension is to be sought in the relationship between language and thought in the course of development. Is it possible that the earlier command of expressive language by girls in fact alters the way in which language functions in learning? Do boys gain an advantage in this one aspect of language acquisition by a delay in their command of speech? It is at least worth exploring a little further the hypotheses that would arise from such questions.

Once language skills enable denotative functioning to operate, situations become controllable through the medium of language. When speech incorporates whole patterns acquired through the imitation of adult models, situations tend to be simplified by the imposition of that choice from a limited range of specific models which best fits the child's wish or intention towards the situation. The more specific the model that is applied, the more readily the situation is resolved in relation to motivation. Conversely, the less specific the model, the less easily is resolution achieved, and the longer the duration of motivation up to the point of frustration. One would also argue a greater likelihood of dialogue in social situations in which adults are led to achieve resolution through the mediation of language. For example, contrast two situations: (a) one child can say, "I want a drink," and (b) another child commands only the one syllable "tea" to stand for any form of eating or drinking in relation to any intention from the denotative to the request. In the (b) case, the adult will exploit the child's listening comprehension to elicit some signal that the intention has been recognized, while in the (a) case, there is simply compliance with or denial of the request accompanied at the most by some conventional phrase. The former situation provokes little discriminating listening attention by the child, while the latter enforces it. Thus, given the differential rates of expressive language acquisition commonly found between sexes, males will for a longer period be exposed to dependence on discriminating listening attention and, it may be argued, will learn to function more effectively in such contexts. By the same token, they will run a greater risk of being frustrated either by their own inability to make appropriate discriminations or by the inadequacy of adult linguistic or functional anticipation of their intention. It would be argued further that boys more than girls are likely to display anger in social situations where adults attempt to comply with their wishes, but they are less likely to display negative emotion in listening situations.

The earlier ability of girls to command a range of speech models would lead to an increase in the range of such models since the discrepancy between the application of a particular model and the intention is likely to lead to adult correction and the substitution of a more fitting model. For boys, the longer lack of precision of controllable speech models is likely to delay the acquisition of more differentiated models.

Such hypotheses and their deductions could be tested through normative studies of the forms of linguistic interaction between adults and infants and through experimental studies in which the forms of adult linguistic intervention are controlled. The most promising outcome of such studies would be a closer understanding of the language learning process and particularly of the active process of listening.

Notes

Abbreviated references, such as Nos. 3, 4 and 5 below, refer to the entry number in Sam Duker's Listening Bibliography 2nd Ed. (Scarecrow, 1968) where the full citation may be found.

1. M. I. Dunsdon and J. A. Fraser-Roberts. "A Study of the Performance of 2,000 Children in Four Vocabulary Tests." British Journal of Statistical Psychology 10:1-16, 1957.
2. M. C. Templin. Certain Language Skills in Children. Minneapolis: University of Minnesota Press, 1957.
3. C. W. Dow, 302.
4. R. S. Hampleman, 510.
5. M. K. Hollow, 578.
6. O. C. Sampson. "The Speech and Language Development of Five-Year-Old Children." British Journal of Educational Psychology 29: 217-22, 1959.
7. W. H. King, 663.
8. J. Caffrey, 161.

An Auditory Language Quantum

J. Buckminster Ranney & Mary Virginia Moore

To listen is to have language. To speak is to have language. To read is to have language. Yet, what is language and how is it measured? The disciplines of linguistics, psychology and speech pathology have all been concerned with language and language development. Many students of language have suggested that some children are primarily hearers, some seers and some touchers.

Hardy[1] has suggested levels or steps of language acquisition which have the potential of being informal measures leading to an auditory language quantum. Hardy's presentation is in terms of audition--hearing and auding. A child must hear--physiologic sensitivity, before he may aud--listen.

The Hardy steps are six in number. The first three steps are concerned with hearing--sensitivity; the second three are concerned with auding--listening. The hearing steps are: I, sensitivity; II, discrimination and III, perception (or recognition). The auding steps are: IV, processing; V, pattern making; and VI, retention. A final step has been added to express the awareness of concepts, VII, conceptualization.

An informal seven point auditory language quantum scale is presented which provides a basis for the evaluation in broad terms of the audition of a language impaired child.

I. Sensitivity

The ability to perceive sound--sensation--is fundamental to any auditory communication. The deaf child, 80/85 dB ASA Values,[2] "fails" the first unit of the scale, for he does not perceive the auditory signal. The measurement of sensitivity may be accomplished in a gross manner by any teacher or patient.

Does the child attend in terms of sensation to a bell, squeaker or a rattle; does he attend to a speaker's voice? If the answer is yes, score one point (on the seven point scale): the problem is not gross sensitivity.

II. Differentiation

The ability to separate the components of one sound from the other is a prerequisite to the separation of the complex signals which form the basis for speech. At a most fundamental level, does the child have the ability to distinguish between a bell, a squeaker and a rattle?

If the child separates the bell from the rattle from the squeaker (or any other appropriate non-speech stimulus) score two points on the seven point scale: the problem is not differentiation.

III. Recognition

The ability to recognize speech sounds as unique from all other sounds is the final step of hearing as a process which leads to auding. Does the child recognize--alert and attend to by turning toward and seeking the source of--the stimulus of the spoken word as speech?

Is the speech signal truly unique for the child? Does he separate from speech all other sounds? The child will score at nearly the half way point on the scale--three of seven points--if the recognition of speech has been established.

IV. Processing

The ability to process sound is crucial in the development of auding. The chief concern of the child is a speech signal, but processing may involve coding of all forms, for example, the telegrapher of old listened to "dits" and "dahs". Simple non-speech and speech stimuli reveal the ability to process.

Does the child have the ability to duplicate, to imitate by manual or vocal action a simple auditory signal? The stimulus may be a tapped pattern; tap, tap tap tap or a phoneme; k, k, k. If the child reproduces by manual or vocal action the sequence of taps or the phonemic pattern, score four points on the scale--four of seven.

V. Pattern Making

If the preceding steps have been established, the child must move from the awareness of sound and the process of sound to the making of patterns from speech stimuli --patterns which, in the Mowrer[3] sense, have meaning. The patterns may be associated with an object or person and, at a more abstract level, a picture of an object or person. The stimulus may be cast as a single word or in a phrase or sentence.

Does the child with an auditory stimulus (speech) recognize the person or object or the picture of the person or object? For example, the stimulus may be, "Show me shoe." Does the child point to a shoe? Or, "Where is mommy?" Does the child look toward his mother? If the answer is yes, score five on the seven point scale.

VI. Retention

The steps I through V are not complete for the development of language auding, because the "process" and the "pattern" must be retained beyond the period of the immediate stimulus if the child is to aud. There is some evidence that the breakdown of the intellectually delayed child passes the steps one through five, but he does not retain the speech signal; hence, he may not score on item six.

Does the child retain the next day or next week without a period of "relearning" auditory symbols such as "no", "ball" and "mother"? Is there spontaneous recognition of the auditory symbol? If the answer is yes, score six points--six of seven.

VII. Concepts

Concepts or abstractions, especially higher level abstractions, pose problems for children and adult listeners as well. A basic level for the child may be represented with the concept of over and under.

If the child demonstrates the ability to understand and express with nonspeech behavior "over" and "under," score seven points--a maximum for the scale. Over and under are recognized as a relatively low level of abstraction. An illustration of a relatively high level of abstraction would be rights and equities.

The achievement and success of children in developing language is dependent upon a multiplicity of factors. The question of auditory language quantum--the potential for the development of language utilizing the auditory pathways--should be evaluated.

The informal evaluation of the auditory language quantum is suggested as one concern in the total evaluation of the child who does not succeed in the acquisition of language skills, listening, speaking, reading and writing. The auditory language quantum is presented on the preceding seven step scale.

The suggested purpose of the scale is to provide a basis for planning a program of rehabilitation for the child with auditory problems. A number on a scale which provides a level of the child's performance is a starting point. The rehabilitation of a child may be initiated at the point on the scale where his auditory language quantum is found, regardless of his chronologic or intellectual age level.

Notes

1. William G. Hardy. "Problems of Audition, Perception and Understanding." Volta Review 58:289-300, 1956.

2. Hallowell Davis and R. Richard Silverman. Hearing and Deafness. New York: Holt, 1960.

3. O. H. Mowrer. "Hearing and Speaking: An Analysis of Language Learning." Journal of Speech and Hearing Disorders 23:143-52, 1958.

Chapter II

Relationships: Listening and Reading

It has long been pointed out that the four language arts or communication skills--listening, reading, speaking and writing--are closely related. It is, of course, obvious that speaking and writing are skills of transmission while listening and reading are skills of reception. Similarly, listening and speaking are oral activities while reading and writing are visual in their nature.

At first glance, it would appear that certain specific common skills would be involved in the two receptive communication modes. For example, both would certainly require more than using one of the five senses, because to see is not necessarily to read and to hear is not the equivalent of listening. It has been proposed that the mental assimilation processes involved in going beyond the physical acts of seeing and hearing may be similar. It is commonly assumed that the processes of concentration or attention, of memory, of gathering meaning, of applying critical judgment would be very similar. Much has been written in support of the propositions so briefly stated in this paragraph.

Others differ sharply and say that there is no hard, convincing evidence to bolster up the conclusions just mentioned. In fact, these writers say, there is more evidence to the contrary.

The first article in this chapter, which I wrote some years ago, attempts to present some evidence, in the form of findings from a number of studies, for the belief that there is indeed a close relationship between the two receptive modes of communication. There was, when I wrote this article, and there is now no feeling whatsoever on my part that the truth about the relationship between listening and reading had been finally and irrevocably established for all time to come. Further discussion and future research may indeed contradict some of the views expressed here.

A scholarly and very persuasive presentation of an opposite viewpoint is presented in the next item in this chapter. Dr. Thomas G. Devine, a professor in the School of Education at Boston University, has made a number of major contributions to knowledge about listening, beginning with his 1961 doctoral dissertation on the subject of critical listening. His review of listening in the 1967 Language Arts issue of the Review of Educational Research is both thoughtful and analytical. The portion of this chapter which Professor Devine has contributed will, I think, be of interest to readers who are concerned about the true relationship between listening and reading.

The third article in this chapter is taken from the 1963 Teachers College, Columbia University doctoral thesis by Dr. Melvin Mart. Here the relationship between communication modalities is treated in a scholarly and informative manner. It is hoped that the excerpts used here will give enough of the flavor of the approach employed to challenge at least some readers to take the time to read the entire document which is available from University Microfilms. The time spent in such perusal will be well repaid.

Dr. Charles T. Brown, Chairman of the Speech Department of Western Michigan University, has kindly allowed me to use several items from his writings in this book. His courses on listening have proven of great value to students and they are in great demand whenever they are offered. The passage from his work which appears in this chapter deals with a number of relationships. It is included because of the light it sheds on the reading-listening questions.

Next, I have reprinted a short passage taken from an undated publisher's promotional leaflet written by Dr. Paul McKee of Greeley, Colorado. This leaflet was written in the form of a letter to a young teacher who had asked about the effect the teaching of listening skills might have on a young child's reading. Professor McKee has made enormous contributions to the teaching of reading for many years. His down-to-earth, common sense style, shown in this short excerpt, certainly makes it understandable that his contributions have been so very effective and persuasive.

The last two articles in this chapter are also concerned with listening-reading relationships but in a different way from the previous material. The first five selections in this chapter focus on the existence of certain relationships; these last two are about ways in which these relationships can be used.

Dr. James J. Fenwick's article is concerned with the effectiveness of using aural instruction in teaching slow-learners with reading difficulties at the ninth grade level. No statistically significant results were obtained. This is not surprising in light of the findings of Thomas Wood Smith.[1] Excerpts from Dr. Smith's work are found in my first book of readings.[2] Probably "poor readers" are not peculiarly poor in reading but are in most cases handicapped in general language or verbal skills. This is recognized by Dr. Fenwick in his discussion of the results he obtained. It might well be that aural instruction for the type of youngster who was the subject for this experiment would be the most profitable mode but almost certainly such aural instruction should be preceded by instruction in listening skills.

The last passage is by Dr. Thomas Dreiling, who describes a successful search for aural testing devices that would be usable in determining the general abilities of a population of nonreaders and poor readers.

Notes

Abbreviated references refer to the entry number in Sam Duker's Listening Bibliography 2nd Ed. (Scarecrow, 1968) where the full citation may be found.

1. Thomas Wood Smith, 1107.
2. Sam Duker (Editor). Listening: Readings, Metuchen, N. J.: Scarecrow Press, 1966, p. 125-30.

Listening and Reading

Sam Duker

Interest in the subject of listening is at the highest point it has ever been. There is growing recognition of the importance of this skill. Increasing numbers of studies are dealing with the nature of listening and with ways of teaching it at all educational levels from pre-kindergarten to industrial training.

One reason for this concern is the growing awareness of the intimate interrelationship between listening and reading. Both are receptive communication skills and as such share many attributes.

A recently published bibliography on this subject, which I compiled, includes about two hundred entries on this interrelationship.[1] The items are concerned with:

1. the correlation between reading- and listening-test results;
2. the effects of teaching listening on reading skills and vice versa;
3. the evaluation of listening skills as a measure of reading potential;
4. listening skill as a factor of reading skill;
5. the relative effectiveness of reading and listening as a means of learning.

Increasingly, experts on, and teachers of, reading are recognizing the importance of knowledge about teaching listening in effective reading instruction. A considerable amount of time and attention was devoted to the question at the 1963 Annual Conference on Reading held at the University of Chicago.[2] Textbooks on methods of teaching reading are devoting increasing amounts of space to this topic.[3,4] Curriculum bulletins are also giving increased attention to listening.[5]

An important distinction must be drawn between hearing and listening. Just as seeing is essential to, but not the same as, reading, so hearing is a prerequisite of listening but not an equivalent. Listening and reading both involve comprehension, interpretation, and evaluation, which hearing and seeing do not. A generally accepted factor in reading readiness is auditory discrimination. This is a skill in hearing, not in listening. Studies of auditory discrimination, important as they are, must not, therefore, be confused with studies of listening.

How close is the relationship between reading and listening?

Twenty-three major studies (1:306) have reported coefficients of correlation between reading and listening. Table 1 lists representative studies made at the elementary-school level.

As Table 1 shows, coefficients of correlation reported range from .45 to .70. The mean of the reported coefficients of correlation is .59. The wide range of findings is probably a result of the differing populations employed as subjects and of the variety of tests used to measure listening and reading skills. However, all these studies show a strong positive relationship between listening and reading.

This relationship is not at all to be unexpected of two receptive communicative skills; but, surprisingly enough, many inferences are often deduced from this relationship that are not justified by these research findings. It is frequently assumed that poor readers are able to profit more from aural instruction than good readers are. One implication of these correlational studies is that in general the poor reader is also likely to be a poor listener. This does not preclude the possibility that a poor reader may not at times listen better than he reads, but his listening skills are not likely to be of a high enough caliber to enable him to learn any more effectively through listening than through reading.

In this day of concern about the education of culturally deprived children it is also commonly taken for granted that reading tests and intelligence tests that require reading are "culturally biased." This assumption is probably a sound one. But oral intelligence tests and listening tests are not less biased, according to the studies discussed here. One example of a misapprehension of the nature of cultural bias is found in action taken in New York City, where as a

Table 1. Coefficients of Correlations between Listenign and Reading

Investigator*	Date	Listening Test	Reading Test	Grade Level	Number of Subjects	Coefficient of Correlation Reported
Biggins......	1961	Wright†	California	2	124	.45
Biggins......	1961	Wright†	California	3	130	.70
Bonner......	1960	STEP‡	Stanford	4	76	.53
Bonner......	1960	STEP‡	Stanford	5	90	.57
Bonner......	1960	STEP‡	Stanford	6	84	.65
Hall.........	1954	Hall†	Gates	5	441	.56
Joney.......	1956	Joney†	Durrell	4	140	.65
Lewis.......	1954	Lewis†	Nelson-Denny	5	200	.68
Many........	1953	Pratt†	Pratt†	6	352	.68
Rankin......	1926	Rankin†	Rankin†	5	124	.48
Rankin......	1926	Rankin†	Rankin†	7	130	.48
Spearritt....	1961	Spearritt†	Spearritt†	6	300	.68
Toussaint....	1961	STEP‡	Gates	4, 5, 6	172	.67
Watkins.....	1960	My Weekly Reader	California	2	300	.46

*Full bibliographic references to these studies may be found in my Listening Bibliography (see Reference 1).

†Unpublished test.

‡Sequential Tests of Educational Progress: Listening. Princeton, New Jersey: Educational Testing Service, 1957.

matter of policy the administration of group intelligence tests has been abandoned and plans have been made to substitute a listening test in the earlier grades.

What will the substitution of listening tests accomplish? Cultural bias is involved in listening tests. In fact, correlational studies give eloquent testimony to the fact that listening tests are as culturally biased as group intelligence tests. Even more direct evidence is provided in a study by Smith,[6] who found that cultural bias is as much a factor in listening as it is in reading. It is verbal comprehension rather than reading alone which is affected by cultural deprivation. Smith's study shows, for example, that the coefficient of correlation between parental occupation and reading is almost identical to the coefficient of correlation between parental occupation and listening. The coefficients were .31 and .33, respectively. Smith found the coefficient of correlation between reading and listening to be .48.

The significance of these correlational studies is generally accepted on a theoretical level. What is desperately needed is a willingness to apply the findings to teaching procedures used in the classroom.

Does the teaching of listening skills improve reading skills? Does the teaching of reading skills improve listening skills?

Nineteen studies have dealt with the effect of instruction in either reading or listening skills on the other (1:312). A selection of studies of this type at the elementary-school level is summarized in Table 2.

The results are not entirely consistent, but many studies show that instruction in listening skills leads to improved reading. Most of the investigators assumed an automatic transfer of learning, a hypothesis that has been shown to be unsound. Taba states the modern theory of transfer as follows:

> ...the ability to transfer learning is achieved not by studying a particular subject, or by specific drill and rote learning, but rather by emphasis on cognitive principles applied either to methods of learning or to the understanding of content, and on ways of learning that stress flexibility of approach and that develop an alertness of generalizations and their application to new situations. Positive

Table 2. Effect of Instruction in Reading or Listening on the Other

Investigator*	Date	Duration of Listening Instruction	Grade Level	Statistically Significant Improvement in Reading	Number of Subjects
Dumdie.....	1961	5 weeks	4, 5	Yes	30
Kelty.......	1953	30 days	4	Yes†	188
McCormack.	1962	6 months	1	Yes‡	88
MacDonnell.	1962	3 months	1	Yes‡‡	64
McPherson.	1951	30 days	2	Yes**	130
Madden.....	1959	20 lessons	5	Yes††	600
Marsden....	1951	8 lessons	5, 6	No	232
Matthews...	1958	6 months	3	No	241
Merson.....	1961	45 lessons	4	No	700
		Duration of Reading Instruction		Statistically Significant Improvement in Listening	
Dumdie.....	1961	5 weeks	4, 5	Yes	30
Madden.....	1959	5 weeks	5	No	60

*Full bibliographic references to these studies can be found in my Listening Bibliography (see Ref. 1).
†For reading for details but not for reading for main idea or for drawing conclusions.
‡For total reading, sentence comprehension, paragraph comprehension but not for word recognition.
‡‡But not a significant improvement in spelling.
**For Reading for details.
††For Reading for main idea, for details, and for drawing conclusions.

> transfer, therefore, depends on both how and what an individual learns.[7]

From the results of the studies just discussed and from Taba's statement it seems most likely that instruction in listening skills which have much in common with reading skills may be extremely effective in improving reading. The greater receptivity that many children might feel toward such an aural program is a potent argument in its favor. It is, however, not likely that any sort of pedestrian listening instruction will have any great effect on reading, but an enlightened approach that emphasizes pupil-discovered generalizations gives promise of great effectiveness. That kind of approach is well described by Taba:

> ... As can be seen from the discussion of how concepts and generalizations are learned, the more abstract the principles and generalizations, the greater the possibility of transfer. But the actuality of transfer depends on whether or not curriculum materials and educational processes are addressed to transfer--on the extent to which both the curriculum and the ways of reacting to its content stimulate the discovery of basic principles, give practice in applying principles and develop a set for learning, an expectation that whatever is learned will be used in new and different ways.[7]

Are listening skills a measure of reading potential?

An evaluation of listening ability may be an effective and dependable measure of reading potential. This hypothesis describes an interesting relationship between listening and reading. For years we have operated on the theory that the best predictor of reading potential was a device designed to measure intelligence. There can be no doubt that intelligence-test scores may reveal an important factor in reading potential, but some studies indicate that listening ability is an even more significant factor in predicting reading potential.

In a very carefully conducted study of aural and visual vocabulary, Armstrong[8] reports the following results for two hundred children in Grades 1 through 8:

Age	Mean Number of Words Visually Known	Mean Number of Words Auditorially Known (Includes Number in Column 2)
6-6	848	3,048
7-6	1,184	3,476
8-6	1,900	4,240
9-6	4,040	5,120
10-6	6,040	6,600
11-6	6,080	6,640
12-6	7,240	7,480

Armstrong concluded that the size of a child's auditory vocabulary "is direct evidence of potential improvement in ability to read and visual vocabulary is itself a measure of reading achievement" (8:107).

In a study of forty-six pupils in grades 2 through 4 Barbe and Carr suggested that listening ability may be a better predictor of reading potential than mental age, despite the high coefficient of correlation between listening ability and mental age.[9]

Furness draws the same conclusion from an analysis of the basic role of vocabulary in both listening and reading.[10]

In a study of 110 children in grades 2 through 4 Owen found a closer relationship between reading-test results and measures of listening than between either listening or reading scores and intelligence-test results.[11] He suggests that the best prognosis of reading potential is obtained by using both intelligence and listening tests.

Schultz found an oral vocabulary test more significant in predicting reading potential than either a written vocabulary test or an intelligence test.[12]

Both Spache[13] and Triggs[14] have discussed the value of the Auditory Comprehension Section of the Triggs Diagnostic Reading Tests as a measure of reading potential.

In a particularly well-planned and well-executed study Toussaint found that a test of listening in combination with other tests provided the best measure of reading potential.[15]

All the studies just cited support the value of listening tests as a tool in predicting reading potential. It is difficult to overestimate the usefulness of an instrument of this kind to the teacher of reading.

How is listening related to reading?

Several factor-analysis studies are of interest to the student of reading who is concerned about the role of listening skills in the reading process (1:308).

Of particular importance is the study by Holmes and Singer which is based on test data from a sample of four hundred high school students.[16] In an original and very carefully performed study, the authors analyzed the variance of speed of reading and were able to account for 55 per cent of the variance. Using the California Auding Test developed by Donald P. Brown and John G. Caffrey as a measure of listening, Holmes and Singer found that 14 per cent of the variance was accounted for by listening ability. Thus, more than a quarter of the variance that was accounted for was attributable to listening.

In "power of reading," 75 per cent of the variance was accounted for. Here again listening played a major role, since 16 per cent of the variance was attributable to this factor. Thus more than 21 per cent of the variance accounted for was found to be due to listening. This study furnishes dramatic evidence of the role played by listening skills in the reading process. The vital importance of the skills to the teacher of reading cannot be exaggerated. An analysis of various subgroups shows similar results. Table 3 summarizes the findings.

The data in Table 3 furnish many avenues to future research, but they leave no doubt that listening ability plays a vital role in determining reading success or failure.

Other factor-analysis studies such as the excellent one by Spearritt leave no doubt of the existence of listening ability as a separate distinct ability.[17]

What kind of presentation is most effective for learning--a presentation that calls for reading or a presentation that calls for listening?

Innumerable studies during the past sixty years have compared the effectiveness of written and oral instruction.

Table 3. Summary of Holmes and Singer's Findings for Subgroups

Group	Number of Pupils	Coefficients of Correlation: Listening and Reading Speed	Coefficients of Correlation: Listening and Reading Power	Mean Scores: Speed of Reading	Mean Scores: Power of Reading	Mean Scores: Listening	Contribution of Listening to Variance of Speed of Reading	Cont. of List. to Var. of Power of Reading
Boys........	211	.55	.73	20.06*	66.89	31.85	12.4%	17.6%
Girls	189	.66	.78	22.13*	70.48	31.98	22.9%	14.7%
Bright†	108	.37	.42*	27.73*	80.89*	37.94*	3.0%°	5.6%
Dull‡	108	.45	.69	15.43*	53.32*	25.67*	negligible	16.88%
Fast**	108	.34	.....	30.93*	78.98*	37.32*	3.8%††	.....
Slow‡‡	108	.42	.....	12.47*	54.58*	25.63*	5.0%	.....
Powerful°°	108	...	.41***	26.54*	85.35*	38.52*	.....	9.4%
Non-powerful†††	108	...	.44	15.06*	45.87*	23.84*	.....	2.4%

*Difference significant at 1 per cent level.

†Those earning scores in the upper 27 per cent of the distribution on the verbal ability of the Thurstone and Thurstone Primary Mental Abilities Test.

°Only 20 per cent of the variance was accounted for in this analysis.

‡Those earning scores in the lower 27 per cent of the distribution on the Thurstone and Thurstone Primary Mental Abilities Test.

**Those earning scores in the upper 27 per cent of the distribution on the Diagnostic Examination of Silent Reading Abilities, Rate of Comprehension Scale, by Dvorak and Van Wagenen.

††Only 22.4 per cent of the variance was accounted for in this analysis.

‡‡Those earning scores in the lower 27 per cent of the distribution on the Diagnostic Examination of Silent Reading Abilities, Rate of Comprehension Scale, by Dvorak and Van Wagenen.

° ° Those earning scores in the upper 27 per cent of the distribution on the Dvorak-Van Wagenen Diagnostic Examination of Silent Reading Abilities. According to Holmes and Singer: "Comprehension denotes only a knowledge of, but power implies a working knowledge and use of information and concepts derived from reading." (16:212.)

***This was the highest coefficient of correlation reported between any two of the fifty-four factors involved in this analysis. Holmes and Singer conclude: "The most valid predictor of power of reading for the powerful group is auding ..." (16:220). (The authors use the term "auding" in the same sense that I use the term "listening.")

†††Those having scores on the lower 27 per cent of the distribution on the Diagnostic Examination of Silent Reading Abilities, Rate of Comprehension Scale, by Dvorak and Van Wagenen.

There are a number of excellent summaries of this research. No useful purpose would be served by still another one. I shall, therefore, confine myself to a few brief comments on these reviews.

Excellent reviews of the literature are to be found in the introductions to doctoral theses by Carver in 1935,[18] Krawiec in 1936,[19] and Hampleman in 1958.[20]

Day and Beach made a very fine analysis of thirty-four studies.[21] They report that half the studies favored written instruction and half favored oral instruction. Explanations for the seeming conflict may be found in eleven generalizations:

1. A combination of visual and auditory presentation of material leads to more efficient comprehension than either an auditory or a visual presentation of materials.

2. Meaningful, familiar material is more efficiently presented aurally; meaningless, unfamiliar material is more efficiently presented visually.

3. The greater the intelligence of the receiver, the greater the relative advantage of a visual presentation.

4. The greater the reading ability of the receiver, the relatively more effective a visual presentation.

5. The relative efficiency of a visual presentation increases with age. At the age of six visual presentation is less effective than aural presentation. At the age of sixteen a visual presentation may be more effective than an aural presentation.

6. Unusually difficult material is more effectively received with a visual presentation; particularly easy material is better understood with an auditory presentation. The relative effectiveness of the visual presentation increases with increasing difficulty of the material.

7. When comprehension is tested by an immediate recall of the material, a visual presentation is favored. If a test of comprehension is made after a considerable delay, an auditory presentation is favored.

8. The relative efficiency of a visual presentation

diminishes as the interval of delayed recall increases.

9. One of the most significant advantages of a visual presentation is the relatively greater referability, or opportunity for reviewing the material, that it affords. The less the referability afforded by a visual presentation system, the less its advantage over an auditory presentation.

10. Material that is organized and related--such as prose or factual information--is better understood with an auditory presentation; material that is comparatively discrete and unrelated--such as a code--is more effectively received with a visual presentation.

11. The comprehension of material can be tested either by the ease with which material is learned or by the amount that is retained after a period of time. As a rule, measures of learning tend to favor a visual presentation, while measures of retention are higher after an auditory presentation.

A more technical treatment of experimental comparisons of vision and audition is found in Cheatham.[22] He suggests:

> Studies should be made in which vision and audition are compared directly. Variations should be made along comparable dimensions for the two senses, at the visibility-audibility and legibility-intelligibility levels of discrimination, using the same criterion of response for both sense modalities. A suggested criterion would be the efficiency of response in a motor task which would allow a moment-to-moment measure such as time-on-target. Such a measure would be sensitive enough to reveal small differences in efficiency as a function of sense modality and the dimensions of stimulation.

The latest review was made in 1959 by Witty and Sizemore.[23] They concluded that differences in efficiency in learning depend not so much on the particular type of presentation as on a large number of other factors.

Certainly the research on the relative learning value of auditory and visual presentation reveals sharply conflicting findings. This disagreement is not easily resolved, but it can be explained on the basis of the differences in learning materials presented, the diverse characteristics of the populations used as subjects, and the varying means of testing employed.

We have here a persuasive illustration of the desirability and necessity of coordination of research. The tremendous amount of time and effort spent on this research could have yielded more worthwhile results if the researchers had not worked in a completely individual fashion but had made some effort to coordinate the studies.

The effective planning of reading instruction is made impossible when the interrelationships between reading and listening are ignored. When all who are concerned with the teaching of reading take into account the importance of the role of listening in reading instruction by using the findings of the research discussed in this article, reading instruction will almost certainly be more advantageous to the learner.

Notes

Abbreviated references, such as 6, refer to the entry number in Sam Duker's Listening Bibliography 2nd Ed. (Scarecrow, 1968) where the full citation may be found.

1. Sam Duker. Listening Bibliography. Metuchen, N. J.: Scarecrow Press, 1968.

2. H. Alan Robinson (editor). "Reading and the Language Arts." Supplementary Educational Monographs, No. 93. Chicago: University of Chicago Press, 1963.

3. Nila Banton Smith. Reading Instruction for Today's Children. Englewood Cliffs, New Jersey: Prentice-Hall, 1963.

4. Emerald V. Dechant. Improving the Teaching of Reading. Englewood Cliffs, New Jersey: Prentice-Hall, 1964.

5. Reading and Language in the Elementary School. Gary, Indiana: Gary Public Schools, 1962.

6. Thomas Wood Smith, 1107.

7. Hilda Taba. Curriculum Development. New York: Harcourt, Brace and World, 1962. p. 125.

8. Hubert C. Armstrong, 36.

9. Walter B. Barbe and Jack A. Carr, 61.

10. Edna L. Furness, 448.

11. Jason C. Owen, 925.

12. Jennye F. Schultz, 1056.

13. George Spache, 1116.

14. Frances O. Triggs, 1196.

15. Isabella H. Toussaint, 1188.

16. Jack A. Holmes and Harry Singer, 580.

17. Donald Spearritt, 1117.

18. Merton E. Carver, 191.

19. Theophile Krawiec, 681.

20. Richard S. Hampleman, 510.

21. Willard F. Day and Barbara R. Beach, 275.

22. Paul G. Cheatham, 204.

23. Paul A. Witty and Robert A. Sizemore, 1302.

Reading and Listening: New Research Findings

Thomas G. Devine

That reading and listening are related has long seemed apparent. The nature and extent of the relationship have been explored on both the theoretical and the research levels for at least two decades. Investigators regularly note that both kinds of behavior are related in that (a) both are concerned with the intake half of the communications process, (b) each seems to be a complex of related skills components, (c) the same higher mental processes seem to underlie both, (d) high correlations exist between test scores in reading and listening, and (e) the teaching of one seems to affect the other. As the literature on reading and listening has grown, certain assumptions have become commonly accepted. The need for researchers to test basic assumptions and to relate them to some general research theory has become increasingly obvious.

It is the purpose of this paper to reexamine two widely held assumptions about reading and listening in the light of recent research studies. Both seem basic to an evolving general theory of listening and of language and thinking. Yet neither is supported by recent studies.

First is the belief that instruction in listening (or reading) affects pupil competence in reading (or listening).[1] The theoretical basis for this assumption has seemed obvious to many investigators: reading and listening are both reflections, at the language or applied level, of the same higher mental processes. "Recognizing a writer's main ideas" and "recognizing a speaker's main ideas" are closely related to a postulated higher mental process, "recognizing main ideas in discourse." It has been implied in the literature that a teacher who develops in pupils the listening skill, "distinguishing between a speaker's opinion and factual statements," is also developing the related reading skill, "distinguishing between a writer's opinion and factual statements," because both skills seem to reflect, at the language level, the same postulated higher mental process, "distinguishing between fact and opinion."[2]

Recent research does not support the assumption. Lewis[3] provided weekly instructional units in listening to 85 college freshmen for nine weeks, compared their pre- and post-experiment scores on a reading test with those of 82 students in a matched control group which received no listening instruction, and found that the experimental treatment did not significantly affect reading scores. Hollingsworth[4] used two commercially-developed listening programs in a study involving 298 eighth grade pupils. After ten weeks of instruction neither of the experimental groups following the two listening programs scored significantly higher on a standardized reading test than a matched control group. Reeves[5] gave thirty tape-recorded listening lessons to 228 fourth-grade pupils in a fifteen-week study, compared their pre- and post-treatment reading test scores with those of a matched group of 216 pupils, found no significant differences between mean gain in reading scores. Skiffington[6] provided twenty-six taped auding exercises, for nine weeks, to a group of eighth-grade pupils, compared its reading test scores with that of a matched control group and discovered that, while scores in paragraph comprehension and alphabetizing were significantly higher for pupils who received the lessons, reading scores in rate, rate-comprehension, directed reading, word meaning, sentence meaning, and use of index were not. With the exception of Skiffington who found significant differences in <u>total</u> reading achievement (due to the weighting of paragraph comprehension and alphabetizing), the investigations cited found no evidence that the teaching of listening affects reading competence.

This research evidence does not invalidate the assumption that listening (or reading) instruction affects competence in reading (or listening). None of these studies was designed to test the hypothesis provided by Devine.[7] It is still not known whether instruction in <u>specific</u> listening skills (e.g., listening for organizational patterns, listening to recognize inferences, listening to recognize a speaker's bias) affects the development of <u>related</u> reading skills (e.g., reading for organizational patterns, reading to recognize inferences, reading to recognize a writer's bias). These studies do make clear, however, that (a) it is difficult, if not impossible, to suggest that teachers teach general listening (or reading) to help pupils become better readers (or listeners), and (b) research is needed to discover the effect of instruction in specific listening (or reading) skills upon reading (or listening) achievement.

The second basic assumption about reading and listening to be reexamined in the light of recent research is that listening and reading test scores correlate highly. Reported coefficients of correlation have always been positive and high. For example, Ross[8] reported a coefficient of .74; Brown[9] found coefficients of .82, .76, and .77 at various grade levels; Duker[10] reported an average coefficient of .57. These coefficients have been obtained by correlating scores from standardized tests of reading and listening.

However, recent studies have raised serious questions about the listening tests used to establish correlations. Anderson and Baldauf[11] analyzed the Sequential Tests of Listening Comprehension Test (Form 4), and concluded that heavy loadings in verbal comprehension suggested that achievement on the test may be a matter of verbal comprehension and not listening as a distinct ability. Kelly[12] studied both the STEP Listening Comprehension Test and the Brown-Carlsen Listening Comprehension Test, and concluded that the construct validity of each was questionable because neither test correlated significantly higher with the other than with reading and intelligence tests. It may be that much of the existing statistical evidence commonly accepted in studies of the reading-listening relationship is invalid. If the two most widely used listening tests in research are measuring something other than listening, coefficients of correlation between reading and listening need to be reinterpreted.

What is needed is not simply more research, but more research designed to test some general theory of language and thinking. Reading and listening, speaking and writing, are related to each other, and to thinking. At the moment no general theory governing the interrelationships is commonly held, and few are advanced in the literature. Researchers in the language arts need to emulate researchers in the physical sciences and realize that progress comes more rapidly when each independent study contributes to a testing out of a general theory than when each rests uncritically upon a variety of often untested assumptions and has no relation to a general theory.

Notes

Abbreviated references refer to the entry number in Sam Duker's Listening Bibliography 2nd Ed. (Scarecrow, 1968) where the full citation may be found.

1. Sam Duker, 325.

2. Thomas G. Devine, 287.

3. Robert F. Lewis, Jr., 725.

4. Paul M. Hollingsworth, 577.

5. Harriet R. Reeves, 993.

6. James S. Skiffington, 1091.

7. Thomas G. Devine, 287.

8. Ramon Ross, 1021

9. Charles T. Brown, 129.

10. Sam Duker, 325.

11. Harold M. Anderson and Frank J. Baldauf, 51.

12. Charles M. Kelly, 655.

The Relationship Between Achievement and Verbal Communication of Secondary School Children

Melvin Mart

The literature will be reviewed in accordance with the theoretical framework of the present investigation: i.e., those studies concerned with the interrelationships of the communication modalities will be discussed separately under each of the categories.

Receptive Modalities

It has been stated that most of us do our learning primarily through listening and reading, which are similar and related skills.[1] The relationship has been shown to be quite high even when intelligence is held constant, indicating that reading and listening comprehension are related in some way other than through general intelligence.[2] Young,[3] working with 4th, 5th and 6th graders, reported that no children were found to be in the highest quarter in one of these phases of language comprehension and in the lowest quarter in the other. He concluded that, in general, children who do poorly in comprehending through reading do poorly in comprehending through hearing.

Henneman[4] likewise has questioned the general superiority of either mode, but has said that if any superiority in comprehension exists, it varies as a function of the tools and learner, of the medium or context differentials, or of acquired skills. The receptive modalities were regarded as both alike and different; alike in their assimilative character which includes understanding and interpreting symbols, and in their development of certain skills and attitudes; different in that the listener has but one opportunity to comprehend whereas the reader may reread that which he does not understand.[5] In addition, it has been stated that listening is usually a group activity unlike reading which is usually an individualized one, and that listening demands adjustment to the pace of the speaker whereas in reading the only adjustment is to the pace desired by the reader.[6] Factors common to reading and listening comprehension were listed by Dow[7] as follows: meaning, motivation, organization (needed in the expressive skills as well), purposes, retention and recall, vocabulary, and tone or intent. Toussaint,[8] in her classified summary of listening, reported a study of 4th and 6th graders in which listening comprehension was reported to be superior to reading comprehension.

Coefficients of correlation have been reported in several experiments.[9] They range in size from .51 to .78, but are not directly comparable to the results of the present 7th grade sample because of the wide range of grade levels represented, i.e., from third grade to college freshman.

Considerable interest in the problem of transfer of training across modalities has been evidenced and conflicting evidence presented. The results of Weissman and Crockett's[10] study indicated that positive transfer does occur from auditory training to visual discrimination though the mediating processes are not clear. One investigator, using 4th, 5th, and 6th graders, obtained results which show the transfer from listening training to reading to be of a temporary nature,[11] but results in a later study were different, and he indicated that reading improves when children are given training in listening.[12] Lewis stated, however, that the reverse is not the case; i.e., listening does not improve when only reading is taught. Positive transfer to reading as a result of listening training was explained in terms of auditory familiarity which leads to lower visual thresholds,[13] but this rationale was contradicted by Postman and Rosenzweig[14] who suggested there is more transfer from visual training to auditory discrimination than conversely. They explained transfer in terms of the probable mediating mechanism: that is, subjects tend to repeat the visual stimulus during training subvocally which mediates the transfer to auditory discrimination; but, on the other hand, auditory training does not produce a subvisualization of items which facilitates transfer to visual discrimination.

Differences have been reported between reading and listening abilities in terms of difficulty of the material presented. Artley[15] found that reading comprehension becomes superior to hearing comprehension as the difficulty level of the material increases, and this agrees with Goldstein's[16] conclusions reported 10 years before. The latter investigator implied that listening may be more advantageous for comprehension of easy material whereas for difficult material, it does not matter which mode is chosen.

There seemed to be general agreement concerning the relative effectiveness of the receptive modalities. Judd[17] traced the rate of silent reading and found a range of 10 words per minute in grade 1, 130 in grade 4, and 250 in grade 7. Russell[18] established the 7th grade as the point where silent reading by pupils catches up in effectiveness with the teacher's oral presentation, and this was confirmed by Furness[19] who stated that up to and including grade 5 children learn more from having things read to them, the relative effectiveness is equal in grade 7, and reading is more effective after the 9th grade. Lewis[20] concluded that improvement in listening stabilizes about the end of the 6th grade as children achieve a fair degree of proficiency in reading.

Intelligence plays a role in the differences between receptive abilities, and studies have shown agreement as to its effect. The difference in favor of listening comprehension has been found to be greater for the less intelligent groups, and the greater difference in favor of listening comprehension of easy than of hard material has tended to be more marked for the less intelligent group.[21] Within each mode the more intelligent groups score relatively higher on the difficult than on the easy passages; the reverse holds true for the less intelligent groups. Henneman[22] confirmed that brighter students tend to be better readers than listeners, and Larsen and Feder[23] found superiority in reading comprehension over listening comprehension quite marked for those high in scholastic aptitude, while those low in scholastic aptitude comprehend almost as well by listening as by reading.

Informal Modalities

Most investigators have considered the informal symbolic processes of listening and speaking to be mutually interdependent. For example, Nichols and Lewis considered effective listening and effective speaking to be inseparable, and the best classroom speakers were thought to be those who most successfully improved their speech by listening to their classmates.[24] Poor enunciation by speakers was believed to decrease the amount of information listeners acquire from a talk, and a well organized oral discourse to produce more effective listening.[25] Successful oral communication was thought to be as much a function of the skill of the listener as that of the speaker.[26] Bird also believed that listening skills must be taught along with speaking skills if the total process of human communication is to be improved. The dependence of speaking skill development on hearing, which reveals the spoken word to the brain, was noted by two investigators.[27]

The importance and interrelationship of the informal modalities have been repeatedly stressed. Buys and Fishback estimated that 85% of all human communication and 90% of all human learning take place via the medium of speaking-listening. These investigators also regarded thinking as the process of one speaking with himself and hence "it is proper to say that a child learns to think only while and after he has been taught to speak."[28] The authors supported the idea that skill in listening can be taught, and that listening is to the receiver what thinking is to the sender; hence, listening is thinking.[29] Because of the paucity of reliable evidence concerning the relationship between listening and speaking ability, Stark[30] studied specifically the relationship between listening comprehension and two aspects of speech competency. He concluded that there is a positive correlation between listening comprehension and both aspects of speech competency, but a significantly greater correlation exists between listening and communicative speech competency (content, organization, sentence structure, vocabulary, usage, and fluency) than between listening and vocal speech competency (volume, pitch, quality, rate, stress, phrasing, and diction). Stark found intelligence to be substantially related to listening ability and communicative speech competency and only slightly related to vocal competency. In terms of self-perceptions, it was reported that people tend to think better of themselves as listeners than as speakers, and also that they are less able to discriminate between good and poor ability in listening than in speaking.[31]

Summary

It was the purpose of this study to determine and to compare the degree of relationship among the several symbolic processes, and then to relate academic achievement, including English, social studies, mathematics, and science to these symbolic processes which were classified either as receptive (listening and reading) and expressive (speaking and writing), or informal (listening and speaking) and formal (reading and writing). Both specific and composite scholastic achievement averages were related to each of the receptive and expressive, or informal and formal communication modalities.

Previous studies concluded that the codified communication modalities: (1) reading, (2) listening, (3) writing, and (4) speaking were intimately related, and that the basic relationships should be stressed in education. There seemed, however, to be a lack of systematic research focusing on the type and degree of the interrelatedness of the symbolic processes, or research relating these relationships to academic achievement.

Two hypotheses were tested in terms of the two problems of the study. First, it was hypothesized that though there is a positive relation among listening, speaking, reading, and writing, the magnitudes and patterns of relationship vary. The hypothesis was as follows: A stronger relationship will exist between any two language modalities if these two modalities are similar in terms of either informal or formal or receptive or expressive characteristics, and a less strong relationship will exist if any two modalities are not so related. Second, it was hypothesized that composite scholastic achievement will have the strongest relationship to reading, the weakest relationship to speaking, and intermediate relationships to both writing and listening.

The N was 109 7th grade students in a school district in Suffolk County, New York. The reading, listening, and writing tests were administered in a uniform order in a group situation while the speaking tests were individually administered. School records were used to obtain intelligence, socioeconomic status, age, sex, and academic achievement data. Final grades for the current school year constituted the measure of scholastic attainment for the investigation.

A 26 variable matrix of Pearson product-moment intercorrelations was computed. The nine primary variables were the four communication modalities tests, the four separate scholastic achievement indices, and their composite. Supplementary analyses were directed toward identifying other factors that may relate to or influence communication and achievement patterns: such factors, for example, as intelligence, socioeconomic status, age, and sex.

All hypothesized strengths of interrelationship among the communication modalities were in the predicted direction, but only the correlations of the receptive processes were significantly higher than those of the two nonsimilar combinations. The null hypothesis was rejected also for the receptive vs. expressive, and receptive vs. informal classifications. For the second hypothesis of this study, results again were in the predicted direction, and though the correlation of writing with composite scholastic achievement was higher than that of reading, the difference was not significant.

There would appear to be a need for schools to reflect the interrelationships of the language elements in terms of a better balanced emphasis on all the verbal communication processes with particular reference to more extensive development of speech competency. Finally, this study suggests the importance of developing more objective and sensitive techniques for measuring interpersonal, verbal communication processes.

Notes

Abbreviated references refer to the entry number in Sam Duker's Listening Bibliography 2nd Ed. (Scarecrow, 1968) where the full citation may be found.

1. Thomas R. Lewis and Ralph G. Nichols, 728.

2. Harry Goldstein, 480.

3. William E. Young, 1320.

4. Richard H. Henneman, 556.

5. Maurice S. Lewis, 722.

6. Thomas R. Lewis and Ralph G. Nichols, 728.

7. Clyde W. Dow, 303.

8. Richard S. Hampleman, 510 cited in Isabella H. Toussaint, 1187, p. 129.

9. Oscar M. Haugh, 533, p. 498.
   Hubert C. Armstrong, 36.
   Robert P. Larsen and D. D. Feder, 693, p. 250.
   Thomas R. Lewis and Ralph G. Nichols, 728.
   Harry Goldstein, 480, p. 51.
   John Caffrey, 161.

10. Stuart L. Weissman and Walter H. Crockett. "Intersensory Transfer of Verbal Material." American Journal of Psychology 70:283-85, 1957.

11. Maurice S. Lewis, 721, p. 117.

12. Maurice S. Lewis, 722, p. 456.

13. D. W. Forrest. "Auditory Familiarity as a Determinant of Visual Threshold." American Journal of Psychology 70:634-36, 1957, p. 636.

14. Leo J. Postman and Mark R. Rosenzweig. 'Practices and Transfer in the Visual and Auditory Recognition of Verbal Stimuli." American Journal of Psychology 69:209-26, 1956.

15. A. S. Artley, 42.

16. Harry Goldstein, 480, p. 57.

17. C. H. Judd. "Reading: Its Nature and Development." Supplementary Educational Monographs, Vol. 2, No. 4, 1918, p. 145.

18. R. D. Russell, 1038 cited in William E. Young, 1320, p. 36.

19. Edna L. Furness, 450.

20. Maurice S. Lewis, 722.

21. Harry Goldstein, 480.

22. Richard H. Henneman, 556.

23. Robert P. Larsen and D. D. Feder, 693, p. 250.

24. Thomas R. Lewis and Ralph G. Nichols, 728.

25. Mildred A. Dawson, 270, p. 231.

26. Donald E. Bird, 80, p. 105.

27. Evelyn Stahlem and Victor Garwood. "Needs of Auditorily Handicapped Children." Education 80:480-83, 1960.

28. William E. Buys and Woodson W. Fishback, (Eds.) "Communication in the High School Curriculum. Speaking and Listening, Grades VII-XII." Subj. Field Service Bulletin D-1. Springfield, Ill.: The Illinois Curriculum Program, Office of the Superintendent of Public Instruction, 1961, p. 3.

29. Ibid., p. 6.

30. Joel Stark, 1125

31. Paul W. Gauger, 468.

Relationships Among Listening, Reading, Intelligence, and Scholastic Achievement

Charles T. Brown

An analysis of previous studies comparing reading, listening, intelligence, and achievement in school led to the following conclusions, which in turn suggested the hypotheses for this investigation:

1. Listening tests, in part, are measures of intelligence.
2. Listening and reading involve different skills. This conclusion has been based largely on the fact that listening and reading scores at the high school and college levels do not correlate highly.
3. The data concerning the relative importance of reading and listening to scholastic achievement are contradictory.

The hypotheses for this third study were as follows:

1. Listening and intelligence are highly correlated.
2. Listening and reading are highly correlated.
3. Listening is more closely related to intelligence than it is to reading.
4. Listening is more closely related to scholastic achievement than reading is.

Procedure

The listening scores obtained in the two previous studies, the California Test of Mental Maturity, the reading scores of the Stanford Achievement Test, and the battery median of the Stanford Test (with reading scores eliminated) provided the data for the same subjects as those in the first two of these three experiments. The steps in handling these data were as follows:

1. The adjustment on a correlation chart of all reading scores and all listening scores to a common mean. The

writer analyzed the chart for the line of best fit and calculated the correlation ratio.

2. The computation of intercorrelations among the variables. The statistical procedure for determining the interrelationships among the independent skills involved in listening, reading, and intelligence and the relationships of each to scholastic achievement was partial correlation. In this phase of the experiment the writer used only sixth grade scores, primarily because the sixth grade achievement tests had the largest number of subtests on which to establish a median.

The first analysis by partial correlation was a study of the relations of listening, reading, and intelligence. Listening and reading were correlated with intelligence held constant, listening and intelligence were correlated with reading held constant and reading and intelligence were correlated with listening held constant.

The second analysis was a study of the relation of the independent skills in listening, reading, and intelligence to scholastic achievement, as measured by scores on achievement tests. The writer computed all of the possible first- and second-order correlations--that is, examined each pair of variables (such as listening and achievement) with first one of the other variables (intelligence <u>or</u> reading) held constant and then with both of the other variables (intelligence <u>and</u> reading) held constant.

The third analysis was like the second except that the criterion for scholastic achievement was the average of the teachers' grades, including those in reading, for one year. The purpose was to see how the roles of listening, reading, and intelligence change, if at all, when teachers' grades rather than scores on an achievement test form the criterion.

Results

1. The first hypothesis, that listening and intelligence are highly correlated, was supported. The correlations between listening and intelligence scores were .76 in the fourth grade, .69 in the fifth, and .76 in the sixth. None of the differences among these correlations was significant.

2. The second hypothesis, that listening and reading scores are highly correlated, was supported. The correlations were .82 in the fourth grade, .76 in the fifth, and

.78 in the sixth. Differences among these three were not significant.

A further analysis of the six charts correlating listening and reading (separate charts for the Amish and the non-Amish students for each of the three grades) also confirmed the hypothesis. Although the means of the six groups differed, the patterns were identical in all six groups. In all instances most of the scores fell into the first and the third quadrants--i.e., the ones in which listening and reading are positively related. The distribution, however, appeared to be curvilinear, and a test of best fit, with values plotted on logarithmic and semilogarithmic paper, indeed showed the distribution to be an exponential curve in which listening values were the exponent. The standard error of estimate was 2.65, and the correlation ratio was .77.

Table 1

First-Order Partial Correlations of Listening, Reading, Intelligence Scores for Fifty-one Subjects in the Sixth Grade

Correlated Variables	Constant	Partial
Listening and reading	Intelligence	.45
Listening and intelligence	Reading	.39
Reading and intelligence	Listening	.56

Table 2

First-Order Partial Correlations of Listening, Reading, Intelligence Scores with Achievement Scores for Fifty-one Subjects in the Sixth Grade

Correlated Variables	Constant	Partial
Listening and achievement	Reading	.14
Reading and achievement	Listening	.57
Listening and achievement	Intelligence	.16
Intelligence and achievement	Listening	.61
Reading and achievement	Intelligence	.43
Intelligence and achievement	Reading	.48

Table 3

Second-Order Partial Correlations of Listening, Reading, and Intelligence Scores with Achievement Scores for Fifty-One Subjects in the Sixth Grade

Correlated Variables	Constants	Partial
Listening and achievement	Intelligence and reading	-.05
Reading and achievement	Intelligence and listening	.41
Intelligence and achievement	Listening and reading	.47

Table 4

First-Order Partial Correlations of Teachers' Grades with Listening, Reading, and Intelligence Scores for Fifty-One Subjects in the Sixth Grade

Correlated Variables	Constant	Partial
Listening and grades	Reading	.52
Reading and grades	Listening	.11
Listening and grades	Intelligence	.41
Intelligence and grades	Listening	.40
Reading and grades	Intelligence	.11
Intelligence and grades	Reading	.51

Table 5

Second-Order Partial Correlations of Teachers' Grades with Listening, Reading, and Intelligence Scores for Fifty-One Subjects in the Sixth Grade

Correlated Variables	Constants	Partial
Listening and grades	Intelligence and reading	.40
Reading and grades	Intelligence and listening	-.09
Intelligence and grades	Listening and reading	.40

3. The third hypothesis, that listening is more closely related to intelligence than to reading, was not supported. The differences among the correlation coefficients are not significant, and the tendency is contrary to the hypothesis (see Table 1).

4. The fourth hypothesis, that listening is more closely related than reading to scholastic achievement, was supported when the criterion for achievement was teachers grades (see Tables 4 and 5) but rejected when the criterion was scores on the achievement test (see Tables 2 and 3). Both of these findings, based upon the differences between the relevant correlation coefficients, are significant at the one per cent level.

Discussion and Conclusions

The four sets of findings provide the basis for some interesting speculation regarding the various interrelationships of a number of skills that are thought to be basic to elementary education. Here correlations between listening ability and intelligence are higher than they are for high school and college students. Whether this means that listening becomes more of a learned and less of a native ability with maturing or whether these findings are artifacts arising out of the nature of the tests cannot be determined. In fact, whether the high correlation of intelligence and listening is anything more than a product of invalid measuring devices has been challenged.

Similarly the finding of coefficients between listening and reading that are higher than those reported for high school and college students is subject to more than one interpretation. The decline in the correlation figure may be nothing more than an effect of school dropouts, which makes the range of ability smaller for older students than for those who are younger. On the other hand, the much greater stress upon reading than upon listening may cause an actual increase in the disparity between listening and reading skills as the individual advances in education. Data supporting the second explanation are not yet conclusive, but the concerted effort to teach good reading in the elementary school may be responsible for the curvilinear relation between listening and reading.

Finally, the findings that listening is significatly correlated with teachers' grades but not with scores on achievement tests whereas the situation is reversed for reading suggest two possible explanations. Either teachers and achievement tests rate two different complexes of abilities or the measuring devices themselves are of questionable validity. In other words, the achievement test may in fact be more of a test of reading than of "achievement," or again teachers' grades may reflect reactions to the courteous behavior that probably accompanies good listening as well as to achievement strictly and properly defined. A realistic hypothesis, assuming that the terms listening, reading, and achievement are acceptable at face value, is that listening is more important than reading to scholastic achievement when the criterion is teacher's grades but that reading is more important than listening to scholastic achievement when the criterion is the score on an achievement test.

On Listening

Paul McKee

Education, like most professions, does have "magic" words, and I suppose that today listening is one of them. At least the term is used frequently in educational circles, often with a good deal of vagueness, and no doubt some persons have the idea that any instructional program is bound to be a good one if it makes some use of listening.

You ask whether I think giving boys and girls experience in listening has much value in teaching them to read. Well--I doubt that it has, if the experience is nothing more than just listening in general to people talk or read. But if that experience is directed toward the teaching of certain understandings and skills, I think it can contribute quite a little to the child's growth in the power to read independently. Let me give you a few examples of what I think is profitable experience in listening.

When the young child enters the first grade, all his experience in making meaning of language has been in listening; he understands language only when it is a language of sounds, and a speaker's voice intonations as well as the words he uses help the child understand the talking he hears. In order to learn to read, the child must realize that his reading matter is "printed talk," just another way of saying what he has heard and understood many times before, and he needs to learn to transpose a printed line into the sounds he would hear if someone said that line to him. All this means that if the child is to understand what his reading matter is saying, he must develop the habit of thinking the required voice intonations as well as the names of the words when he looks at that print.

There is one type of experience in listening that can help a child do this. When you are reading aloud to your pupils before they have begun to learn to read, and you find in the dialogue of the story a short speech of one of the characters that could be easily misunderstood unless the correct voice intonations were used, stop your reading. Help your pupils recall what has happened so far in the story and, if necessary, decide how the character feels. Tell them that you are going to read the character's speech in three ways, and ask them to listen to decide which way shows best what the character means. Then read the speech in a monotone, using no stress or pauses to indicate meaning. Read it again, using the voice intonations needed to show what the character means. Read it a third time, using voice intonations that show a meaning not intended by the character. When you have done this, ask different pupils to tell which of the three readings shows best what the character means. In much the same way when you are reading a story aloud after your pupils have begun to learn to read, print on the board a character's short speech which you know they can read. Then ask different pupils to read the line aloud to show what the character means. I know nothing more useful than this type of listening experience in equipping boys and girls to "hear," as they read to themselves, the familiar spoken language which the print stands for. It will help them to avoid word-calling, to make meaning in their reading, and to build a sure basis for good oral reading.

A second type of experience in listening can help the first grade child get ready to use context and the beginning consonant sound of a word to figure out the pronunciation of strange words which he will meet in his reading. You can give him this experience by doing two things. First, to help your pupils understand that some of the words in a sentence can be used to help decide what another included word is, you can say, for example: "Listen while I read a sentence aloud. I'll leave out one word. As you listen, use what the other words mean to decide what word I left out. Here is the sentence: Tommy washed his face and hands with soap and hot ______. What word did I leave out?" Second, to give pupils practice in using both oral context and the beginning consonant sound of a word to decide what that word is, you can say, for example: "Listen while I read a sentence aloud. I'll leave out one word. That word begins with the same sound as slap, sled, and slow. As you listen, use that beginning sound and what the other words mean to decide what word I left out. Here is the sentence: Tommy couldn't keep his eyes open because he was so ______. What word did I leave out?"

At least two other types of experience in listening are profitable simply because the thinking that anybody must do in order to understand printed language is so similar to that needed in understanding spoken language. First, let me remind you that a good program in reading teaches boys and girls to read for certain specific purposes, such as reading to find out what the main idea of a selection is, reading to get all the details that a selection gives on a certain topic, reading to note particularly the sequence of events, and reading to draw a conclusion based on information given in a selection. There is now little doubt that practice in listening for these purposes improves pupils' ability to read for the same purposes. All you need to do to give pupils practice in this kind of listening is to read suitable short passages to them and ask them to listen for some one of the purposes I have mentioned.

Second, keep in mind the fact that a good intermediate grade reading program teaches pupils study skills and the skills that will help them overcome meaning difficulties they may meet in their reading. For instance, they should learn how to use the context to get the meaning of a strange word, how to decide in which of several possible senses a particular word is being used, how to interpret figures of speech, to visualize scenes and events, to think stress correctly, to decide whether a statement is important for a particular purpose, to distinguish between a statement of fact and a statement of opinion, to decide what the topic of a paragraph is, and what the main topics of a selection are. After you have used a definite lesson to explain what is meant by one or another of these skills and to illustrate its correct use, you will, of course, want to give practice in using the skill. Certainly much of that practice would need to make use of suitable reading matter. However, a child can get good practice in the skill by using it in listening as you read a suitable short passage aloud. I should expect such practice in listening to reinforce that given in reading and to improve the child's use of the skill in his reading.

It seems to me that giving children the right sort of experience in listening can contribute to the development of their power to read.

Slow-Learners and Listening

James J. Fenwick

The origins of this research can be traced to a strong conviction held by the author that slow-learners at the secondary school level are typically penalized in their efforts to learn by the use of teaching methodologies which emphasize reading as a requisite skill in the mastery of course content. Empirical evidence from the author's experience in the classroom suggested that many slow-learners, while possessing marked reading retardation when measured by standardized test scores, had developed compensatory abilities in aural-oral skills which enabled them to function on a cognitive level substantially higher than that normally indicated by scores from either achievement test batteries or individual measures of intelligence.

This study was premised on the hypothesized superiority of aural instruction over visual instruction for ninth grade, reading handicapped slow-learners. Accordingly, subjects, identified as ninth grade reading handicapped slow-learners, were randomly and proportionately assigned to four experimental groups and one control group in order to provide data to be used in testing the respective hypotheses. The experimental groups were composed of subjects receiving instruction in four different ways: (1) aural-carrel; (2) aural-group; (3) visual-carrel; and (4) visual-group. Every subject received a minimum of three identical treatments in each instructional situation using a thematic series of specially designed lessons with matching criterion variables.

Control subjects were tested on each of the criterion variables used with the experimental subjects <u>but</u> received no prior instruction in terms of individual lesson content. In this way it was possible to insure that subjects in the experimental groups were dependent upon the lesson materials and instructional modes for their learning. Substantial differences were found between the mean scores of experimental and control groups, significant at the .001 level.

Raw score data for all subjects were carefully analyzed using analysis of variance techniques corrected for unequal frequencies and disproportionality. The resulting $\underline{F}$ test values were found to be nonsignificant in every instance. Slow-learner subjects learned equally well in relation to both aural and visual instructional approaches.

Three sub-types of slow-learners, low-average, low, and those with reading handicaps only (as reflected by standardized verbal scores significantly lower than corresponding quantitative scores), performed equally well in each instructional situation. Moreover, no significant differences occurred between male and female subjects in relation to either the aural or visual mode.

Aural and visual instruction. It is interesting to observe that although no significant evidence was provided in the present study to sustain either the major or the minor hypotheses, the resultant raw score means tended in this direction in both instances. As the reader will recall, the aural mode was hypothesized as a superior instructional mode as contrasted to the visual approach. Subjects receiving aural instruction did earn higher mean scores than subjects receiving visual instruction. In like manner, the listening carrel was predicted to be the one most effective instructional approach of the four modes tested. Subjects receiving the aural-carrel treatment did have the highest raw score mean, even though statistically nonsignificant.

In evaluating possible reasons why the hypotheses, as originally formulated, were not sustained, it is instructive to consider several potential intervening factors. Specific skills are associated with effective listening just as they are with effective reading. Although, by definition, the subjects in this research were handicapped in the latter category, one might well ask the question "Does it necessarily follow that these same subjects might also be handicapped in terms of effective listening skills?" The answer may be "yes."

Empirically, it seems tenable to continue to defend an earlier premise (see above) that many slow-learner, reading handicapped students do have aural-oral skills which enable them to function on a cognitive level substantially higher than that normally indicated by scores from either achievement test batteries, or individual measures of intelligence, especially when these measures rely on well developed reading abilities. However, this does not mean that these aural-oral skills cannot be further sharpened in such a way that the true learning capacity of the student might be more nearly realized in terms of those situations depending primarily on instructional strategies involving the aural approach. This point is further supported by the fact that classroom emphases typically rely heavily upon developing reading skills, even for the slow-learner, at the expense of concentration upon the development of refined listening skills. At this point, the slow-learner, reading handicapped child suffers most.

This discussion leads directly to the possibility that additional training in how to listen effectively could pay real dividends for the slow-learner with reading handicaps since it would mean building upon his strongest capacities, rather than those which can be objectively demonstrated as constituting his "Achilles' heel." Therefore, it would be most interesting to replicate the present study with subjects who had received instruction in effective listening. The author suspects that if the research reported in this dissertation were replicated with this added condition, statistically significant learning differences might well result.

Developing Measures of Aptitude for Poor Readers

Thomas Dreiling

Beginning in 1963, the GATB[1] has been administered routinely to every new inmate at the Oklahoma State Penitentiary who could read and write. The test results were utilized by the classification committee for job selection and by the Oklahoma Division of Vocational Rehabilitation for vocational counseling.

A 1964 penitentiary report noted that the average formal grade completed by incoming inmates was the 8th grade. Those who had not achieved this level were handicapped by their slow rate of reading and writing. The illiterates were given the Revised Beta to afford some indication of their I.Q. level. For both groups, the illiterates and slow readers, test results were somewhat dubious and unreliable. Through a screening process, the illiterates' names were eliminated before GATB testing. It seemed quite obvious that a majority of the slow readers could not compete with the average reader and consequently were penalized by their handicaps on each timed test in which reading was required.

In view of the handicap of many of the incarcerated inmates, the obvious problem was to afford some means of assessing the aptitudes of the slow readers and illiterates who could not perform adequately on reading or writing tests. In order to utilize nonreading tests, it seemed desirable that such tests should parallel as closely as possible those subtests in the GATB that required reading ability.

The problem of this study was to combine a group of relatively simple nonreading tests that measured general and specific aptitudes which would be appropriate and adequate for assessing these measures for incarcerated inmates and for the administration and exploration of their factor structure.

The purpose of this study was to make preliminary exploration of the factor structure of these tests as a first step in the development of specifications for the tests in terms of factor structure and possibly leading to the reporting of factor scores useful in improving prediction of the slow reader and illiterate. The study was frankly exploratory and was designed to assist in generating hypotheses which might be tested in later studies.

An experimental study leading to the development of a non-reading version of the General Aptitude Test Battery was carried out using 150 male inmates at the Oklahoma State Penitentiary as subjects. Each subject had been administered the GATB within 90 days previous to the study.

The Ammons Full Range Picture Vocabulary Test, Form A; Part 6 of the Revised Beta Test; Coin Matching Test; Coin Series Test; and the Matrices Test were adminisered in order to ascertain and explore the possibility that these tests might serve as substitutes for reading tests currently in use in the GATB. The results were subjected to factor analysis utilizing the varimax multiple rotation technique.

The findings and conclusions obtained from this study were:

1. The Ammons Full Range Picture Vocabulary Test showed high factor loading on a factor interpreted as General Learning Ability which might serve as a substitute for reading requirement tests now in use in the GATB that measures factor G, Learning Ability.

2. The Ammons Full Range Picture Vocabulary Test showed high factor loadings on the same factor that showed a high loading for the V, Verbal factor of the GATB.

3. The Wechsler Adult Intelligence Scale Arithmetic subtest did not show a significant loading on the same factor as did N, the Numerical in GATB. Numerical showed a high loading on another factor. This observation seemed to sustain the notion that arithmetic reasoning and fundamentals of arithmetic were not measured by the same factor.

4. In the present study, the research Coin Matching Test in use by the United States Employment Service showed more promise for measuring numerical ability than did the research Matrices Test.

5. Part 6 of the Revised Beta Test and Aptitude Q, Clerical Ability both showed high factor loadings on the same factor. Because of the lack of alphabet items, the Revised Beta Part 6 seemed to represent more closely a nonreading test of the likes-opposites type that was generally thought of as measuring clerical aptitudes.

In summary, it appeared that certain nonreading tests in use today might well serve as substitutes for reading tests in the present form of the GATB, B-1002, and may tap similar or identical aptitudes. Such a nonreading version of the GATB would afford reliable measurement of vocational and occupational aptitudes for slow reading or illiterate individuals.

Note

1. General Aptitude Test Battery. GATB, B-1002. Grades 9-12 and adults, 1952-63. Available through Science Research Associates, Inc., Chicago, Ill.

Chapter III

Relationships: Listening and Other Psychometric Factors

The four articles in this chapter are concerned with relationships to listening which go beyond listening's relationship to reading which was discussed in the previous chapter.

Professor Milton W. Horowitz, the senior author of the first passage in this chapter, is a professor in the Department of Psychology at Queens College of the City University of New York and a member of the graduate faculty of that University. He has written extensively in many journals and has spent much time in the experimental investigation of many aspects of communication including listening. Briefly put, the question to which an answer was sought in this paper was whether the mode of acquisition, reading or listening of material, had an effect on the best mode of reproduction, writing or speaking. Readers should find this scholarly article of more than casual interest.

Dr. William B. Legge investigated the interrelationships of listening, intelligence and school achievement using children of the fourth, fifth, and six grades as subjects. The usual approach in studies of this kind has been to use correlation techniques but in his dissertation Dr. Legge used a different procedure: he compared the lowest quartile in each of the factors with the highest quartile. A strong likelihood exists that for actual teaching purposes such an approach is much more informative and predictive than the correlational approach. A number of statistically significant relationships were discovered and are reported in this interesting excerpt.

The next excerpt is from an article by Charles T. Brown, who is referred to in the introduction to the preceding chapter. The relationship between listening abilities and number of siblings is explored in this passage. Several studies have been done on this topic, which is understandable as, a priori, the opportunity for experience in listening would seem to be quite different in a large family than in a small one.

The final selection in this chapter by George H. Zimmerman poses an intensely interesting question: What is the relationship between the skill of listening to verbal material and the skill of listening to music? Mr. Zimmerman takes the position that the skills are similar. More and more evidence is coming to light in support of this belief. For example, Dr. Justyn L. Graham[1] reports, in his 1965 Colorado State College thesis, that listening scores on the Hollow Listening Test (which deals entirely with verbal material) showed a statistically significant improvement over the pre-test after a period of instruction in the skill of listening to music.

Note

Abbreviated references refer to the entry number in Sam Duker's Listening Bibliography 2nd Ed. (Scarecrow, 1968) where the full citation may be found.

1. Graham, 486.

Listening and Reading, Speaking and Writing: An Experimental Investigation of Differential Acquisition and Reproduction of Memory

Milton W. Horowitz and Alan Berkowitz

We deal in this research with two processes for the acquisition of a memory trace (listening and reading) and two processes for the reproduction of the trace (speaking and writing) and ask a straightforward question: Does one of the former processes favor acquisition and does one of the latter processes favor reproduction and, if so, in what ways?

Let us examine the latter two processes first. When Ss are given simple, open-ended cognitive tasks[1] such as "What does a good teacher mean to you?" or, "What does a good citizen mean to you?" and are asked to speak or write their minds until they have exhausted their information on the topic, a great many differences show up between the two modes of expression.

For example, spoken expression produces significantly more material both absolutely and per unit time, is more repetitive in words, produces more ideas, more subordinate ideas, more ancillary ideas, and exhibits many other differences as well. Further, the essential differences between spoken and written expression show up when time for thinking, time for speaking and writing, and amount of material are controlled. Indeed, even more facile modes of writing, e.g., typing and stenotyping, differ significantly from speaking along most of the same dimensions. The question arises whether similar cognitive differences will also manifest themselves in the free recall of a given amount of meaningful material, i.e., a closed-end cognitive task.

Reprinted with permission of author and publisher: Horowitz, M. W., & Berkowitz, A. "Listening and reading, speaking and writing: an experimental investigation of differential acquisition and reproduction of memory." Perceptual and Motor Skills, 1967, 24, 207-215.

The processes, listening and reading, have been given extensive, but not similar, experimental investigation. A great part of the work done with listening has dealt with the relationship to listening in terms of test results, their relationship to intelligence, and the degree to which listening can be taught in the same manner that reading comprehension or reading skills are taught.

Listening and reading represent, of course, the cognitive and perceptual counterparts of the two major sensory modalities, audition and vision. It has been estimated that 85% of our knowledge is derived from visual sources and, in light of this, it seems, other things being equal, that reading should maintain a distinct advantage over listening in the acquisition of cognitive material.

It is clear, certainly, that differences between these two pairs of modalities are important for both practical and theoretical reasons. For the authors, however, listening seemed to bear a similar relationship to reading that speaking did to writing: listening seemed, on a logical basis, to be freer from the stimulus, more prone to distort the material it conveyed; it seemed a "looser" modality, and, in general, without sounding too mystical, a more direct and less complicated process, more in tune with thought processes as they occur "naturally" than did reading. In short, speaking on the motor and reproduction side, and listening on the sensory and acquisition side, seem to be more naturally (less artificially) related to thought processes than do writing and reading.

What is the rationale for the use of a closed-end cognitive task in this experiment? First, and most important from the point of view of listening and reading, no controlled test between them seemed possible on any other basis. That is, the nature of the test dictated a finite, and fairly small, body of material that could be taken in a sitting, that is either listened to or read. For speaking and writing, the rationale is somewhat similar but more complicated. For one thing, neither the speaker nor the writer can ever be entirely sure that he knows what he means, or understands what he thinks he understands, or remembers what he thinks he remembers, until he has spoken it or written it. Hence, in this sense, one must speak or write before one can truly say that one "remembers."

Allied to this fact is an early (and perhaps primitive)

point of view that held that thinking was tied biologically to the larynx. From such a point of view the differences between spoken and written expression are no more than one would expect from a mode (speaking) that is tied directly to thought processes and another mode (writing) that is merely connected artifically in the fingers, wrist, and arm.

A more modest point of view, however, reminds us that speaking and writing are simply the channels through which thought is expressed. In channeling thought processes, they distort or otherwise mold the thought to their own peculiar manifestations, i.e., put their particular stamp on them. Clearly, there is no way to differentiate between these alternative views of cognitive process and mode of utterance when using open-ended tasks. Under these circumstances the differences could result from the underlying cognitive process (and its favored or natural mode of utterance) or the mode of utterance itself, channeling and distorting the same cognitive processes differently.

However, when closed-end cognitive tasks are used, the modes of expression are severely curtailed. There is less freedom for speaking to do other than directions and material dictate. That is, both modes are made more similar by the means of control. Any differences, therefore, could be attributable to a genuine and "natural" alliance between the mode of expression and the cognitive material.

Method

Materials and Ss

An ideal medium for examining these variables is a well studied passage used extensively in memory experiments, The War of the Ghosts. This closed-end cognitive task has several advantages. As above, it controls many of the conditions contributing to differences found previously between spoken and written expression and, thereby, allows thought processes to be examined more directly through their different manifestations in speaking and writing. It was, further, completely new material for our Ss and was short enough (332 tokens) to be easily read and listened to in one sitting, but too difficult and too long to be committed completely to memory.

Fifty-six students in elementary psychology were assigned to one mode of acquisition (listening to a tape recording of the story or reading it) and to one mode of expression (speaking or writing). Control was exerted only to the extent that the same number of Ss were subjected to each of the four conditions. Ss were seated comfortably at a table. For listening the following instructions were read:

> You will hear a passage entitled The War of the Ghosts on the tape recorder. I will play it for you twice. You should listen to it as carefully as you can, because you will be tested for accuracy of recall. Are there any questions?

After S had listened to the story the following instructions were given:

> Now I would like you to speak (write) what you have just heard. There will be no time limit so you should be as detailed as your memory permits. When you have spoken (written) all you can remember indicate this by saying 'I'm finished.' Are there any questions? Please begin.

For the readers the instructions were modified in the following manner:

> Before you is a story which you will be asked to read twice at your own rate of speed.

The time spent in listening and reading was controlled by determining by pre-test the average reading time used by S (2 min. 55 sec.). The tape recording of the material was then adjusted to produce the same average time exposure for the listeners. Previous research had shown that great variations in speaking rates could be used without distortion of the story and without the perception that the speaker was hurrying.

Otherwise, instructions were identical for all Ss. S heard or read the story twice and immediately afterward was asked to reproduce it. Spoken expression was tape recorded and both spoken and written results were typed and coded to prevent prior knowledge of conditions from influencing the scoring procedure.

Scoring

All reproductions were analyzed for number of types,

tokens, type/token ratios, and for cognitive units, i.e., ideas, subordinate ideas, ancillary ideas, and signals which had been used previously in other, similar research (Horowitz & Berkowitz, 1964; Horowitz & Newman, 1964)[2]. To get a different and more precise measurement of memory processes, however, the story was divided into 62 meaningful cognitive units. These were defined as the smallest organized, meaningful "bit" of information that conveyed a sense of action, or pointed to a person or thing, that could stand alone but was not necessarily a complete thought or sentence. For example, the beginning of the story was divided as follows:

> One night/two young men/from Egulac/went down to the river/to hunt seals/

Each coded reproduction, with the original as a model, was divided similarly into appropriate units. Thus, protocol WG 22 was scored:

> One night/two men/from Kalama/went out seal hunting/in their canoe/

Each reproduction was then scored for total cognitive units, for omissions, distortions, and additions. For a unit to be scored as a distortion the action represented, or the meaning of the unit, had to be changed. In the example above "two men" would not be a distortion even though the word "young" was omitted, nor would "two warriors" be scored as a distortion. "From Kalama" is a distortion since the original reads "from Egulac."

Additions, to the scorer, meant additions of actions, or meanings (such as "in their canoe" above) as well as signal material that was inserted. Signals that could be scored as linguistic introductions to units (e.g., "Wait. I just thought of something else.") were not included in this scoring. Communicative and organization signals were counted as part of the unit to which they belonged.

Finally, each unit was rated for "stylistic excellence" on a 90-mm. rating scale so that a total score representing omissions, distortions, and faithfulness to the original work was derived. A perfect score for a unit was 90, multiplied by 62 units, gave a total possible score of 5580.

Results

The statistical measure employed for all units was analysis of variance. Discussion of results, therefore, can conveniently be divided into differences found between mode of acquisition (listening or reading) and mode of reproduction (speaking or writing). Mode of reproduction is discussed first.

Table 1 gives F values for the significance of difference of form (types, tokens, and TTRs) in speaking and

Table 1

Mean Types, Tokens, Type/Token Ratios (TTR) for Spoken and Written Expression and the Significance of Differences Between Them

	Types	Tokens	TTR
Speaking	106	236	.45
Writing	108	208	.52
F	.32	3.44	19.27
p	N.S.	.07	.001

writing. Although differences between types were not significant, spoken expression produced a significantly larger body of material and a lower type/token ratio. Speaking produced a mean of 236 tokens whereas writing produced only 208 mean tokens. This difference is significant at approximately the .07 level. This difference agrees well with previous findings. Written expression produced a higher TTR (M = .52) than spoken expression (M = .45). The F value is 19.27 ($p < .001$) and indicates the greater diversity of expression of writing, or conversely, the greater tendency of speaking to be repetitive lexically. It is possible that some of this difference is a function of the fewer tokens produced in written expression. It is known, for example, that the TTRs tend to decrease as tokens increase. This is due to the greater repetition of smaller words (e.g., and, of, by, in, etc.) and, consequently, types fail to increase commensurately with the increase of tokens. It is clear, however, that the greater part of this result is a differential function of the modes themselves, since even with the greater numbers of tokens, spoken expression produced fewer types. Further, previous research with open-ended cognitive tasks has clearly shown this same tendency (with both time and tokens controlled) to be inherent in the mode itself.

The analysis of cognitive units (ideas, subordinate ideas, ancillary ideas, and signals) shows that spoken expression produces significantly more subordinate ideas (redundancy) ($F = 3.19$, $p = .08$) and signals. The subordinate idea analysis is an indication of repetitiveness, cognitively, and indicates that in <u>idea</u> production as well as in lexical production, spoken expression tends to be repetitively prolix and less diversified than written expression. There were no significant differences between these two modes in either ideas or ancillary ideas. However, written expression produced no signals and the mean for spoken expression was 4.22. About 70% of these were startle signals.

Finally, speakers produce significantly more additions to their memory of the story $M = 6.2$ as opposed to an M of 3.7 for the writers ($F = 7.31$, $p < .01$). However, the modes speaking and writing do not differ significantly in number of omissions, distortions, thought units, or total style score. However, two significant interactions deserve mention; speakers who read the story produced significantly more omissions, more additions, and fewer ideas than speakers who listened to the story.

Differences in the memory trace directly applicable to the two modes of acquisition are pronounced. *Ss* who listened to the story produced a larger corpus, more ideas, fewer omissions of important units, and a stylistically superior reproduction. In so doing, however, they also produced more distortions than *Ss* who read.

Table 2 indicates the F values and probability levels for the significance of differences between listeners and readers for types, tokens, and TTR. Listeners produced significantly more types (M for listeners = 109.3, M for readers = 99.8, $p < .08$), more tokens (M for listeners = 240.0, M for readers = 203.3, $p \cong < .02$), and had a significantly lower TTR (M for listeners = .46, M for readers = .50, $p \cong .05$).

Although there was no significant difference between the two modes of acquisition for signals (M for listeners = 3.43, for readers = 5.00) listeners did produce significantly more ideas (p .05) and total ideas (ideas + subordinate ideas + ancillary ideas) ($p < .07$). Subordinate ideas and

Table 2

Mean Types, Tokens, Type/Token Ratios (TTR) for Listeners and Readers and Significance of Differences Between Them

	Types	Tokens	TTR
Listening	109.3	240.0	.46
Reading	99.8	203.3	.50
F	3.14	5.69	4.34
p	.08	.02	.05

total units (all ideas plus signals) did not differ significantly.

Table 3 summarizes the data for the other cognitive analysis. Listeners produced fewer omissions and more distortions than did readers. Listeners had a far greater mean total style score than readers (2289 vs 1838) as well as a larger number of total units remembered (M for listeners = 40.8, for readers = 36.1, $p < .07$). There were no differences in number of additions.

Table 3

Mean Differences and Their Significance Level Between Listeners and Readers for Additions, Distortions, Omissions, Style, and Total Units

	Additions	Distortions	Omissions	Style	Total Units
Listening	4.6	8.1	25.3	2289	40.8
Reading	5.2	6.9	31.5	1838	36.1
F	0.36	4.41	5.78	7.36	3.45
p	N.S.	.05	.02	.01	.07

Discussion

It is clear that many differences exist between the two modes of reproduction (speaking and writing) and the two modes of acquisition (listening and reading). In general, these differences are both linguistic and cognitive and bear out the essential similarity of behavior (on the variables tested) of speaking and listening on the one hand, and reading and writing on the other. Since a closed-end task was used, many of the conditions that could account for differences previously discovered between speaking and writing were eliminated. That is, the need to fill in silent intervals; the need to elaborate already given material (prolificacy); the seriousness of the commitment; the correctness as well as the permanence of the record--all were eliminated by the conditions of the closed-end task. Since many of the differences previously found between speaking and writing were re-established in this study, it seems clear that these differences must be largely attributable to the nature of the thought process in alliance with the mode, rather than to the nature of the mode, itself. This in itself is an exciting fact. The differences that persist may be characterized as follows: Thought processes reproduced through spoken expression tend to be looser, wordier, more repetitive (both in words and in cognitive content), and tend to produce more additions than thought processes reproduced through written expression.

Many of the differences that characterize speaking and writing also characterize listening and reading, the two modes of acquisition. Listeners, whether reproducing by speaking or writing, are also looser, wordier, and more repetitive than readers. Further, listeners seem to be more accurate in terms of fewer omissions, although they were more prone to distort the material they reproduced than were readers. The greater accuracy of listeners is also attested by their significantly greater style score (faithfulness to the original) and greater number of units recalled.

Two interactions, mentioned only in passing in the results section, are also worth discussion. Speakers who read produced significantly more omissions, more additions, and fewer ideas. Speakers who listened to the story displayed a far more accurate memory than speakers who read it. This can be interpreted as either a facilitation of memory for speakers who listened or as an interference process for speakers who read. The latter possibility seems to fit better with the protocols of our Ss as well as E's bias. It seemed difficult for Ss who read the story to put it into appropriate words. The authors tend also to the conviction expressed above and bolstered by the data, that listening is, in the acquisition of memory, highly similar, both biologically and psychologically, to speaking in the reproduction of memory and reading is closely allied to writing. The latter two processes seem less natural, more artificial, more difficult, more stimulus bound, more inhibited and careful and circumspect and correct (in the sense of fewer distortions and additions) from nearly all points of view. Further research planned and in progress will elaborate and verify these differences.

Notes

1. An open-ended cognitive task is one in which the amount of material produced is a function of factors other than the material itself. That is, S can speak (write) as long as his free recall, his ingenuity in adding relevant or semi-relevant ideas, his skill in utterance, etc., hold out. Practically speaking, there is virtually no limit to the amount of material that could, conceivably, be produced. In contradistinction, a closed-end cognitive task is one in which the original amount of material learned is specifically defined and limited and, conceivably, could be learned and reproduced accurately and *in toto*, if S were given sufficient time or trials.

2. Horowitz, M. W., & Berkowitz, A. "Structural advantage of the mechanism of spoken expression as a factor in differences in spoken and written expression." *Perceptual and Motor Skills*, 19: 619-25, 1964, and Horowitz, M. W., & Newman, J. B. "Spoken and written expression: an experimental analysis". *Journal of Abnormal and Social Psychology*, 68: 640-47, 1964.

Listening, Intelligence, and School Achievement

William Bruce Legge

Definition of Terms

For the purpose of this study, listening was defined as hearing with meaning, or hearing plus interpretation or comprehension of spoken language. This writer acknowledges Caffrey's[1] use of the term auding to refer to the same idea, but also postulates the unnecessary stipulation of a new term for one which, in the writer's opinion, carries sufficient meaning for purposes of communication.

Those subjects classified high-intelligent and low-intelligent were those who ranked in the upper and lower twenty-five per cent of the population respectively in each of the fourth, fifth, and sixth grades included in the study as measured by the intelligence test appropriate for the specific grade levels.

High-achievers and low-achievers were those who ranked in the upper and lower twenty-five per cent of the population of the fourth, fifth, and sixth grade pupils included in the study as measured by the achievement test appropriate for the specific grade levels.

Over-achievers and under-achievers were those in the population who departed upward or downward from their mental ages by as much as one-half of one year on grade placement scores as determined by results of achievement testing.

Hypotheses to be Tested

The hypotheses to be tested in this study fell into four major areas. These hypotheses were stated in directional form.

In comparing listening abilities of children categorized by intelligence test scores, the directional hypothesis was:

1. High-intelligent fourth, fifth, and sixth grade pupils are significantly higher in listening ability than low-intelligent pupils in each of these three grades.

In comparing listening abilities of high-achievers and low-achievers, the directional hypothesis was:

2. High-achieving fourth, fifth, and sixth grade pupils are significantly higher in listening ability than low-achieving pupils in each of these three grades.

In comparing the listening abilities of over-achievers and under-achievers, the directional hypothesis was:

3. Over-achieving fourth, fifth, and sixth grade pupils are significantly higher in listening ability than under-achieving pupils in each of these three grades.

In comparing the listening abilities of girls and boys, the directional hypothesis was:

4. Fourth, fifth, and sixth grade girls are significantly higher in listening ability than boys in each of these three grades.

Methods and Procedures

Population Used in Study

The subjects comprising the population for the study came from all fourth, fifth, and sixth grades from three elementary schools in the Bloomington, Illinois public school system. The three schools were identified as being schools with very nearly the same socioeconomic pupil populations. Inasmuch as socioeconomic considerations are not a part of this study, choosing schools with similar populations was an attempt to control or to reduce the extent of this variable.

Instruments Used in Testing

The listening test of the Sequential Tests of Education Progress, form 4A, was used to test all subjects participating in the study. This test was designed to measure the ability of subjects to comprehend main ideas and to remember significant details, and to evaluate and apply the material presented. Materials for test items, of which there is a total of eighty, include directions and simple explanation, exposition, narration, argument and persuasion, and aesthetic material (both poetry and prose). The results of this test combine into a single score.

The Stanford Achievement Test was administered to the population participating in the study in October, 1965. Appropriate forms for the various grade levels were used. This test purports to measure the important knowledges, skills and understandings commonly accepted as desirable outcomes of the major branches of the elementary curriculum. At the fourth and fifth grade levels, sub-tests in Word Meaning, Paragraph Meaning, Spelling, Work-Study Skills, Language, Arithmetic Computation, Arithmetic Concepts, Arithmetic Applications, Social Studies, and Science are found. The sixth grade level contains the same sub-tests except for Work Study Skills.

The intelligence test used in this school system was the Pintner General Ability Test. The test designed for use in the intermediate grades contained eight subjects--Vocabulary, Number Sequence, Analogies, Opposites, Logical Selections, Arithmetic Reasoning, Classification, and a Best Answer test. The results of this test combine into a verbal quotient and a non-verbal quotient. Only verbal quotients were used in this study.

Methods of Collecting Data

The listening tests were administered to subjects in the eighteen groups during the two week period of October 25 through November 5, 1965. Every effort was made to make the testing situation as ideal as possible.

Results of achievement testing done in the school district during the week of October 18 through 22, 1965, were collected. These tests were administered by individual teachers in the various classrooms.

Intelligence tests were also administered on a group basis by teachers in the classrooms. Intelligence tests were administered to the fifth grades in October 1965. The fourth grades and sixth grades participating in the study were administered intelligence tests in October of 1964.

Classification of Subjects

High-intelligent and low-intelligent subjects at each level were determined on the basis of intelligence testing completed in the school system in October of 1964 and in October of 1965. The upper twenty-five per cent of the pupils at each of the three grade levels who had intelligence test data available constituted the high-intelligent group for each of the three grade levels. The lower twenty-five per cent of the pupils at each grade level who had intelligence test data available made up the low-intelligent group.

High-achievers and low-achievers were determined on the basis of scores on total achievement test results. The upper twenty-five per cent of the group at each grade level who had achievement test data available constituted the high-achieving group. The lower twenty-five per cent of each grade level on achievement test results were the low-achieving group.

Achievement test results and expected achievement test levels were used in determining over-achievers and under-achievers at each of the three grade levels. The manual containing directions for administering the achievement test contained expected achievement test levels for subjects in each of the fourth, fifth, and sixth grades on the basis of the subjects' placements on the Otis Quick-Scoring Mental Ability Test. As Otis scores were unavailable for the subjects in the study, a conversion of Otis scores to Pintner scores was made on the basis of the results of a study completed at the Bureau of Pupil Guidance in the Chicago Public Schools by Lund[2] and others. Expected achievement levels for subjects in each of the three grades were then established.

Over-achievers were those subjects who deviated upward by as much as one-half of one year on achievement grade placement from their expected level. Under-achievers were those who deviated downward by as much as one-half of one year on achievement grade placement from their expected intelligence level.

Testing differences in listening abilities of girls and boys was done because of many writers' views that girls score higher on language arts related tests than boys.

Results

Table 1

Comparisons of Listening Scores of the High-Intelligent and Low-Intelligent Fourth, Fifth, and Sixth Grade Subjects

	Listening test mean score	Standard error of the mean	*t* ratio
Fourth Grade--			
High-Intelligent Group (*N* = 28)	61.036	1.436	
Low-Intelligent Group (*N* = 28)	41.607	1.978	3.698*
Fifth Grade--			
High-Intelligent Group (*N* = 36)	68.861	.660	
Low-Intelligent Group (*N* = 36)	48.361	1.636	6.587*
Sixth Grade--			
High-Intelligent Group (*N* = 33)	69.424	.670	
Low-Intelligent Group (*N* = 33)	55.576	1.439	8.730*

*Significant at the .05 level

Table 2

Comparisons of Listening Scores of the High-Achieving and Low-Achieving Fourth, Fifth, and Sixth Grade Subjects

	Listening test mean score	Standard error of the mean	_t_ ratio
Fourth Grade--			
High-Achieving Group (_N_ = 36)	62.610	1.229	
Low-Achieving Group (_N_ = 36)	40.306	1.885	9.873*
Fifth Grade--			
High-Achieving Group (_N_ = 36)	68.770	.667	
Low-Achieving Group (_N_ = 36)	45.722	1.604	13.269*
Sixth Grade--			
High-Achieving Group (_N_ = 39)	69.692	.590	
Low-Achieving Group (_N_ = 39)	52.231	1.411	11.420*

*Significant at the .05 level

Table 3

Comparisons of Listening Scores of the Over-Achieving and Under-Achieving Fourth, Fifth, and Sixth Grade Subjects

	Listening test mean score	Standard error of the mean	*t* ratio
Fourth Grade- -			
Over-Achieving Group (*N* = 49)	56.612	.880	
Under-Achieving Group (*N* = 5)	45.800	7.632	1.325
Fifth Grade- -			
Over-Achieving Group (*N* = 57)	63.842	1.044	
Under-Achieving Group (*N* = 27)	57.926	2.075	2.237*
Sixth Grade- -			
Over-Achieving Group (*N* = 43)	65.488	1.096	
Under-Achieving Group (*N* = 38)	60.974	1.685	2.067*

*Significant at the .05 level

Table 4

Comparisons of Listening Scores of Girls and Boys in the Fourth, Fifth, and Sixth Grades

	Listening test mean score	Standard error of the mean	*t* ratio
Fourth Grade- -			
Girls (*N* = 70)	53.786	1.578	1.462*
Boys (*N* = 76)	50.853	1.239	
Fifth Grade- -			
Girls (*N* = 72)	57.625	1.201	1.534*
Boys (*N* = 73)	60.425	1.374	
Sixth Grade- -			
Girls (*N* = 74)	63.338	1.098	.416*
Boys (*N* = 80)	62.725	.932	

*Not significant at the .05 level

In summary, the following findings resulted from the tests of the hypotheses formulated for this study:

1. Two groups each from the fourth, fifth, and sixth grade populations used in this study were categorized on the basis of intelligence test scores and compared on listening abilities as measured by a standardized listening test. The results showed that those subjects in the study who were higher in intelligence were also significantly higher in listening ability.

2. For achievement and listening ability, again two groups each from the fourth, fifth, and sixth grade populations used in this study were categorized on the basis of

standardized achievement test scores and compared on listening abilities as measured by a standardized listening test. The results showed that those subjects in the study who were higher in achievement test scores were also significantly higher in listening ability.

3. In regard to the listening abilities of over-achieving and under-achieving subjects at each of the three grade levels considered, over-achievers and under-achievers were determined according to the criterion previously described. The listening abilities of over-achievers and under-achievers at each of the three grade levels were then compared. Over-achievers had significantly higher listening abilities than under-achievers at the fifth and sixth grade levels, but not at the fourth grade level.

4. As regards sex differences and listening ability, girls were not found to have significantly higher listening skill than boys, as measured by the standardized listening test used in this study.

Conclusions

1. The first hypothesis, stating that high-intelligent pupils in grades four, five, and six are higher in listening ability than low-intelligent pupils in these grades, was accepted. These findings were consistent with the results of correlational studies by Hollow,[3] Ross,[4] Bonner,[5] Rose,[6] Kramar,[7] and Heilman[8] which revealed significant positive relationships between listening ability and intelligence. However, these findings are somewhat different from previous studies because this study was concerned with testing differences between groups of pupils, not relationships.

The results of testing the hypothesis in the major area of intelligence and listening ability show that the *t* ratios increase and that the standard error of the mean decreases as the grade level increases. This finding suggests that those lower in listening ability may be slower in developing mental abilities than those who are higher in listening ability. The data also suggest that as children proceed through the intermediate grades differences between high-intelligent and low-intelligent pupils become more distinct insofar as listening abilities are concerned. Educators are well aware that the mental capabilities of children are not fully developed by the end of the intermediate grades. Nowhere in the literature surveyed was this increasing difference in the intelligence levels and listening abilities noted.

Intelligence is nurtured and influenced by verbal stimulation, so the findings indicate that those who are poorer listeners may not actually "receive" as much of the verbal sensory stimuli they are subjected to as may the better listeners. Therefore, the intelligence levels of the lower groups of listeners may not develop at the same rate as in the case of those higher in listening ability.

2. The hypothesis stating that high-achieving pupils in grades four, five, and six are higher in listening ability than low-achieving pupils in these grades, was accepted. These findings were consistent with the correlational studies cited previously which were completed by Hollow,[9] Ross,[10] Still,[11] Steeg,[12] and Blewett,[13] which reported significant positive relationships between listening ability and achievement. These findings were similar to the studies by Brown[14] and Kielsmeier,[15] though they were completed at levels other than the intermediate grade level of the elementary school.

The highly substantial differences in the listening abilities of the high-achieving and low-achieving groups indicate that the ability to listen well has definite and positive implications for scholastic achievement. Again, the trend of the difference is upward as the grade levels increase. It may be that some children acquire skill in listening and others do not. The fact that nothing is done to improve the listening abilities of this latter group may result in a widening achievement gap between them and the better listeners as they both progress in school.

It should be noted that differences in the listening abilities of high-achieving and low-achieving subjects are a good deal larger than the differences in the listening abilities of high-intelligent and low-intelligent subjects in the fourth, fifth, and sixth grades. This leads to the conclusion that in this study listening ability is more highly related to scholastic achievement than it is to intelligence. This finding is inconsistent with the results of Hollow's[16] study which indicated that correlations found between intelligence and listen-skills were of the same general order as were correlations between selected school subjects and listening ability.

3. The hypothesis stating that over-achieving pupils at each of the fourth, fifth, and sixth grade levels are higher in listening ability than under-achieving pupils at each of

these grade levels, was rejected at the fourth grade level and accepted at the fifth and sixth grade levels. This result at the fourth grade level may have been due to the small number of under-achievers at this level, which made for a large standard error of the mean. When this is the case, a substantial mean difference between the two groups is required in order to obtain the level of significance set for testing. It can be seen by examining Table 3 that the mean difference between the two groups at this level is actually larger than at the other two levels, where significance was obtained. One may conclude that this result was due to the fact that the listening abilities of pupils in the fourth grade were not detrimentally affected yet. It may be that children are in fact conditioned to poorer listening habits as they grow older, particularly if they have little success in school or have no experiences with the improvement of listening skills as a goal. It may be that teachers do not give the same amount of attention to pupils whose achievement levels are in the lower ranges. A deterioration of listening skills for some children in the school situation may be indicated, particularly as they move further along in the grades.

There was no related literature concerned with the matter of over-achievement, under-achievement, and listening ability.

4. The hypothesis stating that girls in each of grades four, five, and six are significantly higher in listening abilities than fourth, fifth, and sixth grade boys, was rejected. The t ratios for each of the three hypotheses failed to reach the level required for significance. These findings were consistent with the results of the study by Bonner[17] and indicated in the study by Still.[18]

The hypotheses formulated for comparing the listening abilities of girls and boys were made directional because many writers hold that girls are superior to boys in language arts skills, of which listening, of course, is one.

It was interesting to note that the listening abilities of the subjects at each grade level were higher in terms of scores on the listening test as grade levels increased. It is widely held that as children's reading skills increase as they grow older, there is less dependence upon listening as a vehicle for learning. The data of this study suggest that this may not be the case. If there is as much verbal activity in classrooms as suggested by Wilt,[19] listening ability probably continues to be a significant factor in scholastic achievement at all grade levels.

Recommendations

The findings and conclusions of this study have resulted in the following recommendations concerning the matter of listening as an influential factor in a school achievement.

1. Both the literature cited previously and the results of this study indicate that listening skill is an influential factor in scholastic achievement. This knowledge, coupled with the results of research which indicate that listening skills can be improved in a variety of ways, suggests that more time be given in school to improving listening skills. It is recommended that these skills not be sought after in an incidental fashion, but rather through planned and sequential instructional experiences.

2. It is recommended that the teaching of good listening habits be begun as early as children begin school.

3. It is recommended that children with poor listening skills be given remedial teaching with a view toward improving these skills.

4. It is recommended that the listening skills of children be ascertained, either by standardized testing or in informal ways, as soon as possible as a prerequisite to improving these skills.

In addition to these recommendations, and partly as a result of them, the following suggestions for further research are made:

1. This study should be replicated both at lower levels and at higher levels to determine if listening skill is developed in a linear fashion, as indicated by this study.

2. How to make children better listeners should be studied further.

3. The matter of factors involved in socioeconomic differences and listening ability is suggested as an area for investigation.

4. Since this study indicates a higher relationship

between school achievement and listening ability than between intelligence and listening ability, it is suggested that a study of school achievement as related to listening ability be made with the variable of intelligence controlled, or held constant.

5. It is suggested that the relationship of listening ability and different subject areas of the school be investigated, as some areas may be more oriented toward auditory input and others more toward visual input.

6. It is recommended that dependence upon listening as opposed to dependence upon reading as vehicles for learning be investigated further.

Notes

Abbreviated references, such as 1, refer to the entry number in Sam Duker's Listening Bibliography 2nd Ed. (Scarecrow, 1968) where the full citation may be found.

1. Caffrey, 160.
2. Lund, Kenneth W. et al., "Equivalent of Intelligence Quotients of Five Group Intelligence Tests," (Chicago, Illinois: Bureau of Pupil Guidance, Chicago Public Schools), Technical Manual E-17 (no date given).
3. Hollow, 578.
4. Ross, 1021.
5. Bonner, 104.
6. Rose, 1018.
7. Kramar, 678.
8. Heilman, 547.
9. Hollow, 578.
10. Ross, 1021.
11. Still, 1136.

12. Steeg, 1128.

13. Blewett, 95.

14. Brown, 138.

15. Kielsmeier, 662.

16. Hollow, 578.

17. Bonner, 104.

18. Still, 1136.

19. Wilt, 138.

Listening Ability and Number and Position of Children

Charles T. Brown

The purpose of this experiment was to determine what relations, if any, exist between the child and his status within his own family. The two specific hypotheses were (1) that children who have older and younger brothers and sisters are better listeners than are either the oldest or the youngest in the family and (2) that children from small families are better listeners than those from large families. The reason for framing the first of these was the writer's belief that he had observed that the middle children develop the listener's role, and the reasons for choosing the second were both his suppositions and the inconclusive results in an earlier study. Children in small families, according to Hollow, made higher listening scores than those in large families, but the difference was not significant.[1]

Procedure

The data obtained in the first experiment in the present series, including responses to an item in which each child indicated the number of brothers and sisters older and younger than himself, formed the basis for the present study. The statistical procedure for examining the first hypothesis was a chi square test to determine whether the respective distributions of the best and the poorest listeners differed significantly from chance distributions. The statistical procedure for examing the second hypothesis was a *t* test applied to the average number of children in the families containing respectively the upper and the lower halves in listening ability. Amish and non-Amish groups were treated separately, and for the latter of these the listening scores of those with two or fewer brothers and sisters were compared with those with four or more.

Results

1. The hypothesis that middle children are more likely

to be the better listeners was not supported. First, of the forty-four best listeners, thirteen were the eldest in the family, twenty-three were middle children, and eight were the youngest. Tested by chi square against the chance distribution of 10, 24, and 10 (based upon the fact that the average number of brothers and sisters was 3.56), these figures fall far short of significance. Likewise, the eldest and the youngest did not differ significantly. Second, the distribution of the poorest listeners does not differ significantly from chance. Here the actual figures are that eight were the eldest, thirty-one were middle children, and five were the youngest, and the chance distribution, based on an average of 4.59 brothers and sisters, is 8, 28, and 8 for eldest, middle, and youngest respectively.

2. The second hypothesis, that the children of smaller families are better listeners than those of larger families, was supported only for the non-Amish. The mean difference of 0.87 between the number of brothers and sisters of students in the best and the poorest quartiles is significant by a one-tailed test at the five per cent level (t = 1.975). Among the Amish, the comparable mean difference of 0.74 by the one-tailed test is not significant at the five per cent level (t = 0.925).

A second method of evaluating the data confirms the preceding findings for the non-Amish group. (This method could not be applied to the Amish-Dutch families, for only four children had two or fewer brothers and sisters.) The difference between the mean score (61.26) of those with two or fewer brothers and sisters and the mean score (56.91) of those with four or more brothers and sisters by the one-tailed t test was statistically significant at the five per cent level (t = 1.719).

Discussion and Conclusions

Although the age of the child in relation to his brothers and sisters was not related to listening ability, the size of the family was significant for the non-Amish. The scores for the Amish children revealed the same tendency, but the differences were not significant statistically. Although this evidence concerning the possibility of a relationship between listening and family size is not yet conclusive, some speculation as to possible reasons would do no harm. One possibility is that the heightened noise and confusion in a large group leads to the development of a protective insulation or a non-listening attitude that the child transfers to the classroom. More precise information regarding the causes for relatively poor listening by children coming from large families could lead to the development of remedial procedures.

Note

Abbreviated references refer to the entry number in Sam Duker's Listening Bibliography 2nd Ed. (Scarecrow, 1968) where the full citation may be found.

1. Hollow, 578.

Listen!

George H. Zimmerman

An increasing number of articles appears in educational journals on the subject of listening as it pertains to the language arts curriculum and a child's mental growth. Growing alarm is expressed that teacher's tend to overlook the teaching of "listening." Administrators are concerned about children's inability to identify central ideas or follow a sequence of ideas in a given message.

Writers mention "listening to music" that is for appreciation only, but claim that listening to the spoken word requires a different kind of listening. We take exception to this point: Listening to music and listening to the spoken word require exactly the same mental processes.

Everyone has daily opportunity to listen to music; each listener has his individual response. Some tap their feet. Others grow inwardly excited. Some react by doing both, and in addition can identify the instruments, the style of the composition, and perhaps even name the composer and describe the structure of the music. Some people love to have music accompany their daily chores, and while each "hears" music, not all listen to what they hear.

Music is a time art. It presents no visual symbol, no objects to grasp, touch, or feel, no chart to guide the memory. Whatever we listen to we must immediately associate, compare, discern, evaluate, and retain for recall in either its exact or modified form. Listening is not relaxing. Hearing may be, but listening is not. It is an active process in which the mind is constantly alert to what is being presented. As musical ideas pass before us in succession, we must constantly reconstruct a mental composition. In addition, we transmit our feelings, we shape our thoughts by drawing upon our imaginations, our inner sense, and then even wax poetic before our fellow listeners. This is no passive process.

Music's motives, phrases, and tone colors will go by unnoticed unless the mind has been taught to "latch on" to the various qualities of sound as they pass in time. Unless we are able to recall, we are unable to listen, to discern and to reconstruct the formal aspects of a given composition. How often do we play a record, talk while the record is playing, then tell the class to listen for something that has gone by before we have guided the student to recognize what is being listened for.

We are all aware that we can think faster than a speaker talks, or than music is produced. As the music is being performed, here are some questions to think about. How is this music being produced? How are the basic elements of rhythm, melody, harmony, texture, tone color being put together? How and why does a given musical idea appeal to our emotions? How does it communicate to me? How does this music fill the very world in which we live?

The capacity to listen intelligently to music goes beyond musical experiences. In our listening we relate what we hear to our every day life experiences.

Let us go to the language arts area for analogy. It is said that a child gets no more out of reading the printed page than he can bring to that page through his own personal experiences. Some people say you have to be motivated. Motivation comes from within the individual, not from without. Stimulation is that outside force. A child looks at the letters in sequence which go to spell "f-a-r-m." He may be able to pronounce the letters individually and say the word correctly, "farm." However, unless he can bring some kind of mental image to the word, he does not really know what the word means. With the word "farm," he must be able to associate such things as barn, cattle, pigs, tractors, or silo. The greater the experience with "farm," the greater will be his individual appreciation for "farm." Total experience gives him the real meaning of the letters which together spell "farm." This may sound somewhat far-fetched, but it is also exactly what is required for all-encompassing musical listening. We must have rich experiences in our own individual backgrounds with which we can associate musical sounds and moods. We must have attended concerts, ballets, theater, and have had a host of other experiences to make us become more aware. One understands only in that degree to which he can individually relate. Therefore, listening is more than paying attention. It is three-way proposition: the composer, the performer, and the listener, each with his personal experiences.

A child will take away musical satisfactions in direct proportion to the experiences he brings to his listening. Parents and teachers play a cooperative part in providing a rich supply of these experiences to which children can associate musical experiences, giving them a storehouse to draw upon.

Provide children with a wealth of fine songs to sing from the heart, and rhythms to dance to. This is far greater in importance than being able to identify a printed symbol out of context: a clef, a double sharp, or an Italian tempo marking.

Encourage children to become aware of everything around them, to be proud of their innate poetic natures, and to feel free to grasp and express the beauties of the world. Our task as teachers is to guide children in developing this awareness of beauty and the workings of music, and to help children stimulate their own imaginations in ways that will enhance their own ability of communication.

Provide a cultural atmosphere where these expressions of beauty are both natural, sought after, and anticipated. Do parents sing at home? Do they possess a record collection which the family may sincerely enjoy? Do summer vacations provide a varied world of opportunities? If children have seen an Indian Pow-Wow during a family vacation, for example, they will be able to make necessary associations. Concerts, recitals, theater, ballet, travel, church--all of these make up that variety of cultural and spiritual community opportunities. Are children aware of these?

Children live in a nation of their own, the Imagi-nation. We must draw upon the poetic natures of children in such a way as to involve their total experiences in their listening to music--with an active mind and body. Listening is not a passive process.

A class of eighth graders were sitting, attentively "appreciating" music in the traditional sense--hearing, yea even "listening." The teacher announced he would play one of the variations from Richard Strauss's tone poem Don Quixote. The adventurous tale was vividly told--up to a point. In this particular variation, if they "listened" they might hear the bleating of the sheep. Not real sheep of course, but musical sheep. The precise spot was located and the record played.

"Listen to the sheep! Now what do you hear?"

"I don't hear nothing."

"You're not listening! Let's try again."

"Me? I still don't hear nothing."

"Once more. Now what do you hear?"

"I hear horns!"

And why not? That is exactly what he heard. Not sheep! How many times is this similar situation repeated in appreciation classes in the name of "listening?" This situation was truly approached backwards.

Music is everything. It is part of everyday living. Birds sing. Wind sings. And children are aware of this. When one child places his confidence in another, he can express himself most naturally in poetic phrases. He can also make a valid analysis of his world of sounds. Stimulate the imagination of listener rather than instruct him in exactly what he is supposed to hear. Let the individual's own imagination interpret what he hears, then provide an atmosphere for children to share their ideas with their classmates. If children fail to understand, they should be encouraged to ask questions and receive clarification. This is part of listening. To ask a good question is not a mark of inferiority, but rather of keen intelligence.

Each teacher is a teacher of listening whether it be in music or another academic area. One of the most effective methods we have in teaching good listening habits is to be a good listener ourselves. When we ask a child a question, we should carefully listen to his answer. We rarely ask a question to which we do not know the answer. It is as if one would ask a question for the express purpose of showing the ignorance of the one being asked. If we ask a child to listen to a certain portion of music, regardless of how many times we may have heard the same portion, we must listen as attentively as we expect him to listen. We must be patient and permissive. We must allow sufficient time to listen--together!

There are many occasions when there is unquestionably too much sound with us--sounds from radio, television, record player, etc. To combat this barrage of sound, children and adults learn how to "tune out" those sounds they don't want to hear. We actually learn when to "stop listening," and it becomes increasingly difficult to teach children to "tune in" when they should be listening.

What then are the prerequisites of a good atmosphere for listening? Mental and physical vitality, a well ventilated room, well modulated sound (volume, dynamic range and clarity), and congeniality. Allow children a suitable time and place for listening to what they would like to hear for themselves. Teach children to care for and respect the delicacy and operation of recording equipment, the handling of the tone arm, and the adjusting of the volume. They will accept this responsibility happily.

The listening climate should be enthusiastic, unhurried, and void of emotional tensions. Hard seats in long rows are not the most conducive to good listening: Try small groups of chairs about a listening table in one corner with record player and available albums for the children's choosing.

Children should know what they are to listen for. Is this casual or critical listening? Are we listening for a structural pattern? Make listening sessions stimulating. Draw upon a wide variety of experiences to arouse interest: art, music, puppetry, poetry, literature, dance, and a wealth of other resources. Children will be attentive while they are listening if there has been good preparation and stimulation for their listening.

Disregard the unimportant in giving listening directions; avoid cluttering data. In this way a child will become selective in his listening and be alert to pertinent musical material as it develops. Help a child to hear the rise and fall of melodic patterns by singing them, by hand signs, by picturing the pattern on the chalkboard or the flannel board. If the melody is embellished, can the child discern the skeletal melody beneath the embellishment? When a melody returns--cast in a different musical surrounding--is he able to recognize the original material in its new garb? This will only come with repeated listening, and slow, meticulous guidance.

Poor attention while listening to a musical composition may be the result of insufficient background, inadequate readiness, or limited experience. This can be corrected through more imaginative teaching and greater permission for total involvement of the listener in the music being performed. Will the music hold the listener's interest or is it some "favorite of the teacher" which is beyond the child? Are the musical phrases too long and involved? Are there frequent changes of pace? Are the listening experiences frequent enough for the listener to train himself in organizational listening skills? Is he fully aware that there are patterns, repetitions and modifications of material which bring order to all art? These are guideposts for both listening and memorization.

The beauty of a Haydn quartet or a Mozart symphony lies not in the choice of the thematic material alone, but also in the genius of the composer who skillfully weaves the emotion and the intellect of the listener from one idea to another. Through discerning listening habits one can glory in these points of musical genius and thrill to the total musical texture. There is order in all art and beauty in that order and design. May we each grow in our new musical enjoyment through listening for that order.

Little children find it exciting to listen to footsteps coming down the hall, to pick out distant sounds in an apparent silence, to listen to hear if unseen streets sound wet or dry. This is a type of critical listening. Let us begin in simple, humble, yet exciting realms, and grow in our listening acuity as we grow in years.

Chapter IV

The Teaching of Listening

In considering the way in which listening should be taught it is appropriate to look first at the aims of such instruction. Too often we become absorbed in investigations concerning ways of teaching, what we should teach, and so forth, without first asking ourselves exactly what it is that we want teaching to accomplish in a particular instance. A curriculum bulletin of the campus laboratory school at the University of Northern Iowa, formerly Iowa State College, and before that Iowa State Teachers College, contains an excellent statement of the expected outcomes of listening instruction. It is particularly gratifying to be able to include this material as the first selection in this chapter, because it was during a summer spent teaching at Iowa State Teachers College at Cedar Falls that I first began my serious research into the subject of listening about twenty years ago.

The second portion of this chapter is included through the kindness of the Los Angeles Division of Instructional Services and is taken from one of the Division's curricular publications. This passage should be of great value not only for its specific suggestions concerning the teaching of listening but also for its skillful analysis of the nature of listening.

One of the most unique and exciting ventures into new approaches of teaching was the Midwest Program in Airborne Television Instruction which was developed principally at Purdue University in the late 1950's. The concept was that a wide area could be penetrated by instructional material telecast from high-flying airplanes. This is not the proper place to discuss the results of the project but mention is made of it because the next selection in this chapter, by Dr. Boyd A. Purdom, analyzes the teaching effectiveness of the video-taped listening lessons which had originally been prepared for and used in the Airborne Television Instructional Program.

Guy Wagner has been at the University of Northern Iowa for at least twenty years as director of the curriculum laboratory among many other responsibilities. During this period he has been a prolific writer on a variety of practical matters faced on a day to day basis by classroom teachers. It is not surprising that one with such an obviously practical bent should devote considerable attention to the teaching of listening. One of Professor Wagner's activities has been the collection of various kinds of games that can be used for instructional purposes, and he has written a most useful and widely used book which lists and describes games useful in teaching listening. Another of the many writing activities in which Professor Wagner has engaged is a monthly column in Education. The selection in this chapter is excerpted from one of these columns. It presents a down to earth, practical analysis of the nature of listening instruction and can be read with profit by anyone intending to engage or already engaged in the teaching of listening.

In the next selection Professor Charles T. Brown of Western Michigan State University reports on an investigation designed to determine whether the listening ability of children is or is not enhanced by having commercial television at home. While the sample is relatively small, the investigation is unique in its use of a very ingenious means of selecting a group which did not view commercial television at home. The sample was selected from children in Amish homes in which the strict observance of religious customs prevented any exceptions to the non-viewing of television.

The last selection, by Dr. Van Wingerden, is the report of a survey of teaching practices with reference to listening, reported by a substantial number of teachers in several counties in the State of Washington including the urban King County in which Seattle is located. A number of such surveys have been made and reported over the years in both master's and doctoral theses. The present study reports a greater incidence of listening teaching than any of these. This can be interpreted in two ways: first, as an accurate report of the actual state of affairs existing with reference to the teaching of listening in the classrooms of the teachers responding to the survey; or second, as an exaggerated statement of the fact but a strong indication of intentions and of a belief that listening should be so emphasized. It does not really matter how the data are interpreted for, in either event, it presents rather solid evidence of the increased attention to listening which classroom teachers regard as desirable.

Listening

From a Curriculum Bulletin of
The Malcolm Price Laboratory School,
University of Northern Iowa

Because listening often is more important to a pupil in his daily activities than reading, the language arts program stresses this skill. When it is adequately developed, it can help the pupil to increase his awareness, gain information, find enjoyment, and develop appreciation.

The listening process involves seven steps: the person communicating (1) has his purpose in mind and (2) produces the oral symbols which will carry his ideas across. The person receiving the communication (3) hears the oral symbols, (4) recognizes and interprets them, (5) selects what he wants, (6) to comprehend or retain so that he can (7) respond or react.

Listening and reading have similar psychological bases and, consequently, share related problems. Whatever is done to improve the pupil's skill in listening also contributes to his skill in reading, though reading requires the extra mastery of printed symbols.

From nursery school on, the language arts program utilizes the every-day listening activities of the pupil as instructional opportunities, considering always his interests or needs and his ability to understand. To know when to listen and when not to listen; to listen actively, attentively, and courteously; to become sensitive to the spoken word and its meaning; and to ask for explanations of what is heard but not understood are important goals for the pupil.

Desirable Outcomes in Listening

During or by the end of the Kindergarten-Primary years, the child--

Responds to simple verbal questions, directions, and statements.

Listens with comprehension to short discussions.
Listens critically, recognizing gross discrepancies and distinguishing fact from fancy.
Recognizes words that rhyme.
Hears and matches tones.
Listens and responds to rhythm in music.
Locates the source of a sound.
Identifies voices of his peers and others.
Listens in order to reproduce sounds, such as animal noises.
Becomes sensitive to rhyme and rhythm in poetry.
Appreciates beauty in the language or poetry.
Begins to see word pictures in poetry and prose.
Can hear most likeness and differences in beginning, final, and medial sounds.
Follows sequential development of a story.
Remembers order of events in correct sequence up to five steps.
Derives meaning from intonation.
Identifies with the characters in literature.

Shows increased attention span.
Grows in awareness of the value and the use of words.
Shows enrichment of ideas.
Listens for a specific purpose: details--funny part-exciting part--word pictures--sequence--main ideas--comparisons.
Learns to be a good member of an audience.
Increases ability to make inferences.
Listens in order to relate, compare, and to apply information.

Senses effective speech on the part of others.
Recognizes oral clues.
Begins to determine the purpose of the speaker.
Recognizes onomatopoeic terms.
Raises pertinent questions in discussion.
Perceives cause and effect relationships.
Responds emotionally, sensing the feeling of the speaker or story character.

During or by the end of the intermediate years, the child--

Shows increasing desire to learn through listening, as an individual and as a member of a group.
Shows increasing responsibility for listening efficiently and effectively.

Responds to more complicated verbal questions, directions, and statements.
Listens to peers, as well as to instructors and other speakers, to get information and knowledge and to develop understanding.
Recognizes and respects the needs of others for group listening.
Accepts responsibility to raise questions when the ideas of the speaker have not been understood.
Shows increased skill in offering constructive criticism when reacting to reports, comments, etc., of classmates and teachers.
Follows an argument, a discussion, a problem-solving situation, etc., in order to contribute effectively to the development of group understandings.

Responds emotionally to good poetry and prose.
Develops sympathetic understanding of people of other times and other places through listening to good literature.
Develops understanding of life through vicarious experiences in listening.
Begins to develop discrimination between good and poor literature.
Begins to develop awareness of the use of words in influencing the listener.
Shows increased awareness of shades of meaning of words.
Identifies, enjoys, and uses figures of speech.

During or by the end of the <u>Junior High School</u> years, the student--

Recognizes the relationship between the type of listening (active or passive) and the purpose for listening.
Takes increased responsibility for practicing the skills needed for improved listening.
Understands the relationship between the purpose of the speaker and the responsibility of the listener.
Accepts differences in regional and national speech.
Asks questions if he does not understand the speaker's ideas.
Practices--when it is appropriate to do so--getting general impressions for later recall, instead of writing down "facts" for memorization.
Maintains mental alertness in all listening situations.
Understands that freedom of speech implies freedom to listen.

During or by the end of the Senior High School years, the student--

Develops skill in the four main types of listening: purposeful, accurate, critical, and responsive.

Knows how to exercise emotional control in listening situations by postponing personal worries, by refraining from condemning the speaker or his thesis, and by waiting to formulate questions or critical comments until speaker has said all he has to offer.

Separates the relevant from the irrelevant.

Assumes responsibility as a listener for giving attention to the speaker.

Develops ability to offer constructive criticism to peers after hearing them interpret a piece of literature. (That is, makes suggestions as to rate, pitch, force, general voice quality, etc.)

Separates the central purpose of a speech from the material used to support the central purpose.

Sorts out well-supported facts from generalizations in a persuasive speech.

Distinguishes between facts or reliable opinions and mere emotion-laden utterances.

Shows further recognition of and imitation of acceptable English usage by well-known speakers in either formal or informal situations.

Displays increased recognition of and respect for good oral interpretation of literature.

Recognizes the common propaganda devices as exemplified in advertising and campaigning.

Compares interpretations on recordings and tapes, and observes what is usually done when a piece of literature is adapted for radio, television, or film.

Listens to poetry with increasing depth of interpretation and appreciation.

The Art of Listening

From a Curriculum Bulletin of
The Division of Instructional Services
Los Angeles City Schools*

Instruction

A talk or speech is an enlarged conversation. The listener is necessary to make two-way communication possible. He is responding silently throughout.

Effective listening is important in modern society. A University of Michigan Research Center survey found that 58 per cent of the public's political information in a presidential campaign came from radio and television, while only 27 per cent came from newspapers and magazines. (Presumably, the other 15 per cent came from conversation!) General Dynamics Corporation places great stress on the ability of its engineers to communicate orally, since 25 per cent of their working time is spent in oral conferences. The Air Force presents up to 90 per cent of its material orally, and officers and enlisted men must listen with an efficiency approaching 75 per cent. Certainly, any skill which provides us with so large a percentage of our information and which occupies so much of our communication time deserves study and improvement.

Because certain basic principles underlie effective listening, skill in listening can be learned, improving comprehension and increasing one's store of information and ideas. Development of ability to be receptive to a point of view different from one's own and to respect a speaker who has the courage to say unpopular things is a large step toward maturity.

Listening should be introduced early in the course, and techniques should be used throughout the term in order to provide the student with constant practice in this phase of the

---

*Speech 1 and 2:
Instructional Guide.
Publication No. SC-619, 1966.

communication process. Varied types of oral presentation in the class, growing out of other units of study, offer practice in varied listening situations and techniques. It will be noted that many of the objectives of other units can be met only through an understanding of the role of the listener. The speaker should prepare his talk with the problems of the listener in mind; the listener should be prepared to compensate for the ineptness of a speaker.

Objectives

1. To understand the role of the listener in the communication process.

2. To understand the obstacles to effective listening and to learn how to avoid them.

3. To understand types of listening and to set standards for objective listening.

4. To improve skills by developing techniques of listening.

5. To learn to listen courteously to a speaker even though in disagreement.

Content

1. The nature of listening

a. Hearing

Hearing is prerequisite. For most students, it is not a problem.

Fewer than three per cent have disabilities which pose a problem in the classroom. For this group, selective seating should remove most of the difficulty.

If the speaker talks too softly to be heard, indicate by signals or by a quiet, courteous request that he should speak more loudly.

If physical conditions are unfavorable, do what you can to improve them, such as closing a door or window, changing your seat, or requesting disturbers to be quiet.

b. Comprehending

Research has indicated that there are ten barriers to effective listening. These barriers and what to do about them are as follows:

Barrier	Remedy
(1) Adopting a casual attitude toward listening	Adopt an alert posture; take notes; squirm in your seat; question yourself about the content of the speech.
(2) Failing to develop interest in the topic and in the speaker.	Force yourself to develop an interest by realizing that: -Listening is a quick way to grow culturally. -Listening is the easiest way to acquire information. -Listening provides an easy way to social maturity.
(3) Being overstimulated for or against the speaker	Despite your approval or disapproval of a speaker's delivery, posture, gestures, or mannerisms, give your attention to what he is communicating and attempt to judge it objectively. A positive listening attitude, by providing "feedback," improves any speaker's communicative efforts.
(4) Failing to listen to difficult material	Practice listening to lectures, discussion groups, and famous current speakers, and to current affairs programs on television or radio. Practice attending and listening to sermons and lectures.

(5) Becoming distracted by emotion-laden words and ideas in the speech	Stop debating the speaker when he makes remarks or uses words with which you disagree. Hear him out. Hear ALL of his message, and then answer him if need be. Rise above personalities.
(6) Being unable to take effective notes	Develop new attitudes, more effective techniques: -Don't listen for the details, but for the main ideas which the details support. -Learn to take fact-principle type of notes. -Don't try to outline all speeches. (Only one-fourth of speeches are outlinable!) -After the speech, write a précis. -If the speaker uses a manuscript or book available to you, annotate it as you listen.
(7) Failing to adapt thought speed and speech speed to each other We speak 125 words per minute.	Remedial measures may be: -Maintain eye contact with the speaker. -Watch for visual cues to meaning. -Use pencil and paper. -Play the "guessing game." Try to anticipate the speaker's purpose, message, action step.

We may think up to 900 words per minute.	-Identify the methods of support he is using.
Our mind wanders as we listen to only 125 words per minute.	-Ask yourself what are the implied meanings of the speaker's statements. Relate what he says to what you know. -Take fact-principle notes
(8) Creating or enduring distracting physical conditions	Physical actions may be: -Suggest to the speaker that he speak more loudly. -Change your seat. -Try to quiet disturbing individuals by "sh-sh." -Remove distractions. -React physically to the speaker by sitting still and looking and listening with full attention.
(9) Being unable to identify the central idea	Thought patterns to adopt: -Listen in terms of the "Motivated Sequence" or "The Borden Formula." -Identify the pattern of organization. -React according to the pattern, anticipating the purpose and the development, according to the pattern which should be indicated in the "Need" or "Why Bring That Up?" step.

(10) Being unable to discern whether facts are offered in support of an assertion	Analyze notes; compare with other persons'; discuss speech after it is over.

2. <u>Types of listening, according to purpose</u>

The classification of purposes has not become as standardized for listening as for speaking. However, the following comparison may help in developing the purposes.

	Speech Purposes	Listening Purposes
a.	To entertain, or to interest	Enjoyment
b.	To stimulate, or to impress	Inspiration, heightened feelings
c.	To inform	Understanding
d.	To convince, or to prove	Belief (Should I believe in this?)
e.	To persuade, or to gain action ..	Action (Should I take action?)

3. <u>What the speaker can do to make listening easier</u>

The speaker and the listener may not have the same basic purpose in mind. Research at U.S.C. indicated that the listener could not determine the speaker's purpose until he reached the "Action," or "So What?" step. Hence, listeners may develop a different purpose, and only a very intense action statement will provide even the possibility of recalling them to the speaker's purpose. However, the speaker and listener may maintain the same purpose from the beginning if the speaker has clearly developed his speech, adequately supported it, outlined it according to the "Motivated Sequence" or the "Borden Formula," and maintained a good level of empathy with the audience.

4. <u>What the listener can do: directed listening</u>

Learn how to analyze a speech efficiently by recognizing:

a. The central theme of the speech.
b. The pattern of development used.
c. The main ideas and major premises.
d. The forms of support used.

e. The soundness of reasoning in the speech.
f. The adequacy of facts or evidence presented.

5. Note-taking while listening

a. Taking notes improves listening ability by

-Increasing your attentiveness, preventing side-tracking.

-Increasing chances of your reviewing what you heard; therefore, remedying weaknesses in listening, improving ability to learn from the spoken word, and improving memory of what is heard.

b. Good practices in note-taking.

(1) Keep notes clear.

-Use complete thoughts--sentences or headline-type sentences.

-Use indentation, underlining, or other means of grouping main points or ideas that belong together.

(2) Keep notes brief.

(3) Review notes to clarify the ideas.

c. Procedures in note-taking

When it is well-prepared formal talk:

(1) Listen for

-The main thesis; keep it in mind as you listen.

-The transitional words or phrases that introduce each new step or point to be made.

-The generalizations, or points made by illustration, example, explanation.

-The conclusion reached.

(2) Summarize in your own words the main points

and chief details.

(3) Write out the conclusion.

When the organization of the talk or group discussion is not apparent:

(1) Divide paper into two columns--facts vs. principles or main ideas.

(2) As you listen, put notes in the proper column, and carefully study these notes soon after they are made in order to reorganize them for use.

Activities

Approach

1. Ask students to make a time chart of writing, reading, speaking and listening activities for 24 hours or longer.

2. Have the students discuss the barriers to effective listening and evaluate their own listening habits.

3. Present simple directions to the class. When these directions have been executed, present more complicated directions, as the class gains skill.

Development

1. Listen to a speech, or read one, and write out the speaker's purpose.

2. Write out a speaker's central idea or ideas.

3. Identify in writing a speaker's organizational pattern.

4. Present a recorded news broadcast and check to see if the information was received in the same way by each student.

5. Present recorded poetry or dramatic readings by artists to illustrate the role of appreciative listening and the techniques which heighten its effectiveness.

6. Make your own recordings of current magazine material.

7. Use exercises under the Critical Thinking unit to develop

an attitude of critical listening.

8. To test the ability to use fact-principle note-taking, play a recording of a lecture by some good speaker (Dr. Albert Burke, Dr. Frank Baxter, current television personalities) and have the notes taken by the students compared with those taken by the teacher, which have been duplicated for distribution.

9. Present 10-20 minute excerpts from speeches and have the class members tested on this material to evaluate their ability to remember vital ideas.

10. Present a recording of a 10-minute speech carefully timed to be spoken at 125 words per minute. Have the students then list the listening techniques they followed. Note particularly whether they apply the means of compensating for the difference in speed of speaking and thinking.

11. Present recordings of speeches with definite patterns of development; i.e., problem-solution, cause-effect, topical, chronological-story, dramatic scene, etc. Have the students identify the pattern after the "Need" step has been given, record what they think the speaker's purpose will be, and whether they will be favorably or unfavorably moved toward this purpose.

12. Have each speaker prepare two questions about his own speech. Then, after each speaking program, as a form of test, the class will answer the questions.

13. The class members act as critics, either of individual speakers or of part of the speech presented, using the following guidelines:

    a. How I saw you (poised, tense; earnest, indifferent; etc.)
    b. How I heard you (clearly, poorly, unevenly, etc.)
    c. What I heard (main idea, purpose)
    d. Organization (success of pattern of development used)

Developing Listening Skills

Boyd A. Purdom

It was the purpose of this study to investigate the effectiveness of a listening skill development program produced by the Midwest Program on Airborne Television Instruction (MPATI). The program was analyzed in terms of its effectiveness in developing skills of listening comprehension, interpretation, and evaluation.

It was also the purpose of this study to provide additional information concerning the assumption that listening can be improved through instruction. Finally, the study was designed to provide data on the relationship between the development of listening skills and the use of educational television.

The MPATI listening unit. The Midwest Program on Airborne Television Instruction (MPATI) was developed to provide sufficient quantity of educational opportunity for a fast growing school population, along with increased quality of instruction, and to provide both quantity and quality within a feasible cost.

MPATI telecasts educational courses on videotape from an airplane flying at high altitude over east-central Indiana to schools and colleges in six states of the Midwest region. Financing of the program began with an appropriation of 4.5 million dollars by the Ford Foundation and from other contributions by private industry. The total project cost well over ten million dollars.

After consulting with state school officers, city and county superintendents, and representatives of colleges and universities, the Curriculum Policy and Planning Committee drew up a proposed list of subjects at all educational levels to be included in the final curriculum and formulated policies to govern course selection. Panels of subject-matter specialists developed "ground rules" for the content of each series of telecast programs.

MPATI conducted a nationwide search for the best possible studio teaching talent. A summer-long workshop at Purdue University brought studio teachers together to work up their courses. There each teacher outlined his series, drafted classroom teacher's guides and planned visual aids and production.

In 1960 Dr. Adah Miner developed the "Learning Our Language" series to improve skills of communication in third and fourth grade children. The first section of this series is a unit on listening skill development. The MPATI listening unit consists of twelve videotape lessons. Two lessons are telecast each week. The classroom teacher is supplied with a syllabus which enables her to supplement the televised lessons. The syllabus also aids the classroom teacher in pre- and post-telecast activities.

The purposes of the MPATI listening unit are to help children realize the importance of listening, recognize the purposes of listening, and learn some of the basic listening skills. The major emphasis of the unit is on developing skills of comprehension, interpretation, and evaluation. The creative aspect of listening is also emphasized.

The content of the lessons is arranged so that each lesson develops one aspect of listening which may require a particular kind of attention and thought process.

The "Learning Our Language" series is one of the most widely used programs that MPATI has produced. A survey of program utilization for the 1965-66 school year reports that the series ranked eighth among twenty-eight programs. The survey also shows that 1,433 teachers used this series with 39,813 children.

The MPATI listening unit. The unit to develop listening skills consists of twelve videotape lessons which are presented two days a week for a period of six weeks. The unit is designed so that it can be used as an integral part of the classroom teacher's total language arts program and still reserve three days a week to meet pupils' individual needs, extend television lessons, or present other phases of the language arts program.

Dr. Miner writes that the major goals of the listening unit are:

1. To develop an awareness of the importance of good listening habits

2. To gain an interest in and a desire to improve listening habits

3. To acquire some skill in the specific listening skills presented

More specific objectives are given in the introduction of the unit. These include an understanding of the role of listening in daily life, discovering the intellectual stimulus and emotional satisfaction which accompany critical and creative listening, discovering that various listening situations require different kinds of listening skills, discovering the purposes of listening, developing some degree of efficiency in listening skills, developing understanding, and developing creativity.

The content of the individual lessons was selected to accomplish the objectives of the unit. In the first lesson children are introduced to the purposes of listening. Various aspects of "good listening" are presented and the children are given a formula that relates good listening to attending, listening, repeating, and questioning. In other lessons word perception skills are introduced and the television teacher attempts to help children discover that words give meaning to our language. Brief oral paragraphs are used to help children grasp the concepts of main idea and sequence. Poetry is used to develop visual imagery and an appreciation of spoken language. To increase skill in listening for specific details, simple and complex directions are given orally by the television teacher and the children are asked to follow the directions.

An imaginary trip to Hawaii is used in one telecast to emphasize the importance of listening for facts. The children are asked factual questions about paragraphs that are read to them by the television teacher. In an attempt to develop imagination and creative ability, children are encouraged to predict or choose outcomes from several oral selections. In one lesson, Dr. Miner uses unusual sounds, jokes, riddles, and humorous poems to demonstrate that listening can be fun. In the final lesson, children learn to evaluate their listening ability by using a listening chart.

The individual lessons are developed so that each one emphasizes one aspect of listening which may require a particular kind of attention and thought process. The unit is organized so that the lessons build logically in terms of complexity of skills and thought processes. The skills are reinforced throughout the unit.

Pre- and post-telecast activities are suggested to the classroom teacher in a syllabus which accompanies the unit. The pre-telecast activities help to prepare the children by discussing the topic of the day's lesson and introducing vocabulary. The post-telecast activities are related to those provided by the television teacher and attempt to reinforce the skills which are introduced. The syllabus also contains ideas and suggestions for the classroom teacher for activities on days when the lessons are not telecast. These activities are also used to reinforce the televised lessons and help the classroom teacher correlate the lessons to other areas of the curriculum. Reference materials are listed to aid the classroom teacher in securing additional resources.

Summary of Findings

The analysis of data provides sufficient evidence that the subjects receiving the MPATI listening program made significant gains in listening ability. The MPATI group made a significant gain score on the treatment by order analysis of total scores and on the analyses of sub-category scores. It was the only group to have consistently significant gain scores on all tests. This evidence not only justifies an affirmative response to the primary purpose of this study, but also adds weight to the body of studies supporting the assumption that listening can be improved by a systematic program of instruction.

The analysis of data also provides substantial evidence that viewing television per se made no significant contribution to the gain in listening ability made by the MPATI group. The form by order analysis of total and sub-category scores failed to produce one significant gain score for the television control group.

The group that was periodically reminded of the importance of listening and encouraged to listen throughout the study made a significant gain score on the form by order analysis of total scores. The gain, however, was not consistent throughout the sub-category tests. Only on the analysis of interpretation scores did this group make significant gain. The gain does indicate that the classroom teacher's attitude toward the importance of listening and the conveying of that attitude to her pupils helps to improve listening ability. It cannot, however, be claimed that all of the experimental group's gain is attributed to the increased awareness and approval of the classroom teachers. The motivation control group was not as consistent in gain as was the MPATI group.

Teaching Listening

Guy Wagner

Some Important Listening Skills

There are many specific listening skills which serve as a team in the development of listening power. Many of these skills should be introduced during the days of early childhood education. Most of them should be in practical use by the close of the elementary school years. Furthermore, many of them need maintenance and further development in the secondary school program. While the English teacher may be primarily responsible for this further development, teachers in all curriculum areas can and should make substantial contributions to their student's continued growth in listening power.

Based upon an analysis of professional references and English textbooks, the following illustrate the nature of listening skills currently being stressed in many classrooms. As presented here, these skills are not arranged in any order of priority or time of introduction, but they do serve to point out that we listen:

(1) to answer questions
(2) for main ideas
(3) for complete sentences
(4) for sound patterns
(5) for picture words
(6) for ending sounds
(7) for correct word usage
(8) to improve the voice
(9) to detect propaganda
(10) for key words
(11) to come to conclusions
(12) to interpret directions
(13) to understand explanations

---

(14) to anticipate what follows
(15) to build word meaning
(16) for contextual meaning
(17) for critical appraisal
(18) to draw conclusions
(19) to recognize sounds about us
(20) to make inferences
(21) to make judgments
(22) to organize ideas
(23) to remember or recall important facts
(24) to recognize oral clues
(25) to recognize a speaker's purposes
(26) to recognize rhyming words
(27) to note sequence of events
(28) for story enjoyment
(29) to summarize, and
(30) to recognize descriptive terms.

Some Teaching Tactics

There are many ways in which useful listening skills and desirable listening attitudes can be developed; and individual teachers who are successful in this respect are likely to use those which are unique to their own teaching, as well as those which may be in more common use. In the writer's experience, the following suggestions may have unusually practical applications.

1. In the first place, children need to recognize that the teacher places a high value on good listening habits. Teachers should make it clear that attentive listening is sincerely appreciated. A comment to the class such as, "It certainly is helpful to have a class that listens so thoughtfully to the opinions of the other children," is a positive approach which gives status to good listening.

2. Capitalize on that last "five-minute period" of the day. This is the time to briefly review the highlights of the day so that the children will have something constructive to tell their parents when asked "What did you do in school today?" This last five minutes not only promotes thoughtful listening--it also is an excellent opportunity to develop good relations with the parents.

3. Develop a good speaking voice and help the children to do likewise. The voices of both teacher and children reflect honest interest in what is being said. A pleasant voice

coupled with evident enthusiasm invites others to listen. Thus it is evident that the speaker, too, plays an important part in developing the art of listening. For this reason, oral reports especially should always be most carefully prepared.

4. Sometimes give tests orally. Instead of having children always given tests which involve reading, have them write answers to test items which you dictate.

5. Avoid being a "parrot." Oftentimes, some of the children will pay little attention to what is being said by their classmates or the teacher. In such instances, some teachers will repeat these statements or questions "so that everyone can hear." Such a practice may encourage some of the children not to listen in the first place. However, there may be times when a pupil comment or question may truly not be understood and in this instance the pupil himself should be called upon for clarification.

6. If a pupil has been absent, have another pupil summarize for him what was done while he was gone. This practice will encourage pupils to listen thoughtfully in order to recall the main points of a report or a discussion. In turn, the absent pupil will be inclined to listen carefully to the summary, and thus the practice is a good experience for both pupils.

7. Afford children opportunities to listen to a variety of sources. Children should not only listen thoughtfully to the teacher and to the other children's "talk." Such sources as playbacks on the tape recorder, television, socio-dramas, assembly programs, radio dramatizations, dialogues, and oral reports should be utilized. Listening to oral reading by the pupils might especially be stressed as it seems to have been largely overlooked in recent language arts programs.

8. Guide the children in making a chart listing the characteristics of a good listener. Such standards as (1) asks intelligent questions and (2) respects the speaker's right to his opinion might illustrate points in The Good Listeners Code.

9. Have the children discuss WHY they should be good listeners. This experience in calling forth their own reasons may help the children convince themselves as to the importance of listening well. It would be especially helpful if they list and debate the whys of good listening.

10. Encourage pairs of children to interview each other about their hobbies. Following these interviews, the children could report the findings of their interviews to the entire class.

11. Ask children to give oral summaries of what has been discussed or reported. This activity fosters interest and gives purpose to the listening situation.

12. Provide the children with ample practice in writing from dictation. Start with short sentences and gradually increase the length and difficulty. Normally, say the sentences only once. If the children wish, they may utilize their personal form of shorthand. After a paragraph has been dictated ask the children to point out the main idea and perhaps a key word.

13. By using the socio-drama, have a group of children dramatize both good and poor listening situations. In terms of the negative, one socio-drama could show an inattentive, restless audience; listeners being disturbed by an inattentive pupil; speakers who do not understand their subject or who use distracting mannerisms or poor voice projection. Of course, dramatizations or socio-dramas in which the "positive" approach is used are very important and should follow the negative presentation. Following these presentations, class discussion should bring out a number of important points connected with effective listening.

14. Use the tape recorder. Many occasions lend themselves to the use of this instrument. For example, a tape recording could be made of a class discussion followed by the pupils noting and evaluating the main points made during the discussion. Then when the tape is played back they could compare the main points which they had listed with what they now hear for a second time.

15. Help children recognize the importance of listening carefully for names when they are being introduced to others. Good listening habits pay dividends in this listening situation--and encourage the practice of listening carefully in order to remember.

16. Be a good listener yourself. By the process of osmosis children often do as they see others do. When the teacher listens with sincere interest to what the children themselves say, the latter will "catch" the habit of both attentive-

ness and courtesy in listening. Perhaps this is the most important method of all in helping children to become courteous, thoughtful listeners.

Listening Ability and Radio and Television Habits

Charles T. Brown

The main purpose of this study was to search for relations between listening ability and habits in listening to radio and television. The three specific hypotheses are as follows:

First hypotheses: Children who watch television develop greater ability in listening than do children who do not watch television regularly. The testing of this hypothesis led into an area previously examined infrequently and indecisively.

Second hypothesis: Children who view television for one or two hours daily learn to listen better than do those who view it several hours a day. One earlier experiment, by Sister Mary Kevin Hollow,[1] produced results contrary to the hypothesis, but for various reasons it seemed worthwhile to test again with different subjects in different environments. Specifically she found that the best twenty-seven per cent of the listeners in her sample watched television about three hours a week more than did the poorest twenty-seven per cent and that the difference was statistically significant at the one per cent level of confidence. The best and the poorest listeners, in general, watched the same programs.

Third hypothesis: Girls listen better than boys do. Here the need for further research rests upon the impossibility at present of finding any lawfulness in the results already announced. Only through added information obtained by further experimentation can a basis be formed for creating a general principle bringing together correct findings, and only through further experimentation can correctness be determined in those areas in which results are contradictory.

Assumptions

The most critical assumptions were that the measuring instruments are satisfactory in respect to validity and reliability. The purpose of the investigation was neither to create measuring instruments nor to evaluate those developed and tested by others. The writer recognizes that all measuring devices are imperfect to varying degrees and that these inadequacies should be considered in interpreting the results. He sought to minimize this problem by choosing only tests of listening, reading, intelligence, and achievement that have been prepared and studied carefully.

Procedure

The children of the fourth, the fifth, and the sixth grades at the Topeka, Indiana, elementary school were given Form 4A of the STEP test of listening. The principal, a sixth grade teacher, and the writer examined all classes the same day. In the morning they administered the first part of the eighty-item, ninety-minute test, and in the afternoon they gave the second part.

The reason for selecting the Topeka elementary school was that approximately fifty per cent of the children (N= 76) came from Amish-Dutch families that do not have radio or television in their homes. Moreover, almost all of these children lived on farms and thus rarely, if ever, had access to radio or television outside their homes. Also living on farms and belonging to approximately the same economic class were eighty-six non-Amish children who reported that they listened to the radio and/or watched television. Samples (N= 51) were further equated by pairing viewers and nonviewers on the basis of scores on the California Test of Mental Maturity given to all students six months previously. The samples differed in social, religious, and educational attitudes with the Amish being more closely knit and conservative.

Each child of the non-Amish group was asked to estimate the time he listened to radio and watched television each day. The Stanford Achievement Test and reading scores also were obtained.

Results

1. The first hypothesis, that children who watch television are better listeners than those who do not, was supported at the one per cent level of significance. First, taking the three grades as a whole, the writer obtained a mean listening score for the children watching television that was about twenty per cent higher than the one for the non-viewers. Second, for samples strictly equated for sex and intelligence

the difference between the means still was highly significant (N for each sample = 48; mean listening score for those watching television, 59.5; for nonviewers, 53.8; t = 4.136).

2. The second hypothesis, that children who watch television two or fewer hours a day are better listeners than those who watch four or more hours a day, was not supported. The means for the two groups were almost identical, and the means for intelligence and for reading also did not differ significantly. Moreover, the subjects in the upper half in listening and those in the lower half did not differ significantly in the average amount of time per day spent in listening and viewing (upper half, 4.1 hours; lower, 3.7).

3. The third hypothesis, that the girls would be better listeners than the boys, was not at all supported. The mean listening score for all girls was higher (2.82, raw score) than that for all boys, but the difference by the one-tailed test was not significant at the five per cent level (t = 1.433). Moreover, a chi square analysis of the numbers of the best (18 boys and 26 girls) and the poorest listeners (27 boys and 17 girls), though tending in the hypothesized direction, also was not significant at the five per cent level.

Discussion and Conclusions

In a practical sense the most striking interpretation of the data is the lack of support for the widespread fears that television is harmful to the academic capabilities of children. Although cultural differences between the Amish nonviewers and the non-Amish consumers of television cast some suspicion upon the finding that children who watch television are superior listeners to those who don't, the results clearly are no cause for alarm. Moreover, when the possibility that the socio-religious factor confounded the results is eliminated, fears regarding the ill effects of television still are unfounded. Data restricted to the non-Amish children indicate that the amount of time spent in viewing television is not significantly related to the child's intelligence or his ability to read or to listen.

On the other hand, the finding that those who watch television are superior in listening scarcely justifies a movement to increase the amount of viewing. Listening well is not the whole objective of education, and perhaps the time spent in front of TV set could be better used in other ways. Data incidental to the hypotheses show that the average amount of time consumed in viewing by the non-Amish children was large, though diminishing by grade (fourth grade, 4.5 hours per day; fifth, 3.0; sixth, 2.7. These figures, particularly when combined with those for listening to the radio, seem large (fourth grade, 4.9 hours per day; fifth, 4.24; sixth, 4.47).

Note

The abbreviated reference refers to the entry number in Sam Duker's Listening Bibliography 2nd Ed. (Scarecrow, 1968) where the full citation may be found.

1. Hollow, 578.

What Intermediate Grade Teachers Say When They Are Asked About Their Teaching of Listening

Stewart Van Wingerden

<u>The Questionnaire: A Survey of Practices in the Teaching of Listening Skills</u>

What grade(s) are you teaching this year?............. ______

What is the approximate enrollment of your class? ...... ______

What is the approximate enrollment of your school? ..... ______

Which one of these three types of classrooms is yours? .. ______

Self-contained........... ______

Departmentalized .... ______

Semi-departmentalized .. ______

How many years have you taught at each of the following levels? (Include this year).

Primary (K-3)......... ______

Intermediate (4-6)...... ______

Jr. High (7-9)......... ______

Sr. High School (10-12).. ______

How many years of college education have you completed?. ______

The following series of questions is concerned with the teaching of listening skills. For the purposes of this survey "listening" is defined as the ability to comprehend what is heard, not merely the ability to hear or pay attention. It is assumed that the five major factors in listening ability are the skills of:

(1) Distinguishing between relevant and irrelevant ideas when listening,

(2) Making full use of contextual clues when listening,

(3) Making logical inferences from what is listened to,

(4) Discovering the central ideas when listening, and

(5) Following without loss a fairly complex though unit when listening.

It will help if you keep this definition in mind whenever the term "listening" is used in the following questions.

Approximately what percentage of the total time you spend teaching listening do you teach by:

Direct, planned instruction .... ____%
(This method would consist of those lessons in which you select a specific listening skill (such as the ability to discover central ideas when listening), set aside a period of time to teach it, plan how you are going to present the lesson, carry out the teaching, and measure the pupils' growth toward attaining the skill.)

As a part of reading instruction............... ____%
(This method would consist of those times when, during regular reading instruction, you make a conscious effort to take a few minutes to teach the pupils a specific listening skill which is closely related to the reading skills being taught at that time.)

Incidental instruction .... ____%
(This method would consist of the unplanned teaching of listening that occurs incidentally at any time during the day.)

Total Listening Instruction 100%

Approximately how often do you teach the following skills:	By direct, planned instruction — Once every						As a part of reading instruction — Once every						By incidental instruction — Once every					
	day	week	2 weeks	month	2 months	year	day	week	2 weeks	month	2 months	year	day	week	2 weeks	month	2 months	year
a. Distinguishing between relevant and irrelevant ideas when listening																		
b. Discovering the central idea when listening																		
c. Making full use of contextual clues when listening																		
d. Making logical inferences from what is listened to																		
e. Following without loss a fairly complex thought unit when listening																		

NOTE: You may want to check a skill under all three methods or, if you do not teach a particular skill, you may leave all three methods blank.

How many hours would you say you spend per MONTH teaching listening skills? (Assume a total of 110 teaching hours per month, or twenty 5-1/2-hr. days.)

(Hours per MONTH (by all methods) ____________

Which of the communication skills do you emphasize most in your teaching? (Mark the one you emphasize most (1), next most (2), etc.)

reading.... ( )
writing.... ( )
speaking... ( )
listening... ( )

When teaching the communication skills, what percentage of time do you give to the following?

reading.... ____%
writing.... ____%
speaking... ____%
listening... ____%

	Always	Often	Seldom	Never
Do you teach listening as a separate subject during a specific time period?.............	A	O	S	N
Do you make written plans for lessons specifically designed to teach listening skills? ...	A	O	S	N
Do you give children grades in listening as you do in reading and other subjects?........	A	O	S	N
Do you divide your class for instruction into listening groups as many teachers divide their classes into reading groups?	A	O	S	N

Will your children probably be given a formal hearing test this year?.............................. Yes No

listening test? .... Yes No
vision test? ...... Yes No
reading test? .... Yes No
arithmetic test? .. Yes No

Have you taken a college course in the teaching of listening?...................... Yes No

Does your district provide:

a. A curriculum guide which offers substantial suggestions for teaching listening? .... Yes No

b. Pupil textbooks which contain materials designed to teach specific listening skills?..... Yes No

c. In-service workshops or courses in methods of teaching listening?...................... Yes No

d. Supervisory personnel, other than the principal, who help teachers with listening instruction?............................... Yes No

Would you please compare your own listening instruction with the examples of TYPES of listening instruction described below. Then check the three statements that follow.

TYPE 1: Point out to the class that they will need to listen attentively if they are to understand the vocabulary used in the story you are about to read to them.

TYPE 1: Remind the children that they should be courteous and listen carefully as one of their classmates gives an oral report on Mexico.

TYPE 2: While teaching the use of context clues in a story in a reader, point out that when listening as well as when reading, we should use the words immediately preceding and following an unfamiliar word to make intelligent guesses about the meaning of the new word.

TYPE 2: As a pupil reads orally an article about Mexico from the Weekly Reader, point out to the class that they will be able to answer the questions at the end more easily if they listen for key words.

TYPE 3: Tell the class that often they can identify the main thought in a talk or report by picking out two or three important words from the report and composing a sentence containing those words. For instance, from the words "Mexico" and "beans" the topic sentence might be, "Beans are a staple in the Mexican diet." Then ask the class to contribute key words and topic sentences for several short "Lectures" you give them.

TYPE 3: Explain to the class that often we can discover the meaning of a strange word that we hear by relating it to the words which come before and after it. For instance, in "The three little white cygnets swam across the pond," the words "little, white, swam" help us to unlock the new word, "cygnet." Ask the children to listen for key words in the context as you tell a story containing several similar sentences.

MOST of my listening instruction is like..1 2 3 (circle one)

SOME of my listening instruction is like..1 2 3 (circle one)

LITTLE of my listening instruction is like..1 2 3 (circle one)

Table 1

Number and Percentage of Respondents Grouped According to Total Hours Listening Is Taught Per Month*

No. of Hours	Teachers Responding	
	No.	%
0	3	1.4
1-9	71	32.7
10-19	45	20.7
20-29	40	18.4
30-39	11	5.1
40-49	9	4.1
50-59	17	7.8
60-69	10	4.6
70-79	3	1.4
80-89	4	1.8
90 or more	4	1.8
Total	217	99.8
No response	49	
Total	266	

*Assuming twenty 5-1/2-hour days or 110 total teaching hours per month.

When asked to estimate the percentage of time they spend teaching the four skills of listening, speaking, reading, and writing, the group as a whole replied that reading receives the largest percentage of time, while writing, speaking, and listening receive much smaller percentages of time (see Table 2).

Table 2

Number of Respondents by Percentage of Total Time Spent Teaching Communication Skills

Percentage of Time Taught	No. of Respondents by Subject			
	Reading	Writing	Speaking	Listening
0	1	3	1	6
1-9	0	7	9	26
10-19	9	63	113	83
20-29	22	105	92	66
30-39	58	51	18	40
40-49	54	11	7	15
50-59	72	2	3	6
60-69	16	0	0	1
70-79	9	1	0	0
80-89	0	0	0	0
90-99	1	0	0	0
No response ...	24	23	23	23
Total	266	266	266	266

Table 3

Ranking According to Emphasis Placed on Teaching of Reading, Writing, Speaking, and Listening

Rank	Number of Respondents by Subject			
	Reading	Writing	Speaking	Listening
First	183	12	12	35
Second	32	100	50	61
Third	19	59	102	54
Fourth	4	69	69	85
No response ...	28	26	33	31
Total	266	266	266	266

Table 4

Frequency Five Listening Skills Are Taught by Three Methods

Skills Taught	No. of Respondents: By Direct, Planned, Instruction							As a Part of Reading Instruction							By Incidental Instruction						
	Daily	Weekly	Bi-weekly	Monthly	Bi-monthly	Yearly	Never	Daily	Weekly	Bi-weekly	Monthly	Bi-monthly	Yearly	Never	Daily	Weekly	Bi-weekly	Monthly	Bi-monthly	Yearly	Never
a. Distinguishing between relevant and irrelevant ideas when listening	45	65	19	19	6	9	81	80	68	17	14	3	5	57	113	46	22	7	2	2	52
b. Discovering central idea when listening	62	59	21	12	9	5	76	101	63	25	9	3	4	39	112	45	8	10	4	1	64
c. Making full use of context clues when listening	47	52	24	11	6	7	96	95	60	23	6	4	3	53	86	48	20	9	5	2	74
d. Making logical inferences from what is listened to	62	40	27	16	7	5	87	84	61	21	12	3	3	60	112	49	16	8	2	2	55
e. Following without loss a fairly complex thought when listening	27	39	34	22	7	9	106	41	49	28	15	3	5	103	63	46	24	9	7	4	91

In general, "little" of the instruction is direct, planned instruction; for the largest number of teachers, the most popular answer for "some" of the instruction was the method described as "as part of reading instruction," and "incidental instruction" was the most common answer for the type of instruction used "most" of the time. Fifty-three per cent of the teachers said that little of their instruction is "direct instruction," 56.6% said that some of their instruction is "as a part of the reading program," and 47.1% said that most of their instruction is "incidental instruction."

Table 5

Percentage of Respondents Using Three Methods "Most," "Some," or "Little" of the Time

Method Used	Percentage of Respondents		
	Most	Some	Little
Direct, planned instruction	23.3	21.5	52.9
Part of reading instruction	29.6	56.6	14.5
Incidental instruction	47.1	21.9	32.6

Table 5 summarizes the responses when the teachers were asked to estimate the percentage of time they spend using the three methods, assuming the three methods make up 100% of the time they spend teaching listening skills. Large numbers said they use direct, planned instruction very little or not at all and many said they use incidental instruction almost exclusively.

Responses Describing What Listening Skills are Taught

What these teachers teach when they say they teach listening and to what extent they are prepared to teach listening was indicated by interpreting their responses to questions about their training, the amount of assistance and encouragement they receive from their districts, and their statements regarding the specific listening skills they teach.

Table 6

Percentage of Respondents Who Administered Certain Formal Tests

Type of Test	Percentage of Respondents			
	Yes	No	No. Resp.	Total
Hearing	74.1	17.7	8.3	100.1
Listening	36.5	50.8	12.8	100.1
Vision	88.0	5.3	6.8	100.1
Reading	86.5	6.8	6.8	100.1
Arithmetic	80.1	12.0	7.9	100.0

Only a relatively small number--23 of the 266 teachers --said they had ever taken college course work intended to help them teach listening. Only a small minority of the teachers are provided with textbook material for teaching listening, with curriculum guides or courses of study containing teaching helps, with supervisory assistance in the teaching of listening, or with in-service workshops aimed at improving instruction in this area.

Most of the teachers teach listening incidentally, implying perhaps that the curriculum as far as listening is concerned is either non-existent or at least loosely organized and sketchy. Table 4 indicates that many teachers teach the five skills defined in this study, that many teachers do not teach these skills, and that there is a great difference from teacher to teacher in terms of what is taught under the label "listening."

Chapter V

Testing Listening Skills

The measurement of listening skills has been a subject on which there have been widely differing views. There are at the present time several published tests of listening skills including the Brown-Carlsen Listening Comprehension Test[1] first published in 1955. This test has been very widely used in business and industry, at the college level, and in the upper years of secondary schools. A considerable amount of reported research is available on various aspects of this test, but the merits of the test must be labeled controversial in the light of the differing opinions expressed in the literature.

Another well known test is the listening portion of the Sequential Test of Educational Progress (STEP),[2] first published in 1957, which in several versions is suitable for use from the fourth grade through the high school level. Like the Brown-Carlsen, the STEP has two equivalent forms for each of the levels. While STEP has been used very widely, the research literature about it is more limited than that on Brown-Carlsen. Reviews of both the STEP and Brown-Carlsen tests by Lindquist and Lorge[3] have suggested serious shortcomings. In 1969 the Durrell Listening Reading Series,[4] a series of tests for elementary school levels, was published. This series was developed in doctoral dissertations by Hayes[5] and Brassard[6] and completed under the direction of Donald D. Durrell at Boston University.

This chapter is concerned with several very important issues concerning the testing of listening. The first article, by Dr. Herbert Friedman of the American Institutes of Research's Washington office, examines a wide variety of tests to determine their combined potential as a test of listening. Friedman was concerned with a specialized form of listening--listening to rapid or compressed speech. This chapter introduction is not the proper place for either an introduction to or a more advanced discussion of this subject. The reader who desires further information on this intriguing phase of listening is referred to the September 1968 issue of the Journal of Communication or to the proceedings of two conferences on compressed speech which were held at the University of Louisville in 1966 and 1969. These proceedings can be obtained from Professor Emerson Foulke of the Psychology Department at the University of Louisville. I now have in preparation a book of readings on compressed speech which will be published by The Scarecrow Press in the not too distant future. In addition, a substantial number of items in my Listening Bibliography are concerned with this topic.

It is important, I think, to emphasize my opinion that the relevancy of Friedman's views to the general area of testing listening is not at all diminished by the fact that his article is concerned with compressed speech.

One of the first educators to grasp the importance of listening, and of the likely relationship between this process and the process of reading, was Professor Donald D. Durrell of Boston University. Consequently, in the decade of the 30's, he developed together with Helen B. Sullivan a listening test for the pre-school and primary grade level which he hoped would be used not only to measure listening ability but also to estimate a youngster's potential capacity for learning to read. Publishers found the concept of a "listening test" somewhat exotic and the test was therefore published in 1937 under the name of the Durrell-Sullivan Reading Capacity Test.[7] This test has been and continues to be widely used. There is considerable literature on various aspects of this instrument. It is interesting that Dr. Durrell's principal tenets concerning the relationship of listening and reading have been carried on into the current series of his tests.

Professor Harry Singer, of the Education Department of the University of California at Riverside, has been an active student of the reading process for a number of years and has made major contributions to the literature in this field. The second article in this chapter describes an investigation he made concerning the Durrell-Sullivan Reading Capacity Test. It will be of great interest to all those pondering the relationship between reading and listening. Further investigations along the lines of Singer's approach should be a fruitful activity for future doctoral candidates.

The last article in this chapter is by Charles M. Kelly who obtained his doctorate at Purdue University after writing a dissertation concerned with listening[8] in which he presented evidence that the actual listening performance of a group of foremen was not very closely related to their scores on the Brown-Carlsen. Much of the criticism of listening tests or, for that matter, of the teaching of listening has been rather shrill. Kelly's criticism has been no less forceful despite its lack of shrillness. In the third selection in this chapter Kelly questions the validity of results obtained by using currently available listening tests. Whether one agrees or disagrees with the article's theme and with Kelly's reasoning and conclusions, he presents a good case. At the end of this article, when it appeared in Speech Monographs, a short but very strongly reasoned reply by Charles T. Brown was given. Without reference to my own feelings as to the merits or demerits of Kelly's or of Brown's views, I have decided that the reader is quite capable of forming his own opinions concerning the Kelly article. Anyone wishing to see Brown's reply can readily do so by consulting Speech Monographs, 34:455-66, November, 1967.

Notes

Abbreviated references refer to the entry number in Sam Duker's Listening Bibliography 2nd Ed., (Scarecrow, 1968) where the full citation may be found

1. Brown, 148.

2. Sequential Tests, 1069.

3. Lindquist, 736.
   Lorge, 753.

4. Durrell Listening-Reading Series. New York: Harcourt Brace & World, 1969.

5. Hayes, Mary T. Comparable Measures of English Language Comprehension in Reading and Listening in Primary Grades. Doctoral dissertation. Boston: Boston University, 1957.

6. Brassard, Mary B. Listening and Reading Comprehension in Intermediate Grades. Doctoral dissertation. Boston: Boston University, 1968.

7. Durrell, 340.

8. Kelly, 654.

Compressed Speech: Correlates of Listening Ability

Herbert L. Friedman and Raymond L. Johnson

Studies at the American Institutes for Research have suggested that listening comprehension at normal speech rate does not necessarily correlate with comprehension at high rates of compression. Furthermore, individual differences in understanding compressed speech become more evident as the rate of compression is increased. These facts suggest that the comprehension of a highly compressed speech signal may be dependent upon certain skills which are less discernibly implicated at normal or near-normal speech rates. The possibility that some special competence is needed to comprehend highly compressed speech is consistent with conclusions drawn from studies of individual differences in perceptual motor skills which have demonstrated changes, as a task becomes more difficult, in the relative contribution which specific skills make to the performance of the task.[1]

The purpose of the study described in this report was to specify sources of individual variation in the comprehension of compressed speech. Accordingly, we attempted, first, to identify some of the correlates of listening comprehension, both at normal and compressed speech rates; second, to inspect the correlation data for patterns of change associated with increases in the rate of compression; and finally, to relate the results of the correlation study to current theories of higher cognitive processes and models of speech perception in order to form hypotheses about some of the implicit processes and mechanisms involved in listening. The study is an extension and refinement of previous work.[2]

Method

Subjects. Twenty-nine male and twenty-three female undergraduates, recruited from two universities in the Washington, D. C. area, were paid participants in the study. Thirty were freshmen and twenty-two, sophomores, and their mean age was 18 years 4 months. All were native speakers of English, with no gross hearing deficiences. None had any prior experience in listening to compressed speech.

Procedure. Students were tested usually in small groups, but sometimes individually, during two-or three-hour sessions spread over a period of a month. The order in which particular tests were administered to students was determined by the exigencies of scheduling, and no attempt was made either to maintain a uniform sequence for all participants or to counterbalance the order of administration. The diversity of the test battery seemed likely to preclude any significant order effects.

Materials. On the basis of results obtained from an earlier pilot study, ten tests were investigated as possible predictors of listening comprehension:

1. The vocabulary section of the Nelson Denny Reading Test (designated ND).

2. An estimate of silent reading rate, as determined from performance on the ND.

3. The Space Relations subtest of the Differential Aptitude Test (DAT) battery, which measures the ability to imagine the way a flat pattern would look if it were folded to form a three dimensional construction.

4. The Sentences section of the DAT Language Usage subtest, which requires the subject to detect instances of incorrect grammar, punctuation, and word usage.

5. The Clerical Speed and Accuracy subtests of the DAT battery, which requires the subject to rapidly match various alphabetic and numeric combinations.

6. The verbal section of the Lorge-Thorndike Intelligence Test.

7. The Brown-Carlsen Listening Comprehension Test.

8. The Phonetic Script section of the Modern Language Aptitude Test (MLAT), which requires subjects to discriminate sequences of speech sounds and learn to associate them with orthographic symbols.

9. The Spelling Clues subtest of the MLAT, which measures a student's knowledge of English vocabulary, and to

some extent taps the same sound-symbol association ability measured by the Phonetic Script section.

10. Best Trend Name Test, which requires subjects to infer the semantic relationship among a set of words. For example, the subject is given the words "horse, push cart, bicycle, car" and is asked to decide whether the relationship among the four terms is best described as one of "speed," "time," or "size." The correct answer is "time" since the sequence describes an order of historical development; horses were the earliest means of transportation, cars the most recent. The ability measured by this test is the "evaluation of semantic relations" in the Guilford structure-of-intellect model.[3] This model is a three-dimensional classification system for describing the contents, operations, and products of human intellectual abilities. The model postulates the existence of 120 discrete intellectual abilities, of which the "evaluation of semantic relations" is one.[4]

The four criterion variables (here designated C_1 through C_4) were multiple choice comprehension tests based on the content of four excerpts from a history of seventeenth century England. The tests previously had been equated for level of difficulty and standardized on a college population. Subjects were tested for listening comprehension immediately after hearing a tape recorded reading of each passage. The first excerpt was presented at a normal speaking rate of approximately 175 wpm. The remaining three passages were compressed on the Tempo Regulator and presented, respectively, at 250, 325, and 450 wpm. All four passages and comprehension tests were presented in a single two-hour session, but the scheduling of this block with respect to ten predictor tests varied from subject to subject. Detailed information about the comprehension tests and their construction may be found in Orr and Friedman.[5]

Results

Primary Study

A multiple regression analysis was performed on the test data to determine the extent to which a selection of these ten tests could efficiently predict listening comprehension at four rates of presentation. As a first step, a correlation matrix was constructed to show the intercorrelations among the ten tests and the four measures of comprehension. All entries in the matrix were examined to identify tests which were strongly correlated with one or more of the criterion measures, but weakly with one another. Tests were also sought which exhibited a pattern of increasing or decreasing correlations with comprehension measures, as rate of compression increased. Six of the tests seemed to merit further investigation. The Nelson Denny vocabulary score correlated relatively high with comprehension, at all four presentation rates. The Sentences section of the DAT Language Usage subtest was moderately related to comprehension only at normal speaking rate; as rate of compression increased, the correlation coefficients were found to decrease monotonically. Three tests, on the other hand, were more strongly related to comprehension at high rates of compression than at normal speaking rate: Phonetic Script, Space Relations, and Best Trend Name. Silent reading rate was found to correlate weakly with the criteria, but relatively strongly with some of the possible predictors, thus suggesting that it might function as a "suppressant variable" in a multiple regression system.

The scores from these six tests were then subjected to a step-wise multiple regression analysis for each of the four rates of presentation. In Table 1 are summarized the results of the analyses. As a general observation, it can be seen that the multiple correlation coefficients tended to decrease in magnitude as rate of compression increased, but the corresponding F ratios were significant at each of the four rates.

As an alternative way to examine the data for a relationship between listening comprehension and performance on the six predictor tests, we used a two-factor experimental design with repeated measures on the second factor.[6] A separate analysis was performed for each predictor. Subjects' scores on the multiple choice comprehension tests were categorized according to their performance on a given predictor test (i.e., whether they fell above or below the group mean for that test), and according to the rate of presentation (i.e., 175, 250, 325, and 450 wpm). Significant differences in listening comprehension were found between the high and low scores on three of the six tests: Vocabulary ($F = 41.611$, $p < 0.01$), Sentences ($F = 14.304$, $p < 0.01$), and Best Trend Name ($F = 4.902$, $p < 0.05$). However, the effectiveness of the Sentences subtest as a predictor of listening comprehension was found to decrease as rates of compression increased. This rate-related loss in effectiveness was reflected in a significant interaction observed between comprehension and Sentences test scores ($F = 3.041$, $p < 0.05$).

Table 1
Prediction of Listening Comprehension at Four Rates of Presentation (N = 52)

		Predictors							Criteria			
		1	2	3	4	5	6		7	8	9	10
	Mean	61.08	40.37	25.85	66.83	12.68	374.81		14.55	13.41	10.14	4.93
	S.D.	16.92	12.31	3.53	18.30	3.88	121.32		4.92	6.24	6.57	3.64
		Intercorrelations							Beta-Weights			
Vocabulary (ND)	1	1.00	.51	.22	.15	.30	.54		.54	.53	.53	.44
Sentences (DAT)	2	.51	1.00	.31	.09	.24	.26		.30	.22	.19	.06
Phonetic Script (MLAT)	3	.22	.31	1.00	.17	.28	.16		-.14	-.09	.04	.03
Space Relations (DAT)	4	.15	.09	.17	1.00	.51	-.05		.16	.13	.16	.06
Best Trend Name	5	.30	.24	.28	.51	1.00	.18		-.10	.04	.07	.36
Reading Rate (ND)	6	.54	.26	.16	-.05	.17	1.00		-.06	-.12	-.26	-.17
						Multiple R			.76	.64	.61	.63
						F Ratio			10.09*	5.32*	4.32*	4.93*
		Validity Coefficients							b-Weights			
C-1 (175 wpm)	7	.67	.59	.09	.20	.32	.28	1	.16	.20	.20	.10
C-2 (250 wpm)	8	.58	.45	.10	.24	.22	.20	2	.15	.11	.10	.02
C-3 (325 wpm)	9	.50	.40	.12	.27	.19	.06	3	-.20	-.17	-.08	.03
C-4 (450 wpm)	10	.54	.28	.33	.34	.42	.18	4	.04	.04	-.06	.01
								5	-.13	.06	.01	.34
								6	.00	-.01	-.01	-.01
						Intercept			.76	-2.13	-5.11	-6.10
						σ Estimate			3.42	5.08	5.57	3.00

*$p < 0.01$, df = 6 and 45.

The results of the multiple regression study and analysis of variance identified the Nelson Denny vocabulary measure as the most efficient predictor of listening comprehension at all four rates of presentation. However, Table 1 shows that the beta weights for this variable became smaller as rate of comprehension increased, suggesting that the general language aptitude which appeared to be involved in comprehension at the normal rate of presentation was relatively less important at higher rates. A similar loss of predictiveness was observed for the verbal section of the Lorge-Thorndike, but the decline associated with increasing rates of compression was even more accentuated than was the case with Nelson Denny vocabulary.

In contrast, the ability measured by the Best Trend Name Test was marginally involved in understanding material presented at normal or near-normal rates, and gained significance as a correlate of comprehension only at the 450 wpm rate, thus running counter to the trend. The pattern of increasing beta weights associated with this test singled out the underlying behavior as a source of individual variation in the comprehension of highly compressed speech.

To define the skill which the Best Trend Name Test measures, the intercorrelations among ten tests were factor analyzed by means of a principal axis solution. Three factors, yielding eigenvalues greater than 1.0, accounted for 70% of the common variance. The rotated factor matrix and list of ten variables is presented in Table 2. The first factor received appreciable loadings on three variables: the reading rate and vocabulary measures of the Nelson Denny Reading Test, and the Spelling Clues section of the Modern Language Aptitude Test. This configuration of variables clearly suggested that vocabulary knowledge was the dominant component. The third factor obtained a high loading on only one variable, the Phonetic Script section of the Modern Language Aptitude Test, indicating that this test is relatively independent of other measures of verbal ability and general academic aptitude.

It was Factor II, however, which was most interesting in terms of the present study. The Best Trend Name Test was one of the variables which defined this dimension, together with Space Relations and Clerical Speed and Accuracy. The common task which underlies these three tests is a rapid comparison of alternative responses to find one which is most similar to a stimulus. All tests involve some variant of matching-to-sample behavior, but the subject is not required to produce a response to match the stimulus; only to compare and choose among a set of responses which are already available. This ability to make rapid comparisons is the defining characteristic of the cognitive operation called "evaluation" in Guilford's structure of intellect model. It is a significant historical note that prior to Guilford's classification theory, the evaluative operation was variously termed perceptual speed, speed of judgment, and speed of association.[7] Clearly, the rate of responding is an essential aspect of this ability. The Best Trend Name Test was not designed as a general measure of evaluative ability, however. It was constructed specifically to assess a person's ability to evaluate semantic relations, the meaningful connections between verbal "units." To perform well on this test, a person must be skilled in the cognitive matching operations necessary to infer the semantic connectedness implicit in a given set of verbal concepts.

Table 2

Rotated Factor Matrix Showing Factor Loadings for 10 Predictor Variables on Three Dimensions

Variables/Factors	I	II	III	h^2
Reading Rate (ND)	0.874	-0.018	0.098	0.777
Vocabulary (ND)	0.633	0.135	0.027	0.776
Space Relations (DAT)	-0.081	0.902	0.071	0.851
Clerical Speed and Accuracy (DAT)	0.160	0.850	-0.149	0.781
Lorge-Thorndike Intelligence Tests (Verbal)	0.448	0.259	-0.009	0.851
Best Trend Name	0.032	0.723	0.234	0.638
Phonetic Script (MLAT)	0.130	0.075	0.957	0.955
Spelling Clues (MLAT)	0.746	0.023	0.086	0.694
Sentences (DAT)	0.090	-0.015	0.230	0.805
Brown-Carlsen Listening Comprehension Test	0.452	0.405	-0.041	0.654

Note: The Lorge-Thorndike Intelligence Test, the Sentences section of the DAT, and the Brown-Carlsen Listening Comprehension Test defined the fourth dimension, but since its corresponding eigenvalue was less than 1.0, it was not included in this table.

Supplemental Study

In attempting to interpret these results, we recognized that a multiple choice test was not an uncontaminated measure of listening comprehension. General academic aptitude certainly affected a subject's level of performance. Even more unsettling in its implications for the present study was the fact that "responses to a multiple choice test sometimes reflect evaluative variance."[8] Consequently, the ability to evaluate semantic relations may have contributed to a person's skill in answering multiple choice questions as much as it entered into the listening skill itself. To avoid this type of confounding, we carried out a brief supplemental study using the same 52 subjects, but employing criterion measures different from the multiple choice tests. The stimulus materials were prepared originally by Miller and Isard[9] for a study of sentence perception, and were of three types: meaningful, grammatical sentences; meaningless, grammatical sentences; and "random" word strings without meaning or grammatical order. These sentences and sentence-like strings were presented at the same rates of compression as the "C" passages, and the subject's task was to listen to each one and then transcribe it word-by-word as accurately as possible. Accuracy in this task was correlated with each of the six predictor variables listed in Table 1, and a step-wise multiple regression analysis was performed. Results were generally consistent with those already reported. At normal speech (about 175 wpm), the Best Trend Name Test was the least predictive of the six. But with compression, the test came to the fore as an effective predictor variable. We concluded, therefore, that the ability to evaluate semantic relations--as measured by the Best Trend Name Test--was a correlate of listening comprehension at compressed rates, and not merely an experimental artifact.

Discussion

Merely to demonstrate a correlation between variables has little value unless it leads to a theoretical description of a mechanism of interaction, one amenable to independent test. The matching or comparison process, of which the evaluation of semantic relations is an example, has been suggested as a basic unit in the study of complex cognitive operations, similar to the way "the reflex serves as a unit of analysis within S-R theory."[10] Matching may be conceived to be a basic unit of behavioral analysis because it is more or less directly measurable and because it has been incorporated as an important design feature in contemporary models of cognitive processing (e.g., Miller and Chomsky[11]). In this concluding section of our report, the ability to evaluate semantic relations (as measured by the Best Trend Name Test) will be related to recent theoretical descriptions of listening behavior in an attempt to interpret our finding that skill in semantic matching is a correlate of listening comprehension at high rates of compression.

Figure 1

Simplified flow diagram of "analysis-by-synthesis" model of speech perception. Asterisk identifies operation which may be related to the ability to elevate semantic relations.

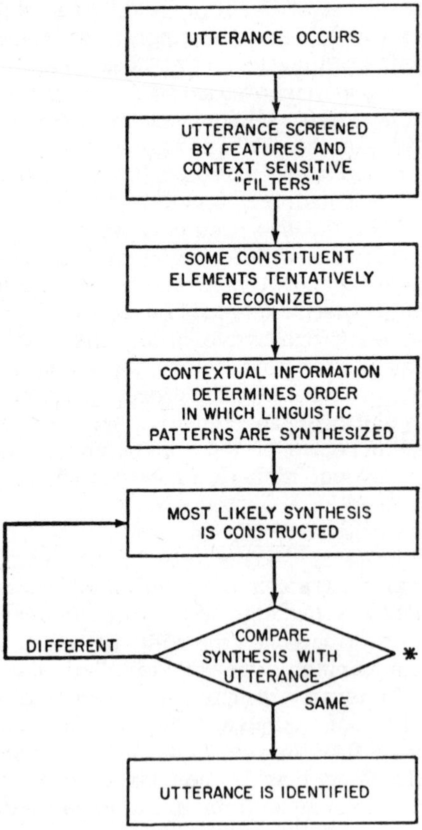

Neisser[12] has outlined an "analysis-by-synthesis" model of speech perception which incorporates, as an important component, an evaluative operation similar to Bruner's[13] "hypothesis testing" and Solley and Murphy's[14] "trial and check" behavior. Listening, according to this model, is a sequential process. (See Figure 1.) The incoming flow of speech first passes through a "filter system" which segments the flow, extracts a few distinctive features, and tentatively recognizes some of the constituent elements or units. The filter system is not only feature sensitive, but context sensitive, and many of the tentative identifications are made on the basis of expectancies derived from contextual cues. Elements which pass through this filter system (the "preattentive phase") are the building blocks with which the listener then attempts to construct or synthesize an utterance internally to match the actual input. The constructive process is not aimlessly trial-and-error, but is guided by contextual information to synthesize the most probable identification first, the least probable last. Thus, context controls the order in which linguistic patterns are synthesized, and these patterns are successively constructed and compared with the actual input until a match is found. The occurrence of a match terminates the synthesis phase and the utterance is perceived.

Analysis-by-synthesis thus involves a "goodness of fit" test which compares the characteristics of the actual speech input with the characteristics of the tentative identification. It seems plausible to equate the ability to perform this comparison rapidly and accurately with the operation designated "evaluation of semantic relations" in the Guilford structure of intellect model, especially at the level of sentence perception and the understanding of connected discourse. The analysis-by-synthesis model specifies that the constructive process can occur on different levels, and yields synthetic units of varying length and complexity, depending on whether the perceptual task is to discriminate individual speech sounds, identify single words, or understand a sentence. As Neisser describes the process:

> Hearing an utterance, the listener constructs one of his own in an attempt to match it. Such matching may go on at "several levels"--that is, in terms of different segment sizes. If a single . . . word is presented, the listener's preliminary speech analysis may pick out a few distinctive features or syllables which suggest a tentative answer; various related words are then synthesized until

> one of them fits. If the stimulus is an entire sequence, a few words tentatively identified by the preliminary system may guide the synthesis of whole constituents as units, or even of the whole sentence.[15]

Presumably, the type of operation necessary to evaluate a synthesis depends upon the level at which the synthesis takes place. Since the evaluation of semantic relations is defined as the comparison of the ways verbal concepts are meaningfully connected, we must assume that it functions at a very complex level in speech perception. The level at which evaluation occurs may itself have implications for the understanding of compressed speech. For the matching operation at higher levels of complexity appears to require more processing time than at lower, less complex levels.[16] Conjunctionally, the technique of compression reduces the amount of processing time which is available to the listener.

By interpreting Guilford's concept of the evaluative operation as one step at one level in the analysis-by-synthesis sequence, we can perhaps offer an explanation for our finding that the Best Trend Name Test was a better predictor of comprehension at high rates of compression than it was at normal speech rate. When the speech signal is degraded in quality (as happens in the case of compression), the listener must repeatedly form, test, and reject hypotheses in search of adequate synthesis. Moreover, the need for greater perceptual processing of degraded information coincides with an increased rate of input. The result is that there is less time available to do more synthesizing. Under these conditions, the ability to perform the evaluative operation, with accuracy and rapidity, becomes a critical factor in the comprehension of compressed speech.

Notes

Abbreviated references refer to the entry number in Sam Duker's Listening Bibliography 2nd Ed., (Scarecrow, 1968) where the full citation may be found.

1. Edwin A. Fleishman. "Factor Structure in Relation to Task Difficulty in Psychomotor Performance." Educational and Psychological Measurement 17:522-32, 1957.

2. H. L. Friedman, D. B. Orr, and C. M. Norris. Further

Research on Speeded Speech as an Educational Medium, Final Report, Part 3. Washington: American Institutes for Research, 1966.

David B. Orr and Herbert L. Friedman. "The Effect of Listening Aids on the Comprehension of Time-Compressed Speech." Journal of Communication 17:223-27, September 1967.

David B. Orr and H. L. Friedman. "Effect of Massed Practice on the Comprehension of Time-Compressed Speech." Journal of Educational Psychology 59:6-11, 1968.

David B. Orr, Herbert L. Friedman, and Jane C. C. Williams. "Trainability of Listening Comprehension of Speeded Discourse." Journal of Educational Psychology 56:148-56, June 1965.

3. Ralph Hoepfner, K. Nihira, and J. P. Guilford. "Intellectual Abilities of Symbolic and Semantic Judgment." Psychological Monographs 80:1-47, 1966.

4. J. P. Guilford. "Intelligence has Three Facets." Science 160:615-20, 1968.

5. David B. Orr and H. L. Friedman. "The Effect of Listening Aids on the Comprehension of Time-Compressed Speech." Journal of Communication 17:223-27, 1967.

6. B. J. Winer. Statistical Principles in Experimental Design. New York: McGraw-Hill, 1962.

7. Ralph Hoepfner, loc. cit.

8. S. W. Brown, J. P. Guilford, and Ralph Hoepfner. "A Factor Analysis of Semantic Memory Abilities." Report of the Psychological Laboratory. No. 37. Los Angeles: University of Southern California, 1966.

9. G. A. Miller and S. Isard. "Some Perceptual Consequences of Linguistic Rules." Journal of Verbal Learning and Verbal Behavior 2:217-28, 1963.

10. M. I. Posner and R. F. Mitchell. "Chronometric Analysis of Classification." Psychological Review 74:392-409, 1967.

11. G. A. Miller and N. Chomsky. "Finitary Models of Language Uses." In R. D. Luce, R. R. Bush, and E. Galanter (Eds.), Handbook of Mathematical Psychology, Volume II. New York: Wiley, 1963, p. 483-88.

12. Ulric Neisser. Cognitive Psychology. New York: Appleton, 1967.

13. Jerome S. Bruner. "Personality Dynamics and the Process of Perceiving." In R. R. Blake and G. V. Ramsay (Eds.), Perception: an Approach to Personality. New York: Ronald, 1951.

14. Charles M. Solley and C. M. Murphy. The Development of the Perceptual World. New York: Basic Books, 1960.

15. Neisser, op. cit., p. 196.

16. Posner, loc. cit.

Listening Comprehension as a Measure of Concurrent Reading Capability

Harry Singer

The Durrell-Sullivan Reading Capacity Test (DSRC), designed to measure reading capacity in grades 3 to 6, is based on the principle that the potential reading achievement of an individual should be equal to his auditory comprehension. DSRC has two subtests. (1) For Word Meaning, the tester pronounces a word which corresponds to one of a group of eight pictures. (2) On Paragraph Meaning, the tester reads a short story, then asks five questions about the story. The pupil answers each question by selecting an appropriate picture from a set of three pictures. The reliabilities for these subtests are high: for grades 3 to 6 they range from .90 to .96 for Word Meaning and from .83 to .93 for Paragraph Meaning.

The principle is dependent upon a basic assumption of uniformity in brain functioning in response to language relationships, whether input is through the visual or through the auditory system. This basic principle and its neurological assumption were explicitly formulated by Sullivan [17] in the first description of the test:

> The principle underlying the use of measures of auditory comprehension as criteria for potential reading achievement is that if the mind is able to handle auditory symbols up to a certain degree of complexity, it should be able to handle visual symbols up to that same degree of difficulty. This principle, of course, assumes a uniformity of brain structure in regard to the handling of symbolic relationships that are involved in language.

Although DSRC has now been in use for some 25 years, there is still very little evidence to support its validity as a measure of reading potential.

Related Research. Whatever it is that DSRC measures

does improve with grade level because there is an average increment of 16 points of raw scores between each year level [Alden, Sullivan, and Durrell, 1]. A correlation between DSRC and Stanford-Binet Intelligence Test (SB) scores for 80 children in grade 4 through 7 enrolled in a public school remedial reading program was .76, but DSRC in comparison with SB overestimated reading potential [Bliesmer, 3]. In a multiple regression equation, DSRC had about equal weight with the California Test of Mental Maturity in predicting scores on California Reading Test [13]. However, for a sample of 87 fourth graders the correlation between DSRC and Gates Basic Reading Tests Types A and D, ranged from only .41 to .54; the highest correlation between DSRC and Primary Mental Abilities (PMA) was .64 between DSRC Word Meaning and PMA Pictures [Bond and Clymer, 4].

Problem. The general purpose of this study is to test by means of a factor-analysis model the basic assumption underlying DSRC that there is uniformity of brain functioning in response to language relationships. Therefore, the following specific questions were formulated. (a) What is the factor analytic structure of DSRC when it is embedded in a matrix of variables selected for their known ability to predict speed and power of reading [Singer, 14]? (b) Is the factor-loading pattern of DSRC similar to that of speed and power of reading? (c) How similar are the factor loading patterns of DSRC and such subskills as word meaning, word recognition, and visual and auditory perceptual abilities?

Further clarification of these questions is necessary. If there is a "uniformity of brain structure" in handling the symbolic relationships involved in responding appropriately to visual symbols of reading tests and to auditory symbols of DSRC, then the factor analytic structure of the visual and auditory tests would be similar. That is, the same factors or mental functions would contribute to the variability of the tests, if not equally then at least proportionately. If so, DSRC would gain support as a valid measure of potential reading achievement.

However, reading ability is not unidimensional, but divides into two major interrelated components, speed and power of reading. Underlying and supporting each component is a complexly interrelated structure of subskills and capacities [Holmes, 7]. Broadly categorized, this general structure consists of interrelated input, mediating, output, and both short-term and long-term memory systems; all of these systems are overlaid with emotional systems and undergirded by physiological systems [Holmes and Singer, 9]. Within the limitations of developmental changes and test battery comparability, this general structure for attaining speed and power of reading has been verified at the college [Holmes, 7], high school [Holmes and Singer, 9], and intermediate grade level [Singer, 14].

These subskills and capacities are predictors at some level in the general structure for speed and power of reading. For example, the following are some of the predictors which occur in the structural model of power of reading in the fourth grade [Singer, 14]. At the lowest level, spelling recognition together with prefixes and spelling recall enter into the constellation of subabilities that make up Word Recognition in Context. At the middle level, word recognition in context, plus suffixes, and mental age contribute to the variance in Vocabulary in Isolation. Finally, on the highest level, vocabulary in isolation becomes integrated with suffixes, mental age, and matching sounds in words to culminate in Power of Reading.

The question then is whether DSRC is also a "capacity" test for one or more of these predictors, particularly the word recognition predictors. This question is quite important because at least from an instructional viewpoint the nature of the reading task changes during the developmental continuum. In the initial stages of reading instruction, development of perceptual and word recognition subskills is emphasized. At this stage, individuals have already matured sufficiently in their reasoning or mediational processing systems so that they could adequately comprehend the relatively simple ideas presented in beginning instructional material, provided that their input or word recognition subsystem were adequately developed for transforming printed stimuli into mental processes. But, during this initial stage there are individual differences in the input system which may be attributable to variation in ability to conceptualize linguistic stimuli, effectiveness of instructional strategies, modality sensitivity and receptivity, or to an interaction of these sources of variance. However, as individuals progress through the grades, they gradually tend to master word recognition processes [Singer, 14]; instructional emphasis then shifts to further development of ability to reason about the increasingly complex ideas presented in the instructional material. Hence, during the developmental continuum of learning to read, there is a shift in instructional emphasis from an estimate of input to an estimate of mediational processing potential.

Method

Sample A battery of 30 tests was administered to 283 fourth graders in a school located in an average socio-economic district in Alvord, California. From comparison of the means of the sample data with standardized test norms on age, I.Q., Speed and Power of Reading, the sample appears to be somewhat representative of the general population of fourth graders.

The grade equivalents for the current sample, according to the norms in the Durrell-Sullivan Manual, are 5.8 on Paragraph Meaning Achievement and 5.4 on Paragraph Meaning Capacity. Not only is the sample higher on achievement than on capacity, but the sample is also advanced approximately one grade level on both tests! However, on the Gates Reading Survey results, the current sample is approximately at grade level. A similar comparison between DSRC and Gates Reading Survey yielded comparable results in a previous investigation [Singer, 14]. These findings suggest that the Durrell-Sullivan norms probably overestimate grade equivalencies.

The cumulative records of the subjects revealed that they had been taught by a wide variety of teachers, had used a heterogeneous set of basal and supplementary readers, and had been registered in many school systems throughout the country. Therefore, the results of this study cannot be related to any particular set of materials nor to any particular methodological emphasis.

Tests. A test battery, listed in Table 1, was constructed of variables which would presumably measure comparable input and mediational processes in the visual and auditory systems for reading and listening, respectively. Reliability coefficients, also presented in Table 1, reveal that all the tests had substantially high reliabilities.

Concurrent validity coefficients between each of the tests and the subtests of DSRC are also given in Table 1. The highest correlation is .64 between DSRC Word Meaning and PMA Pictures. The next highest correlation is .56 between the subtests of DSRC, which means that listening vocabulary and listening comprehension in this sample have only 31 per cent of the variance in common. The correlation of .48 between Durrell-Sullivan Paragraph Meaning Capacity and Paragraph Meaning Achievement is surprisingly low, since Sullivan [17] stated that these tests were constructed with parallel content and comprehension questions. At the correlation level then, DSRC subtests are not highly predictive of any of the variables used in the study.

Factor Analysis. A principal components factor analysis with communalities of 1.0 was used to factor the matrix. The rank of the matrix was specified as the number of eigenvalues equal to or greater than 1.0. Kaiser's normalized varimax rotation technique for maximum interpretability was employed.

Results and Interpretation

The rotated principal component factor loadings, shown in Table 1, yielded five interpretable factors. Factor I was identified as Visual Verbal Meaning because tests with high loadings on this factor require subjects to read for comprehension, vocabulary, and word recognition. Factor II was labeled Auding [Editors note: This word is not in the dictionary but is sometimes used by certain authors as a synonym for "Listening," see Brown, 131.] since the listening tests, such as PMA Pictures, DSRC subtests, and Range of Information correlate highly with this factor. Factor III was named Visual Relationships to represent its saturation of PMA Space, Figure Grouping, and Perception, plus its substantial correlations with DSRC subtests and Word Reversals. Factor IV was defined as Speed of Visual Perceptions by high test loadings of Speed of Reading, Perception, Speed of Word Discrimination, Word Embedded, Figure and Ground, and Cue Symbol Closure. Factor V was called Auditory Perception because of its high correlations with Pitch, Rhythm, and Intensity.

Comparison of the factor loadings of either the Gates or Durrell-Sullivan reading comprehension tests with either of the DSRC subtests reveals that their patterns are not similar. The reading comprehension tests correlate .62 to .75 with Visual Verbal Meaning and .40 to .44 with Auding Factors. The DSRC subtests' highest loadings are .62 to .75 on Auding and .18 to .40 on Visual Relationships Factors. Although both the reading and the listening tests have substantial loadings on Factor II, the quantitative variation in their factor pattern does not substantiate the assumption that brain functioning in performance on these tests is uniform. On the contrary, the evidence supports the contention that the visual and auditory system mobilized for performance on the reading and listening tests although having some common functions and therefore some degree of cortical interfacilitation, are nevertheless

Table 1

Statistical Data on 30 Variables for 283 Fourth Graders

Test Battery	$\underline{r}_{1i}$	Correl. with Capacity for: Words	Par.	Principal Components Rotated Factor Loadings Factors* 1 VVM	2 AUD	3 VR	4 SVP	5 AP
1 <u>Durrell-Sullivan Reading Capacity</u>								
Word Meaning	85**	--	56	18**	75	18	20	16
Paragraph Meaning	87	56	--	16	62	40	10	25
2 <u>Gates Reading Survey</u>								
Speed of Reading	88	40	33	62	39	-19	35	15
Levels of Comprehension	89	45	45	75	40	12	-02	13
3 <u>Durrell-Sullivan Reading Achievement</u>								
Paragraph Meaning	91	52	48	66	44	11	16	24
4 <u>Thurstone Primary Mental Abilities</u>								
Words	91	43	38	76	39	00	00	15
Pictures	70	64	49	28	78	10	07	11
Space	83	25	42	14	19	74	-01	12

	Word Grouping	79	39	42	68	29	30	02	08
	Figure Grouping	84	37	42	20	21	73	09	06
	Perception	94	28	34	27	04	57	40	07
5	<u>Van Wagenen-Dvorak Silent Reading</u>								
	Range of Information	73	49	53	40	67	13	04	04
6	<u>Singer Linguistic Tests</u>								
	Auding Conceptual Ability	76	45	49	51	34	29	10	25
	Meaning of Affixes	77	46	46	71	43	12	04	22
	Word Recog. in Context	93	28	34	80	11	18	-02	15
	Matching Sounds in Words	96	35	32	86	18	17	-01	03
	Blending Word Elements	85	32	32	80	11	23	05	12
	Phonics	92	38	35	75	24	16	02	16
	Syllabication Consistency	83	28	27	71	11	15	13	11
	Auditory Verbal Abstraction	90	30	33	75	14	19	00	09
	Spelling Recognition	90	34	30	83	16	00	19	13
	Speed of Word Perception	80	29	31	57	11	-00	46	14
	Recog. of Affixes and Roots	89	31	25	68	02	24	14	10
	Word Reversals	73	30	40	43	06	48	15	36
7	<u>Holmes Language Perception</u>								
	Word Embedded	92	24	31	59	03	17	44	-01
	Figure and Ground	78	20	08	-01	08	-01	82	-04

Table 1 (Cont.)

Statistical Data on 30 Variables for 283 Fourth Graders

Test Battery	r_{1i}	Correl. with Capacity for: Words	Par.	Principal Components Rotated Factor Loadings Factors* 1 VVM	2 AUD	3 VR	4 SVP	5 AP
Cue Symbol Closure	78	29	27	07	16	29	65	10
8 K-D-H Musical Aptitudes								
Pitch Discrimination	73	21	22	17	21	10	-01	50
Rhythm Discrimination	64	24	25	19	01	15	07	72
Tonal Intensity Discrim.	82	24	34	07	15	02	02	73

*Identification of Factors

1. Visual Verbal Meaning
2. Auding
3. Visual Relationships
4. Speed of Visual Perception
5. Auditory Perception

**Decimals before correlations and factor loadings have been omitted.

separate systems. Hence, at least at the fourth grade level, listening comprehension alone cannot justifiably be used as a valid measure of concurrent reading achievement, and vice versa.

Nor should DSRC subtests be used as a valid measure of concurrent word recognition achievement at the fourth grade level because none of the word recognition measures has any substantial loading on the Auding Factor. Furthermore, the loadings of .18 for DSRC Paragraph Meaning and .16 for DSRC Word Meaning on the Visual Verbal Meaning Factor are quite low. Again, the evidence suggests that two more or less separate systems are operating in performance on DSRC subtests and on word recognition abilities.

Discussion

If the DSRC type of test is taken as a valid measure of an individual's reading potential, then an explanation has to be sought for a significant discrepancy between reading potential and reading achievement, even when achievement is actually higher than potential [Alden, Sullivan, and Durrel, 1]. For some individuals the discrepancy may be validly attributed to inadequate instruction, desire to learn, or to some other causal factor, all of which assume that under optimal conditions there would be no discrepancy. A more general explanation, supported by the results of this study and by the findings of a similar investigation on 60 fourth graders [14], is that at least two separate, though moderately interrelated systems are mobilized for performance in reading and in listening; therefore, an individual could perform better or have higher potential in one than in the other system, possibly as a result of intra-individual variation in mental capacities or asynchronous development of mental functions.

Further support for the interpretation of the separateness of the two systems can be adduced from several studies: Gates [6] concluded that visual perception for words, objects, and geometric symbols are specific abilities; Karwoski, Gramlick, and Arnott [11] inferred that the longer reaction times for objects and pictures than for words was due to the formulation of an intermediary symbol before a verbal response to objects and pictures could be made; Strang [16] explained that verbal and nonverbal mental tests tap different mental processes; Gaffrey [5] at the high school level identified an auding factor, which was distinct from reading comprehension, mental age, chronological age, and interests; and Spearritt [15] at the sixth grade level using the STEP listening test in a battery that included reading, reasoning, and rote memory, also isolated a listening comprehension factor. Consistent with all these findings is the localization theory of neurology [Nielsen, 12] with its implications for the reading process [Holmes, 8] that different areas of the brain are involved in (a) visual perception of objects, pictures, and words and (b) auditory perception of music and language. Moreover, from a battery of tests the best predictor of first grade reading achievement was the visual word discrimination subtests of Gates Reading Readiness [Balow, 2]. It would therefore seem that a valid test of silent reading potential would necessarily be weighted with items or scales that require perception, retention, manipulation and conceptualization of written or printed verbal symbols, with input through the visual mode.

Summary

The validity of the basic assumption supporting the use of the Durrell-Sullivan Reading Capacity Test as a measure of reading potential was investigated by means of principal components factor analysis. Factors were extracted from a matrix of 30 variables that had been selected to measure both visual and auditory input and mediational processing systems for listening and for reading. The varimax rotated factor loadings for a sample of 283 fourth graders did not support the Durrell-Sullivan assumption that there is a uniformity of brain structure in regard to the handling of symbolic relationships in listening and reading tests. The listening tests primarily loaded on an Auditory Factor while the reading tests primarily tapped a Visual Verbal Factor. However, the pattern of loadings suggested that what DSRC actually assesses in the fourth grade is listening comprehension at a concrete or auditory-visual associational level rather than listening comprehension at a more abstract level. Consequently, an alternate hypothesis was advanced that what is mobilized for performance in listening and reading in the fourth grade are two separate, though moderately interrelated, multidimensional systems in which individuals could have higher potential in one system than in the other. Caution should therefore be exercised in the use in the fourth grade of the Durrell-Sullivan Reading Capacity Test alone for assessing concurrent reading capability.

This conclusion should not, of course, be generalized to other measures of listening comprehension, to other grade levels, nor to other curricula without further investigation.

In fact, Holmes and Singer [9] found in a factor analytic study of a similar battery at the high school level that another measure of listening comprehension and reading achievement did indeed correlate highly with the same factor. Further integration in these two systems apparently occurs sometime after the fourth grade level. Moreover, it is possible that emphasis at the elementary level upon the development of listening comprehension may accelerate this integration. If so, then listening comprehension would serve as a more valid group estimate of concurrent reading capability even at the elementary school level, but caution would still be necessary in estimating expectancy levels in particular individuals because of the possibility of (a) intraindividual variation in capacities or (b) asynchronous development of an individual's cognitive systems for listening and for reading.

Notes

Abbreviated references refer to the entry number in Sam Duker's <u>Listening Bibliography</u> 2nd Ed., (Scarecrow, 1968) where the full citation may be found.

1. Alden, Clara L., Helen B. Sullivan and Donald D. Durrell. "The Frequency of Special Reading Abilities." <u>Education</u> 62:32-36, 1941.

2. Balow, I. H. "Sex Differences in First Grade Reading." <u>Elementary English</u> 40:303-06, 1963.

3. Bliesmer, E. P. "A Comparison of Results of Various Capacity Tests Used with Retarded Readers." <u>Elementary School Journal</u> 56:400-02, 1956.

4. Bond, G. L. and T. W. Clymer. "Interrelationship of the SRA Primary Mental Abilities, Other Mental Characteristics, and Reading Ability." <u>Journal of Educational Research</u> 49:131-36, 1955.

5. Caffrey, 161.

6. Gates, A. I. "A Study of the Role of Visual Perception, Intelligence, and Certain Associative Processes in Reading and Spelling." <u>Journal of Educational Psychology</u> 17:433-35, 1926.

7. Holmes, J. A. Factors Underlying Major Reading Disabilities at the College Level. Doctoral dissertation. Berkeley: University of California, 1948.

8. Holmes, J. A. "The Brain and the Reading Process." Reading is Creative Living, Twenty-second Yearbook of Claremont College Reading Conference. Claremont, Calif.: Claremont College Curriculum Laboratory, 1957, p. 49-67.

9. Holmes and Singer, 580.

10. Holmes, J. A. and H. Singer. "Theoretical Models and Trends Toward More Basic Research in Reading." Review of Educational Research 34:127-55, 1964.

11. Karworski, T. F., F. W. Gramlick, and P. Arnott. "Psychological Studies in Semantics: I. Free Association Reactions to Words, Drawings, and Objects." Journal of Social Psychology 20:233-47, 1944.

12. Nielsen, J. M. A Textbook of Clinical Neurology. 3rd. Revised Edition. New York: Harper, 1951.

13. Owen, 925.

14. Singer, H. Conceptual Ability in the Substrata-Factor Theory of Reading. Doctoral dissertation. Berkeley: University of California, 1960.

15. Spearritt, 1117. Summarized in Russell, 1036.

16. Strang, Ruth. "Relationships between Certain Aspects of Intelligence and Certain Aspects of Reading." Educational and Psychological Measurement. 3:355-59, 1943.

17. Sullivan, 1158.

Listening: Complex of Activities -- And a Unitary Skill?

Charles M. Kelly

A definite study of listening behavior might treat such factors as motivation, habit, attention, auditory acuity, memory span, and comprehension; all these, and more, are variables that have been investigated by research scholars in psychology, speech, education, and related fields. Nevertheless, though listening obviously involves a complex of activities, the phrase "listening ability" (or "listening skill") has acquired a special meaning in recent years. It has come to refer to a presumably unitary ability to listen to and comprehend oral communication. Certainly, too, in pedagogical thinking and writing, "listening," as a behavior, is usually defined in reference to those tests, research projects, and training programs purportedly dealing with consecutive discourse and its comprehension, whether between individuals or between speakers and formal audiences. Fundamental to virtually all such study or evaluation of this kind of listening are two premises: (1) listening is a unique, unitary ability; and (2) listening ability, so understood, can be measured by testing the listening comprehension of subjects who know they are being tested.

It is the contention of this paper that there is sufficient evidence to indicate that, for all practical purposes, listening should be considered a complex of activities, not a unitary skill that can be isolated and measured. In other words, it is argued here that our traditional procedures for testing listening are sterile, as customarily used, and that currently published listening tests are not valid measures of a unique skill such as has been posited in much of the literature on listening.

Since this position contradicts most published opinion on the subject, it will be necessary to undertake an extended analysis of the procedures that have been used in testing listening, in determining the validity of listening tests, and, to some degree, in evaluating listening training.[1]

Testing Procedures

The effects of traditional testing procedures on listeners have long been a concern in research. Many of the possible sources of error, when listening is studied, are obvious; several have been demonstrated experimentally. In testing situations some of the "best" listeners may be subjects with high mental ability who normally are relatively inattentive under non-test circumstances, and some of those who are "good listeners" under normal (non-test) conditions[2] may do poorly in the test environment because they were handicapped by inability to understand the difficult material frequently found in the tests of listening. This is not to imply that all our experiments in listening must approximate normal, non-test conditions. If, however, an experiment does not approximate normal conditions, the researcher must find some way to demonstrate the validity of his conclusions when extrapolated to the typical behavior of the listeners.

The extent to which results can be affected by "mental set" was illustrated by Charles Brown, who compared listening comprehension of two groups of subjects under two different conditions.[3] In the first trial, each group took different alternate forms of the STEP listening test (i.e., group 1 took form 1A; group 2 took form 1B) with prefacing remarks before each individual selection. A typical prefatory comment was: "Here is the fourth selection. It is a speech about the . . . . In the main, the questions at the end will test your memory." In the second trial, the two groups took the other alternate form of the STEP with no prefacing remarks before each selection. The observed difference of 5.18 between the two means (48.48 and 43.30) was significant at the .01 level. Brown concluded that the listener's anticipation of the purpose of the message was an important factor in his comprehension.

It should be noted that both listening situations in Brown's experiment were test conditions and that the difference in "experimental set" was induced simply by prefacing remarks. It could be hypothesized that the difference in set between test and non-test conditions would be much greater.

An interesting inference might be drawn from the following report by Caffrey:

> During the auding test one teacher observed a boy ("a very poor student") with his head buried on his arm on the desk, apparently sleeping or doodling on

> the test paper idly; he was the highest score in his class. About the same proportion of good auders was found in so-called "remedial" classes as in regular groups.[4]

A tenable hypothesis here might be that good auders of the remedial groups were good auders because they were motivated by test conditions; they may not have been motivated to be good auders under normal classroom conditions. The difference between the regular and remedial classes under classroom conditions may be motivation, not ability--at least as far as listening is concerned.

Knower reported an experiment which involved (1) subjects who knew they would be tested over the content given in a talk and (2) subjects who were told only that the purpose of the project was for them to rate the speaker. Knower concluded: "Subjects who knew that they were to be tested retained on the average somewhat more material than subjects who were not told that they were to be tested."[5]

What makes this experiment especially significant is the fact that even the subjects who were not expecting a test had an artifically added interest in the talk, since they knew they were to rate the speaker.

The same results were found in another study in which listening tests were given to two groups of nurses; the difference between the means of a "surprise" test and an "announced" test was significant at the .01 level.[6]

Two separate experiments also indicated that mental ability plays a greater role in listening when subjects know in advance that they are to be tested (.05 level).[7]

Although the dangers of the testing situation are obvious, research scholars are caught in a dilemma: if they warn subjects they are to be tested, the subjects are motivated (thus "standardizing" the test conditions and making inoperative many factors that would normally affect comprehension) and the test becomes artificial; yet, if subjects are not warned, reliability suffers and it cannot be considered a "fair" test.

Even in the best studies of listening, in which an attempt was made to normalize conditions, it is difficult to decide how well this was done. Nichols reported in his classic study that "Special effort was made to make the lecture situations as nearly normal and conventional as possible."[8]

In spite of this effort, a board of judges who observed the subjects in the various sections gave the following reports:

> Literature: Audience seemed unusually quiet and attentive....
>
> Economics: Audience was quiet and attentive throughout. The speaker 'pounded hard, and attention did not waiver.' There was some 'strained attentiveness.'
>
> Biology: Audience quiet and attentive....
>
> One further observation was volunteered by one of the judges, Dr. Thurston. She wrote: 'In general, the students were remarkably attentive and cooperative.'[9]

It is unlikely that an "unusually quiet and attentive," or a remarkably attentive and cooperative" audience is typical of "normal and conventional" classroom situations, yet it is to such situations that Nichols' findings are often generalized.

In reporting the construction of a listening test, Brown also recognized the tester's dilemma when he wrote: "Subjective evidence indicates that the test is more interesting than other tests and that students were motivated to genuine effort."[10] Whether or not "genuine" effort results from a greater than average interest in a test is questionable.

Irvin summarized the difficulty in controlling motivation in reporting his own study:

> ...the only attempts to control this 'receptiveness' were these:
>
> 1. An earnest attempt not to offer rewards in the form of grades, etc., to the listener which might be considered an extra motivating factor favorable to receptiveness.
>
> 2. An explanation within the listening training itself of the power of worry, emotional upset, etc., as a deterrent to effective listening.

> At this point in listening research, it must be conceded that receptiveness at the time of listening is a variable that must be considered uncontrollable. Some studies have sought to overcome it by extra motivation devices. However, such devices have tended to destroy the normalcy of the listening activity.[11]

It may be added that not only "devices" may destroy the "normalcy" of the listening activity, but changing the noraml activity to a testing activity may have the same effect and probably to a much greater degree.

This observation is supported by some of the conclusions of experiments in listening comprehension. Contrary to what might be expected, Nichols found evidence that "listener buoyancy and optimism," social ease of the listener, and worries of the listener about personal problems did not importantly influence listening comprehension.[12] Heath found no significant relationship between listening ability and stated interest in the subject of "interest" as measured by the Kuder Preference Record.[13] Results obtained by Karraker indicated that prediction of listening effectiveness on the basis of interest had only about fifty-one chances in one hundred.[14] Do these conclusions seem characteristic of normal listening situations in which one human being attends to the every-day discourse of another?

Listening Test Validity

Publications to date indicate that researchers have failed to produce any statistical verifications of listening test validity. In fact, evidence strongly suggests that currently published listening tests measure the same basic factors that are now reliably measured by established achievement tests not involving listening.

In every research report of which this author is aware, when two different listening tests have been placed into a battery with a good non-listening achievement test, the listening tests have appeared to be no more similar to each other than each was to the achievement test. That is, when the contents of the listening tests are different (thus changing their commonality of format or subject matter), they lose their identity as unique tests, regardless of the fact that they are presented orally.

Petrie discovered that the Goyer Organization of Ideas Test correlated higher with the Brown-Carlsen listening test and with his own listening test than the listening tests did with each other.[15] (His own test consisted of a half-hour lecture, followed by a written examination.)

Statistical data obtained from a battery of tests given to a group of industrial supervisors indicated that the Brown-Carlsen and STEP listening tests measured factors other than listening. The correlation between the Brown-Carlsen and the STEP was .82; the correlation between the Brown-Carlsen and the Otis Test of Mental Ability was .85; and the correlation between the STEP and the Otis was .85.[16] If the Brown-Carlsen and STEP were both reliable measures of unique factors in the listening of these supervisors, they should have correlated higher with each other than with a test of general mental ability; this was not the case.

This experiment was repeated with college students, and basically the same results were found.[17] (Correlations were all lower because of the greater homogeneity of the sample.) The correlation between the STEP and the Brown-Carlsen tests was .46; between the STEP and a Selective Admission Test, .49; and between the Brown-Carlsen and the Selective Admission Test, .46. It is especially noteworthy that the Selective Admission Test consists only of 60 vocabulary items and 50 mathematics problems. Of course, no listening is involved.

Haberland, in investigating the Brown-Carlsen, the Michigan State College, and the Stephens College Listening Tests, noticed a marked relationship between intelligence test measures (Otis and ACE) and listening ability. Yet he also noted: "The tests of listening ability do not agree closely with each other. They yield vastly different results when correlated with scores on standardized tests."[18] (Correlations between listening tests were not reported.) Haberland supplied a large table of correlations; those in Table 1 are illustrative and suggest that factors not associated with listening as a discrete ability can exert a strong influence on listening test scores.

Table 1 indicates (as Haberland concluded) that the Brown-Carlsen test may be the most difficult test, thus being more appropriate for men in regular classes. The Stephens College Test, being easiest, discriminated best for subjects

Table 1

Correlations Between the Linguistic Section of the ACE and Three Different Listening Tests

	Brown-Carlsen Listening Test	Michigan Listening Test	Stephens Listening Test
Freshman Men in Regular Classes	.72	.42	.09
Freshman Men in Remedial Classes	.33	.31	.47

in reading improvement courses. We may conclude from this that the listening test at the proper difficulty level discriminated best, but probably on the basis of general linguistic ability (among other factors measured by the ACE). The fact that all three listening tests were presented orally did not enable them to measure a common, unique variable.

Haberland also arrived at the usual conclusion that, since the Brown-Carlsen test correlated highest with all the linguistic sections of the standardized tests, it was the best listening test. From available evidence, this is precisely the reason it may have been the worst test. A listening test that measures anything but verbal or general mental ability is hard, if not impossible, to find.

Not only do different listening tests lack commonality, but, apparently, sometimes alternate forms of the same test are found not to be sufficiently equivalent. Anderson and Baldauf, in investigating the STEP listening test, found that the correlation between the alternate forms (forms 4A and 4B were given to fifth-grade pupils) was .74. Yet the overall correlation between the STEP and the Stanford Achievement Test was .82. They concluded:

> Verbal comprehension appears to be the largest factor contributing to the intercorrelations between the various achievement variables. Upon examin-

> ing the factor pattern, the heavy loadings on this one factor suggest that achievement on the test may be largely a matter of verbal comprehension and not uniquely associated with listening as a skill....As this test is now constructed, it appears to be of little general utility in an overall standardized achievement battery for use in a public school testing program.[19]

This is the same listening test (STEP 4A) that Brown used when he tried to eliminate the influence of mental ability by matching criterion groups. He paired Amish and non-Amish children in the 4th, 5th, and 6th grades on the basis of scores received on the California Test of Mental Maturity, thus attempting to eliminate this variable experimentally. (Amish were selected because they do not have radio or TV sets in their homes.) On the basis of results from these tests, Brown concluded that "The first hypothesis, that children who watch television are better listeners than those who do not, was supported at the one percent level of significance."[20]

This seemingly hopeful research design raises the question: if these listening tests (the very same form was used by Anderson and Baldauf with fifth-grade pupils) measure primarily general verbal comprehension, why did Brown detect a significant difference, when this factor was supposedly eliminated? A tenable explanation may be that the Amish children are apt to do less well with almost any unusual test. When confronted with a new situation, the person with a varied background should adapt more readily than a person of limited experience, even though both are equated on the basis of a particular mental test.

This explanation appears more reasonable in light of the results of two separate test batteries in which alternate forms of the Brown-Carlsen and STEP listening tests were administered to college students.[21] In both cases, the listening tests given second in a series had significantly lower standard deviations than those administered first. There is bound to be some difference between means and standard deviations of alternate forms administered successively to the same group of subjects, no matter how well the forms are matched. And it is not unusual to find that this difference is in the narrowing of the standard deviation on the second administration, since almost any test is apt to have both ceiling and practice effects (the difficulty of high scorers' scoring higher, and the possibility of lower scorers' improving with practice). However, the more "different" or novel the test, the more pronounced the results; in the studies mentioned, the standard deviation of the STEP decreased by 28 percent (from 7.47 to 5.36) and the Brown-Carlsen decreased by 23 percent (from 6.23 to 4.77) on second administration--significant at the .01 and .05 levels respectively.

Normally, alternate forms should have about the same standard deviations and reliabilities; however, as Thorndike points out, some tests may be so novel that the experience of being tested adds a significant increment to the individual's practice with the task, so that he is a somewhat different individual at the time of a subsequent test.[22] Anastasi suggests that individuals are likely to differ in amount of improvement, depending upon previous practice with similar material, motivation in taking the test, and other factors.[23] The observations of Thorndike and Anastasi, along with the research results just mentioned, suggest that both the Brown-Carlsen and the STEP tests may have been novel even to the college students tested, to say nothing of Brown's Amish subjects.

In evaluating the studies employing factor analysis, the reader must realize that in each case the statistical results are subjectively interpreted by the investigator (validity is always subjectively determined). Naturally, the usual tendency is to view any unique factor which is found in a listening test as a factor of "listening comprehension."

For illustration, let us analyze the three studies cited by Duker in the most recent review of "What We Know about Listening." In an attempt to substantiate his contention that listening comprehension can be measured, he wrote: "Factor analyses performed by Spearritt, Hanley and Karlin leave no doubt that a quality called 'comprehension of verbal materials presented in spoken form,' which may be referred to as 'listening comprehension', may be identified and isolated."[24]

The first observation one makes in reviewing these studies is that those of Hanley and Karlin explored auditory acuity, rather than the type of listening usually associated with the audience situation.

Hanley's thirty-two tests were all auditory and were designed to test such things as the subject's pitch discrimination, loudness discrimination, sound discrimination, and vocabulary. Although most listening tests previously developed appear to be highly related to verbal ability, Hanley found that "the verbal facility factor was identified in this study but appeared to be unrelated to speech perception measures."[25] (Vocabulary recognition was tested by having subjects check appropriate synonyms printed on paper, as words were spoken.) This indicates that the one test that was most closely associated with listening, when a member of an audience, was unrelated to the rest of her study which dealt mostly with auditory acuity under different conditions. Some of her other factors included: the voice memory factor, the Seashore Battery factor (musical talent), and the threshold of detectability of tones.

Whereas Hanley used only auditory tests, Karlin included five visual tests in his battery of thirty-two. The auditory tests were similar to Hanley's and included, for example: tonal memory, pure-tone loudness discrimination, sensory masking (listening through competing noise), and memory for male voices. In order to approximate "complex social situations" he used tests such as: recall of orally spelled-out nonsense syllables, recall of illogically worded phrases, etc. His visual tests included such things as memory for drawings, memory for limericks (presented on a screen), and two general, mental ability tests.

Karlin found nine factors, such as "resistance to distortion of an auditory Gestalt," and "speed of closure." However, the most striking thing about his results is that his "speed of closure" factor included two auditory tests and one visual test; visual memory span was in this factor, while auditory memory span was not. This led Karlin to make what may be a very significant conclusion: "This factor appears to be a form of mental alertness and ability to make the best use of certain stimuli in a limited time."[26] And this leads to the question: once a person is aware of a stimulus, does it make much difference whether or not its presence was sensed by the eyes or the ears? It may very well not make a difference in the testing situation, except that the circumstances of the typical listening test may introduce more random error into the subject's ability to utilize stimuli over a period of time.

Karlin's finding also demonstrates the potential for error in factor analysis. Had he not used any visual tests in his battery (as Hanley did not), he undoubtedly would have discovered a "speed of auditory closure" factor. There is a moral here for those who have factor-analyzed a single listening test, or a battery consisting entirely of listening tests, into the "dimensions of listening comprehension."

By far the best factor analysis of listening comprehension was done by Spearritt, although his results raise as many questions as they answer. Using sixth-grade Australian children as subjects, he administered thirty-four tests which were intended to measure such factors as intelligence, reading vocabulary, different forms of reasoning, listening vocabulary, and listening comprehension. Nine of these were listening tests, all of which were especially constructed or modified for the investigation.

Although Spearritt found a factor which he called "listening comprehension," he noted that, "A separate listening comprehension factor was identified, but it was fairly closely related to verbal comprehension, induction and span of memory factors."[27] Two of the listening tests, "listening vocabulary" and "listening for general significance," had their highest loadings on the general "verbal comprehension" factor (four other listening tests were also included in this factor, but the loadings were smaller than for tests involving no listening). Spearitt speculated that this may have been due to the great importance that word meanings had in these two specific listening tests. Tests having the highest loadings in the listening comprehension were: listening to boys' talk, listening to girls' talk, listening to note details, listening to a short talk, and a modified version of the STEP listening test.

Apparently, Spearitt did find something unique in these listening tests, but the degree of this uniqueness was small and its cause is difficult to determine. It may be possible that he was able to achieve a series of genuine listening comprehension tests through thorough pretesting; all his tests underwent extensive pilot study. For example, he found that neither the STEP 4A, nor the STEP form 3A were at the right difficulty level for sixth-grade Australian children; after pilot testing, he selected three passages from each. A reason for the failure of past listening tests may be the fragile nature of the instrument or the procedure: it may measure little that is unique and need to be at the precise difficulty level of the subjects tested.

Another possible explanation for Spearitt's results is that all his listening tests were especially constructed or modified for the investigation. Any consistent bias, such as the method of testing which is unique to his brief listening tests, could account for differences. As he noted in his dissertation: "The factor structure of listening comprehension tests should also be investigated in 'live' listening situations and with other populations."[28]

Although much of the research in listening testing is debatable, one conclusion cannot be denied: no two test makers have agree statistically. If one wanted to predict how well a group of subjects would do on "X" listening test, but his best instrument for prediction would be almost any good, general achievement test, not another listening test.

Listening Training

Unfortunately, listening training programs to the present time have been evaluated solely by listening tests in which subjects knew in advance that they were being tested. No significant attempts have been made to evaluate the amount of improvement in listening skills retained by subjects in normal circumstances--circumstances unrelated to special instruction and to formal testing. Thus, the extent of the "Hawthorne effect" in studies of listening training is wholly unknown. Studies of other kinds, however, suggest that the effect may be great.

The sensitive nature of testing conditions was emphasized in research done by Baker, who investigated the effect of pre-experimental set in distraction experiments. His study involved a mental and oral task in which the subject added numbers aloud--first without any distraction--then while dance music was being played.

Four different groups were used. Group one was told nothing; the members knew only that they were in an experiment. Group two was shown a fictitious graph representing the results of some "previous work," which clearly indicated that task performance improved when dance music was played. Group three was also shown a fictitious graph of "previous work" which indicated the opposite--performance was hampered by dance music. The graph which was shown to group four indicated that task performance was first hampered and then helped by dance music. Baker's major finding was that the performance of each group conformed to the "mental set" created in advance: group one yielded "mixed" results; group two improved when music was played; group three was hampered by the music; and group four's performance at first was hampered and then was helped by the music. All four groups (with individual members as exceptions) performed in accord with the advance "information" given them. Baker then observed:

> ....our specific problem bears a relationship... to every experiment in psychology [using] ... human subjects who ... [are] old enough or intelligent enough to impose self-instruction or to react to minimal cues inadvertently given by the experimenter and not mentioned by him in his list of the conditions under which the experiment ... [is] performed. This would include all experiments purporting to demonstrate that one educational method of learning is more efficient than any other; that age, economic and social status, or any other condition of the organism produced by drugs, diet, fatigue, or lack of sleep have any effect at all on performance.[29]

Should not this experiment ring a few alarm bells for listening training? What happens when a group of subjects is given "Form A" listening test, followed by listening training, followed by the final "Form B" listening test? Typically, the training is accompanied by pep talks and at least a few practice tests. Could the experimental test induced by the trainer account for most of the significant differences reported in the literature?

It has also been shown that extrinsic rewards alone can improve scores on listening tests. In one study (of two) involving college students, it was shown that cash awards stimulated subjects to earn higher scores on a listening test (.05 point) when there was no listening training involved--only money.[30]

Another disturbing similarity can be noted between the results of administering tests before and after listening training and merely presenting listening tests in a series. It was shown in two separate experiments that, with no training between administrations of the tests, low scores benefited most (in relation to other subjects) from the second administration of a listening test.[31] At least three researchers have reported that those who benefited most from training were the low scorers.[32] Of course, in both kinds of situations the regression effect undoubtedly exerted its influence, but the similarities suggest that some of the improvement found in low scorers may have been due to "practice effect" (improvement due to increased familiarity with a test). Indeed, Rulison indirectly implied that much training is concerned with learning how to take a test when she reported a reaction of a subject in her training group: "Teach more about listening properly rather than just giving tests."[33]

Putting aside the above unsettling considerations and assuming that subjects who scored significantly higher on listening tests following training really had improved in "listening ability," one may still ask: Can it be concluded logically that those whose scores improved would perform better as listeners when no longer in a testing (or experimental) situation? This is a wholly unexplored question.

Conclusions

There can be no doubt that persons differ widely in their abilities to listen under test conditions, but these differences are, it appears, primarily functions of general mental ability and not primarily functions of an integrated capacity that can be called "listening ability." It is equally evident that persons differ widely in listening performance under normal conditions. Whether this kind of performance can be reliably measured, profitably investigated, and improved through training is largely unknown.

We have a massive body of information about the listening behavior of subjects who knew they were going to be tested. This is important information dealing with one type of listening activity. But we have done almost nothing to find out about performance across the general range of situations from panic to boredom.

The most apparent deficiency in research to date is the neglect of a very basic relationship: the typical behavior of persons listening to consecutive discourse under conditions of ordinary life compared to the listening behavior of like persons when taking a test. I suspect, as with other types of similar behavior, this is not a stable relationship. It is apt to have many variables, and researchers would do well to look for tendencies rather than for absolute values.

For example, it is likely that, as a subject's motivation to listen increases, the influence of mental ability upon his comprehension will also increase. In other words, when a listener's attention is maximal (as when taking a test), he probably makes full use of his mental ability to comprehend what is being presented, and his personality traits, past listening habits, etc. are relatively less important. In view of this possibility, a poorly-presented listening test may approximate "normal" listening conditions. We also may find that the correlation between listening comprehension and mental ability increases in relation to the ability of the speaker, since better speakers supposedly stimulate more audience attention.

Similar variations are bound to be found in listening training methods and training effectiveness. Without doubt, a person can greatly improve his ability to comprehend Morse code by many hours of practice, listening to the dots and dashes. An air-controlman (one who directs aircraft from a tower) may benefit from listening to and interpreting long series of short messages. But this does not mean that a student will necessarily be a better listener in a lecture situation if he has practiced listening to speeches in a course in listening; how well he listens may depend primarily on motivation.

Of course, persons may be more strongly motivated to listen if they understand the dynamics of the listening activity and the factors that influence it. Some listening training, therefore, may properly consist mostly of theory, or of "listening skills" developed through the type of practice commonly found in a course in interviewing.

One does not evade coming to grips with the underlying issues relative to a theory of listening by concluding that listening is <u>only</u> a complex of activities. If this conclusion is true, or even plausible--that listening is not a unique, unitary ability--there are very important implications for the planning of future research and development of future training programs. More imaginative (and possibly devious) ways must be discovered to study and evaluate the many different kinds of listening behavior, and training programs in "listening" must be planned and reported with far more specificity than in the past.

Notes

Abbreviated references refer to the entry number in Sam Duker's Listening Bibliography 2nd Ed., (Scarecrow, 1968) where the full citation may be found.

1. The studies cited here are those most significant and relevant to the issues raised. They represent, of course, but a small portion of published and unpublished research on listening.

2. "Normal" is used here to refer to "typical behavior," as discussed by Lee J. Cronbach: "The ... procedural requirement for measuring typical behavior is that the act of observing by the researcher must not alter the behavior observed." Essentials of Psychological Testing (New York, 1960), p. 44.

3. Charles Brown, 128.

4. John Caffrey, 161.

5. Franklin Knower, "Studies in Listening to Informative Speaking," Journal of Abnormal and Social Psychology, 15:82-88, 1945.

6. Charles M. Kelly, 654, p. 40.

7. Ibid., p. 56.

8. Ralph Nichols, 873.

9. Ibid., p. 27.

10. James Brown, 137, p. 143.

11. Charles Irvin, 607, p. 62.

12. Nichols, op. cit., p. 351.

13. Martha Ann Heath, 543.

14. Mary Karraker, 642.

15. Charles R. Petrie, 945.

16. Charles M. Kelly, 654.

17. Charles M. Kelly, 655.

18. John A. Haberland, 503, p. 302.

19. Harold Anderson and Robert Baldauf, 51, 198.

20. Charles Brown, 131.

21. Kelly, 655, p. 142.

22. Robert L. Thorndike, "Reliability." In Educational Measurement. (Edited by Everet F. Lindquist.) Washington: American Council on Education, 1951, p. 576.

23. Anne Anastasi, Psychological Testing. 2nd Ed. New York: Macmillan, 1961, p. 120.

24. Sam Duker and Charles R. Petrie, 335.

25. Clair Hanley, 512, p. 78.

26. John Elias Karlin, 641, p. 45.

27. Donald Spearritt, 1117, p. x.

28. Ibid., p. xii.

29. Kenneth Baker, "Pre-experimental Set in Distraction Experiments," Journal of General Psychology 16:474, 1937.

30. Kelly, 654, p. 50.

31. Kelly, 655, p. 142.

32. A detailed review of three such studies is presented in Petrie, 945, p. 45-47.

33. Kathleen Rulison, 1030, p. 79.

Chapter VI

Critical Listening

The critical abilities of its citizenry are probably the most essential key to the preservation of a democratic system. A general susceptibility to propaganda and an emotional approach instead of the use of judgment have been the hallmarks of those people who have fallen into subjection to a dictatorship.

Critical thinking, critical reading, and critical listening are so closely entwined that it is difficult to speak of one in a way that is irrelevant to the other two. It has therefore been a great temptation to devote a major proportion of this book to the subject of critical listening. Since this would involve major attention to critical thinking also, I decided that in a treatment of listening in general, such an emphasis would not be appropriate. The development of various other important aspects of listening would have had to be curtailed or eliminated. This in no way reflects a feeling that the subject of critical listening is not of the most urgent importance.

The best recent treatment of critical thinking and its relationship to listening is found in the Fall 1969 issue of the Journal of Development and Research in Education. This issue was edited by Sara W. Lundsteen who obtained her doctorate from the University of California after writing an outstanding thesis on the subject of critical listening. Her work was done under the late David H. Russell who was very keenly interested in critical thinking and who wrote a classic book on this subject, Children's Thinking (Ginn, 1956). Unlike too many others who simultaneously complete their dissertation and lose their interest in the topic dealt with, Professor Lundsteen, now at the University of Texas, has continued to be extremely active in developing new ways of helping children think, read, and listen critically. The bibliography of her writings on this subject is quite extensive.

The issue of the Journal referred to in the previous paragraph is highly recommended to all who have an interest in the topic of this chapter. Such a reader will find the bibliographies at the end of each article of particular value. Three of the articles have been excerpted for this book. One of these is the article by Lundsteen which makes up this entire chapter.

Critical Listening and Thinking: A Recommended Goal for Future Research

Sara W. Lundsteen

Assisting the development of language/thinking skills for children appears to be a concern of high priority and a goal of high worth to our culture. Several key ideas appear to point toward an important need. First, is the generalization that all problems are not solved by being able to think critically, but no problem is solved without it. Second, is the disturbing suggestion that years are spent in school crippling children in language/thinking skills rather than assisting them. Nor does the impact of mass media outside the school appear less damaging. In essence, critical listening does not appear to be a skill gained through random learning. The purpose of this paper is to ask and to try to answer these questions: (1) What does research, limited to instructional outcomes at elementary and at high school level, say to the teacher about improving critical listening, and (2) what steps need to be taken next?

In overview, research in critical listening is scarce and often confounded. It employs varied definitions, explanatory fictions, and hypothetical constructs. But there is hope in the form of a number of landmark studies. Apparently the time has come to make a compendium of the research that exists in order to form a knowledge base. The time has come to produce a plan for future investigation on the broadest possible scale.

Definitions. What is meant by critical thinking and by critical listening? The opinion presented in this report is taken from the definition by Russell [17], also found in the descriptions by Guilford [11] and Bloom [2] for evaluation. Russell distinguished this basic mental process from the five others (perceptual, associative, conceptual, creative and problem solving) by insisting (1) that a standard or highly conscious criterion be present in the mind of the thinker at the same time the process takes place; (2) that as the thinker sifts the evidence regarding an object or statement and suspends evaluation, he does then make a critical judgment; (3) finally, that the thinker, who is able to support his judgment with reasons derived from either internal logic or external values in the form of consensual data, acts or concludes on the judgment made. The thinker may doubt, and then make a decision. For example, because a child has concluded that the second-hand or even fifth-hand information that he received about another child does not fit in with his other knowledge, he does not pass on a rumor that he has heard.

The aspect which is usually lacking in research is the formulation and application of the highly conscious standard or criterion. Most tests that are designed to measure the critical or judgmental process measure only isolated beginning aspects or subabilities and never attack directly the application of criteria for judgment and subsequent reaction. For example, it is possible to analyze propaganda at great length and never go so far as to form a highly conscious judgment concerning the effects of that propaganda. It is possible to discriminate contextual clues and irrelevancies to make inferences about the speaker's purpose, to categorize his purpose in an analytical way, to generate purposes for a speaker, but never to judge consciously in a given situation. The meaning of "consciously" is opposed to "snap" or subliminal or prejudiced, solely emotional judgment. In other words, the thinker makes a conscious effort to be objective and to examine facts from that viewpoint.

In order to reach this terminal goal in thinking, which is still only a vague construct, there may be a chain or network of subskills, some of which may be arranged sequentially. Such a sequence of behaviors both covert and overt is one of the unknowns for most teachers in the area of critical thinking. Investigations have touched the supposed chain in different places mainly at the bottom links involving some simple discriminations or analyses such as some of the 46 abilities listed in a recent study of critical reading (Wolf, Huck, and King, [22]). Broadening of this knowledge base is imperative.

The Russell definition or categorizing proposition is

an hypothesis, lacking evidence of a conclusive nature. As a starting point, however, it may be an effective and logical definition to adopt and to attempt to describe in terms of terminal behavior. Definition of a complex process cannot be given in a single sentence or brief paragraph. Perhaps the term, "critical thinking," should be defined first according to broad use Cady [3]: that is, semantic and classificatory use. The second phase of a recommended definition would be operational: that is, "how does critical thinking work?" This phase might evolve from a conceptual model such as Goodman's [9] for reading. A third phase might be in the form of designating measurable behaviors on the part of an organism.

The next discrimination poses the question: when does the process leave the classification of critical listening or critical reading, for that matter? People think critically with or without input. However, evaluations are commonly modified as a message is decoded.

Consider the following example to show modification of thought: "He was a model of trained-incapacity." Where is the line between critical thinking and critical listening? The question is analogous to drawing the line as to where the neck stops and the head begins.

Arbitrarily, this solution is suggested: the covert responses (critical listening) may be inferred from overt performances which could not have occurred (or were unlikely to have occurred) without the covert responses to spoken language. In addition, it might be helpful to discriminate "listening" or to limit attention to a series of events called behaviors indicating comprehension of spoken language symbols as oppressed verbal sounds that are "heard" but not comprehended.

When the mode of reception of the verbal data with which to think critically is purely auditory, there are more difficulties than when reception is by reading. Reading imposes a helpful constraint of a relatively permanent medium. Perhaps the possibility of reviewing the printed message (in the relative absence of time pressure), the possibility for clearer organization or organizational clues, and the absence of personal influence have influenced findings. As early as the work of Carver [5], findings indicated it was easier to persuade a listener than to persuade a reader. But until researchers know what abilities can be categorized as distinctly listening behaviors, know the relevant concommitant variables, know relevant characteristics of the organism, or can specify antecent conditions or responses, scientific investigation for assistance lags. In summary, three major difficulties in definition remain: (1) Terms are not clear. (2) Aspects of the teaching of critical listening or of its outcomes confound the definition. (3) The ideal of including all behaviors of critical listening in a single definition evades control.

Selected Research

One method of classifying selected research for review is by grade groups. A few important studies are reviewed at the primary grade level and at the intermediate and high school levels. Other reviews have examined studies of critical thinking. Except for a few landmarks, the emphasis here is on critical listening.

Primary grade level

The Kellogg study. At the first grade level the only experimental study purporting to deal even in part with critical listening appears to be by Kellogg [13].

The general results were that performance on the unpublished test of listening comprehension was significant in favor of those pupils having the structured program in listening skills, with the exception of the girls in the traditional reading classes. Significant differences were also found on the Stanford Reading Test scores in favor of boys who had experienced the structured listening program.

There were eight skills included under three headings: (1) listening to get information, (2) skills used to detect speech organization, and (3) critical listening. Under critical listening there were supposedly four skills, but for only one was there any judgmental criterion or standard apparent--discerning between fact and opinion. The other skills in the critical category were: making use of contextual clues, recognizing that which is relevant, and making logical inferences from what is heard.

In summary, results suggested that assisted development of critical listening skills implying use of judgmental criteria at first-grade level is feasible.

The intermediate grade level

Two experimental studies designed to improve critical thinking have been selected to represent the intermediate grade level (Saadeh, [19]; Maw, [15]). One investigator conducted a series of studies concerning critical listening at this level Lundsteen [14].

The Saadeh study. Saadeh [19] evaluated the effectiveness of teaching for the assistance of critical thinking in the sixth grade. He defined critical thinking as a careful examination and evaluation of a product of thought whether it was a result of inductive discovery or of deductive proof. Logicians would hesitate to equate induction with discovery and deduction with proof. To Saadeh, critical thinking involves the attitude or set for evaluation and the ability to evaluate internal evidence, followed by a factual judgment of a verbal communication. Except for the exclusion of value judgments, external criteria and the inclusion of reading skill when testing, the definition is similar to the Russell-Guilford-Bloom definition of critical listening.

The Maw study. Maw [15] wished to determine whether or not certain critical thinking abilities of fourth, fifth and sixth-grade pupils improve after use of prepared exercises. Maw collected pupil and teacher reactions to the materials on rating scales and on check sheets. She divided 42 classes from three grade levels between experimental and control groups. For use as the dependent variable, Maw constructed a 71-item test of three parts: (1) inference, (2) deduction, and (3) interpretation or weighing of evidence. She arranged 24 exercises in order of supposed difficulty: (1) selecting relevant facts, (2) judging reliability of data, (3) making generalizations and inferences, (4) recognizing situations in which evidence is insufficient for conclusion, (5) determining cause and effect, and (6) evaluating arguments. The sixth skill was not represented on the criterion test. From analysis of variance on posttest means she found for all grades a significant difference ($p < .001$) favoring the experimental group with the lessons. This study, however, did not appear to teach or to measure specifically the application of judgment in light of a criterion. There was generally an emphasis on problem solving but without critical judgment of hypotheses, or any other portion of the process according to specified standards.

Intermediate-grade studies on critical listening. The next studies are reviewed at length with hesitancy, but at the time of writing they appear to be the only studies at the intermediate grade level, and the reviewer understandably knows them, especially their weaknesses. Lundsteen [14] generally explored effects of instruction on critical listening abilities at the fifth- and sixth-grade level. Instructional sequences dealt with three skills taught and tested as having particular relevance to the listening mode: (1) Detecting the Speaker's Purpose, (2) Analyzing and Judging Propaganda, and (3) Analyzing and Judging Arguments.

Although the teachers did not administer the 18 lessons individually, they used some techniques of programmed instruction: (1) information and questions sequenced with clues or prompts given to pupils just before an answer was elicited, (2) immediate feedback by the teacher, (3) extra examples provided for branching at the end of each lesson, (4) a device whereby pupils were called upon to answer in random order so that all might feel that they had an equal and unexpected chance of being asked to respond during the instruction.

The materials stressed developing criteria or standards by which to form judgments. With given data, the instructional sequence prompted the pupils to process these examples for generalizations or standards. For example, pupils examined arguments that had two qualities present or not present: (1) the argument contained significant evidence, and (2) the argument contained relevant evidence or "stuck to the topic." Next, the pupil examined reasons that the evidence fit the criteria by again processing examples. For instance, the evidence may not have been important because it contained what is known as "false cause" and/or misuse of "expert" opinion. Pupils developed a standard for testing use of cause and use of expert opinion in an argument. The instructional sequence included four other types of fallacy as well as such attitudinal sets of listening all the way to the end of a speaker's message. Also the lessons included concepts that standards would continue to grow and to develop. That is to say, pupils used an arbitrary standard for testing purposes in order to measure the judgmental process in action, but the sequence pointed out to the pupil that he should think critically about standards given to him or even those that he appeared to have a conscious hand in developing. This continual revision of standards may form the core of critical thinking ability.

Frequently, however, these lessons instructed children in an admittedly arbitrary manner, with flaws in the pacing, with concepts coming at too great a speed for assimilation and accommodation, except in the case of the most able pupil. The sequence usually provided too much material for the mythical average of 45 minutes. In light of pupil and teacher feedback on each lesson, the curriculum needed extensive revision.

Because no appropriate test existed, the investigator constructed a 79-item instrument with explicitly stated standards to apply during the judgment process. After item analysis, the investigator computed a test-retest reliability coefficient (.72, N = 100). Five judges furnished reactions for content validity and factor analysis appeared to indicate construct validity. This test, administered by tape recorder, does not make a contribution to individual diagnosis. No standardized, validated test of listening appears to make a diagnostic contribution at the time of the present writing. The test does not diagnose whether or not the weak point of a child's ability to listen critically lies with a lack of basic linguistic competence, a lack of background and lexical knowledge, a lack of power to mobilize and organize skills and meanings through proper processes of attention, or lack of a hierarchy of supportive reasoning abilities.

In a two-group experiment, volunteer classes in fifth and sixth grades (N = 287) were assigned randomly to experimental and to control groups. It was impossible to assign individual pupils to treatment, an admitted weakness. Pretest scores and tests of mental ability showed no significant difference between the control and the experimental groups. These normally distributed samples showed homogeneity of means and variances on all measures used to describe the sample. The experimental groups received nine weeks of instruction, two lessons per week, while the control groups followed the curriculum guide and texts for language arts adopted by the school system. The data were analyzed by factor analysis, correlation, analysis of variance and planned contrasts.

In conclusion, the lessons appeared to be effective in

raising the experimental group scores above those of the control group. Between the control and experimental groups the difference in mean gains was 6.1 score points, out of 79 possible. The one-way analysis of variance was significant statistically ($p < .01$). The relationship between critical listening scores and mental ability (California Test of Mental Ability, Form E, Verbal), critical thinking (Hendrickson, [12]), general listening (Pratt, [16]), and reading (Stanford Achievement Test, Form N, total reading) was positive and substantial (range: .43 to .64). There appeared to be some indirect evidence of the existence of critical listening abilities as part of general listening ability but as distinct from general verbal ability (Russell, [18]).

Content analysis of pupil and teacher responses on rating scales and on check sheets appeared to indicate evidence of transfer from the lessons or at least practical application to critical listening in other in-school and out-of-school activities (N = 146 pupils, 6 teachers). The data from the factor analysis based on intercorrelations of the 16 experimental test variables suggested the existence of four factors or components of critical listening ability which were labeled: (1) General Analysis and Inference, (2) Reasons for Fallacies in Arguments, (3) Value Judgment in Regard to Propaganda, and (4) Factual Judgment in Regard to Arguments. There appeared to be a distinction between the two types of judgments, as suggested by Guilford. In another study (N = 300 sixth-grade pupils) Spearritt [20] identified a factor of listening comprehension that was independent linearly of his factor of verbal comprehension. He suggested, however, further research which has not yet been attempted.

A follow-up study. In a follow-up of her earlier research, Lundsteen studied the degree of permanence of learning and , again, transfer or practical application to in-school and out-of-school activities. One year after the posttest the criterion measure of critical listening was administered to 222 students from the original experimental and control groups. The small attrition in the sample did not appear to indicate any particular bias. Students in the experimental group were requested to write anonymously of the ways in which they had or had not used the critical listening lessons since the experiment had ended. The experimental group which had received instruction in critical listening still scored significantly higher than the control group ($p < .05$) on the criterion test. Students in this group continued to report specific instances which may be interpreted as representing practical significance or transfer of learnings, at least for this particular sample (Lundsteen, [14]).

Critical listening as a subability to creative problem solving. In the latest experimental study of the series, two parts of the lessons-speaker's purpose and propaganda-were revised in accord with a teaching-learning model that abandoned the partial programmed approach used earlier and depended mainly upon a series of progressive questions for which there was no one right answer. Instructional techniques were adapted from the work of Taba [21] in which the strategy was to present data, to focus on a mental process, to seek multiple responses from high, middle and low layers of the class during discussion, to group and to label the data, and to lift thought to a progressively higher level. Revisions were also made in light of heavy vocabulary and concept load as suggested by feedback from the earlier experiment.

An instructional sequence and measurement was also added for hypothesized prerequisite skills of general listening: (1) discriminating main ideas and details, (2) sequential ordering, (3) summarizing, (4) relating ideas, and (5) making inferences. The investigator suggested tentative hierarchies and roughly constructed behavioral objectives. Instruction and measurement for general listening and critical listening skills were investigated separately as major subabilities or links in the chain leading to skill in the creative problem-solving process, thus remedying one failing of earlier studies.

To attempt to improve critical listening in isolation from other major thinking processes was an uneconomical use of school time. Actually all major thinking processes appeared to be meaningfully related to the one process of creative problem solving. In the earlier studies some of the pupils had tended to become carpingly critical, misusing their "new toy" of critical listening. Although instruction designed to minimize this exaggeration was added, the problem appeared to be solved more efficiently when the major emphasis was on employing the creative problem-solving process in meaningful academic or socially oriented situations with critical listening as a related subskill. Consequently, an experiment was designed to contrast the presence or absence of two supposed subskills to creative problem solving: listening and abstract thinking. It was reasoned that (1) the training for problem solving through group discussion would not proceed far without the mobilization of listening skills, and (2) that an increase in available data through improved and evaluative listening skills should logically increase power in creative problem solving because of more and higher quality of auditory input.[1]

The notion of the relative importance of subskills to creative problem solving was tested in a five-group experiment ($N = 683$) in which three experimental groups received a basic instructional sequence within the context of the language arts which was focused upon creative problem solving. In addition, one experimental group received a sequence for extra practice of problem-solving concepts; a second received an additional sequence for assisting growth in listening skills; and a third received an instructional sequence designed to assist growth in abstract thinking. Two control groups received an equal amount of instructional time utilizing the state- and country-adopted language arts program. Moreover, the control program was specified on a questionnaire completed by each control teacher. One of the control groups received posttests only.

Both pre- and posttests were administered via educational television. On the pretests there was no significant difference among the four treatments having the initial measurement battery including the three listening tests. On the posttest overall differences were significant ($p < .01$) for the two critical listening measures. In a supplementary analysis of covariance (IQ) using intact class as the unit ($N = 30$ class means) overall differences still were significant ($p < .01$, $.05$, $F = 5.44$ and 2.71, 4 and 24 df). According to analysis of covariance (IQ), there was no significant difference among treatments for the test of general listening which was part II of a test by Pratt. On the part concerning judgment of speaker's purpose, the mean of the experimental group with the listening emphasis, the highest mean, was significantly higher than both control group means according to Scheffé tests. On the test of judgment of propaganda, the highest mean (which belonged to the listening emphasis) was significantly greater than that of the control groups and the experimental group with the extra emphasis on abstract thinking.

Six months later a retention test was administered to a randomly selected subsample of the pupils. The test on propaganda was selected to represent the listening battery. According to analysis of covariance, there was a significant overall treatment effect for the five groups ($p < .01$, N = 174, a subsample). Simple inspection showed that, again, the highest adjusted mean was that of the experimental group with the listening emphasis.

On the Sequential Tests of Educational Progress, Reading (4A), the unadjusted mean of the experimental group with listening was the highest for the total score and for three of the five subscores which might be interpreted as measuring higher mental processes in reading. These subscores were: the second one, "translating ideas and making inferences;" the third, "analyzing motivation;" and the fifth, "criticizing," ($p < .01$). Scheffé tests between the group with the listening emphasis and the control group with no pretests were significant ($p < .01$). When IQ was used as covariable, however, the highest mean switched to the group with the abstract emphasis for the total STEP Reading test and for the fifth subscore. The listening emphasis retained top rank on the second and third subscore and added top rank on the first, labeled "reproducing." Apparently, the experimental program did not retard the reading skills of the groups receiving the problem-solving/listening treatment.

Although the means of the experimental groups with the listening emphasis were consistently higher on the three tests of creative problem solving than the means of the two control groups, listening emphasis means were consistently lower than the other two means from experimental groups, significantly so on two of the measures according to Scheffé tests. Thus, in this experiment training the subability of listening did not seem to enhance the measured process of creative problem solving as much as training in abstract thinking ability, first, and, next, simply extra problem-solving practice.

Carroll [4] suggested that basic linguistic competence is probably relatively unsusceptible to improvement except over long periods of time and with great effort. Acting as a subability to improve the creative problem-solving process probably falls within this "long-term-great-effort" category. If measurement and instructional sequences were revised, however, this improvement might effect results in future studies. It now seems apparent that both forms of curriculum building and teaching strategy have a contribution to make to assisted development of a mental process (1) the curriculum with opportunity for divergent answers which stimulates pupil autonomy; and (2) the curriculum with programmed instruction with hierarchies of objectives, prompts for continuing success, and immediate feedback about correct answers for individual progress. The next revision of the instructional sequences should have the best of both approaches.

The high school level

The small amount of research accomplished at the elementary level has been adapted, in the fashion recommended by Bruner, more or less successfully, from work at the high school level. An outstanding and influential study in critical thinking at the high school level was conducted by Glaser [8]. This classic has been reviewed steadily since its appearance and as the major emphasis here is on critical listening, this research is passed over. Instead the reviewer examined in detail a study of critical listening by Devine [6] from which several related studies have sprung.

The Devine study. It is believed that the Devine study was the only experimental investigation at the time of its appearance devoted to the assistance of critical listening abilities at the ninth-grade level. The audio tape recorded lessons appeared to effect significant improvement ($p < .01$). The sample included 445 pupils, 220 in the experimental group and a control group of approximately equal age and sex distribution. Groups were matched on four tests. IQ (Otis), critical thinking (Watson-Glaser), listening (Brown-Carlsen) and critical listening (an experimental test developed by Devine). Five critical abilities were selected with the aid of 14 judges. With these abilities in mind the investigator then built a test and ten lessons, both recorded by audio tape. A pupil response booklet was prepared for use with tapes during the four-week period of training. Pupils were not allowed to interrupt the recording to ask questions and to get feedback, to participate in planning related activities, or to contribute related written work.

The measured abilities included: (1) recognizing the bias of a speaker, (2) recognizing the competence of a speaker to discuss a given subject, (3) distinguishing between statement of fact and of opinion, (4) recognizing a speaker's inferences, and (5) distinguishing between report and emotive language. The reliability coefficient for Devine's experimental test was .76 (N = 100) obtained by split-half method and .79 obtained by the test-retest comparison. This 70-item test, which takes 46 minutes to administer, consists mainly of dialogue, some taken from actual newscasts and interviews. The test, however, does not operationalize the definition of the critical thinking/listening process as suggested by the Russell-Guilford-Bloom definition. The test is designed to measure subskills coming before the application of explicit criteria for judgment and conclusions on the judgment made. The correlations between the experimental test of critical listening and the Watson-Glaser Critical Thinking Appraisal and the Brown-Carlsen Listening Comprehension Test were .68 and .61.

In summary, Devine inferred that critical listening abilities can be improved at all levels of mental ability examined. Training in critical listening did not appear to assist pupils to score higher on tests of critical thinking or general listening as measured by the criterion tests. Although the correlations of critical listening, general listening, mental ability, reading, and critical thinking were positive and moderately high, he believed that the associations suggested a distinct set of critical listening abilities.

Devine's study was repeated with pupils in grades seven through ten in schools situated in areas with varying socioeconomic levels (Evans, [7]; Adams, [1]). Results found were consistent with those found originally by Devine.

Recommendations and conclusions

The state of the existing research and the needs growing out of present day conditions suggest five ideas. (1) The first step should be a nationally organized, nationally communicating attack for economical and scientific progress in assisting development of critical thinking/listening skills. Applications of the convergence technique utilized in research on cancer and now being tried in the attempt to develop a theory for the domain of reading may prove helpful in this complementary area.

(2) Until teachers can listen and think critically it will be difficult for them to assist children. Prospective teachers and inservice teachers need training in these skills.

(3) Other research needs include dimensionalizing

variables within the listening/thinking area, arranging possible chains or hierarchies of skills in varying combinations of interactions with an accompanying thrust of measurement as well as a carefully charted pool of the existing knowledge from interdisciplinary research. Perhaps researchers in this area should take time to study logic, if they purport to be interested in logical thinking. Some of the distinctions adopted by some of the researchers would be distasteful to logicians, e. g., "inference versus deductive proof, fact versus opinion."

(4) If clear, scientific and critical thought is based on a categorizational process (it is, or is it not?) or judgmental process (it is good, or it is bad?), the use of this process may become carping, narrow, be merely for the sake of exercise; or it may be relegated solely to the "arm chair" with no constructive action. Such has been the case among some critics of research on critical listening, who sit back and complain that investigation is in such a poor state that nothing can be concluded. An alternative would be that investigators with the skill to be critical of the area should unite in efforts of imaginative and comprehensive planning.

(5) Finally, both children and adults appear to need a broad focus on creative problem solving which gives to the critical process a larger and more significant purpose with meaningful interrelation for the learner and for society as a whole. Concommitantly, programs should teach critical thinking and listening but not in isolation from the wealth of academic and social problems that should have been faced in the curriculum of yesterday, and that must be faced in the curriculum of today and of tomorrow.

Notes

Abbreviated references refer to the entry number in Sam Duker's Listening Bibliography 2nd Ed. (Scarecrow, 1968) where the full citation may be found.

1. Adams, F. Evaluation of a Listening Program Designed to Develop Awareness of Propaganda Techniques. Doctoral dissertation. Boston: Boston University, 1968.

2. Bloom, B. S. Taxonomy of Educational Handbook 1: Cognitive Domain. New York: McKay, 1956.

3. Cady, H. L. Toward a Definition of Music Education. Conference on Research in Music Education, March 1967, Columbus, Ohio. (USOE Cooperative Educational Research Project No. 6-1388.) (ERIC document Ed. 013 973).

4. Carroll, J. B. Development of Native Language Skills Beyond the Early Years. Princeton, N. J.: Educational Testing Service, 1968. (mimeo.)

5. Carver, M. E., 191.

6. Devine, T. G., 285.

7. Evans, H. N. An Evaluation of Seventh-Grade Level of a Series of Recordings for Teaching Certain Critical Listening Skills. Master's thesis. Boston: Boston University, 1965.

8. Glaser, E. M. An Experiment in the Development of Critical Thinking. Doctoral dissertation. New York: Columbia University, 1941.

9. Goodman, Kenneth S. "Reading: A Psycholinguistic Guessing Game." Journal of the Reading Specialist 6:127-35, 1967.

10. Guilford, J. P. "Three Faces of Intellect." American Psychologist 14:469-79, 1959.

11. Guilford, J. P. The Nature of Human Intelligence. New York: McGraw, 1967.

12. Hendrickson, D. Some Correlates of Abilities in Critical Thinking of Fifth-Grade Children. Doctoral dissertation. Berkeley: University of California, 1960.

13. Kellogg, R. E., 653.

14. Lundsteen, S. W., 764.

15. Maw, E. W. An Experiment in Teaching Critical Thinking in the Intermediate Grades. Doctoral disseration. Philadelphia: University of Pennsylvania, 1959.

16. Pratt, L. E., 970.

17. Russell, D. H. Children's Thinking. Boston: Ginn, 1956.

18. Russell, D. H., 1036.

19. Saadeh, I. Q. An Evaluation of the Effectiveness of Teaching for Critical Thinking in the Sixth Grade. Doctoral dissertation. Berkeley: University of California, 1962.

20. Spearritt, D., 1117.

21. Taba, H., S. Levine, and F. Elzey. Thinking in Elementary School Children. Cooperative Research Project No. 1574. U. S. Office of Education, 1964.

22. Wolf, W., C. Huck, and M. King. Critical Reading Ability of Elementary School Children. Cooperative Research Project No. 5-1040. Columbus: Ohio State University, 1967.

Chapter VII

Listening and the Disadvantaged

The present preoccupation with the teaching of the disadvantaged will, I hope, be replaced during the lifetime of this book by an emphasis on ways of eliminating disadvantagement rather than on ways of catering to it.

The first article is taken from the 1967 Ohio State University master's thesis by Arlene K. Feltman. It has already been remarked in one of the previous chapter introductions that a disadvantaged student is unlikely to be handicapped in reading and able at the same time to listen with efficiency. One mark of the disadvantaged is that he suffers from a general language disability. When he first comes to school he very often comes from an environment where he not only did not listen himself but also has not been listened to. His shortcomings in writing and speaking and in reading seem to be more generally understood than his deficiency in the area of listening. This is probably a carryover from the rather general belief, not too many years ago, that anyone who can hear can, and therefore probably does, listen.

The Feltman article describes an experiment with five-year-olds, the principal emphasis of which was to test the effect of rewards on the performance of listening tasks by culturally deprived children. The concept that the key to disadvantaged children's desire to improve their performance might be found in making available suitable rewards has also been suggested by Carver.[1]

The second selection in this chapter is written by Orr and Graham. Dr. David B. Orr, at the time this article was written, was a Senior Scientist in the Washington office of the American Institutes for Research. At present he operates his own educational consultant firm in Washington, D. C. In this article a description is given of the construction of a listening test which it was hoped would give clues to the potential of disadvantaged youngsters to whom it might be administered. Subsequently the statistical work in this study was criticised by Carver.[2] To my knowledge, Orr did not write a rejoinder to these comments but, regardless of its merits or demerits, the article remains one which presents some extremely provocative ideas and concepts.

Notes

Abbreviated references refer to the entry number in Sam Duker's Listening Bibliography 2nd Ed. (Scarecrow, 1968) where the full citation may be found.

1. Carver, Ronald P. "An Experiment that Failed: Designing an Aural Aptitude Test for Negroes." College Board Review No. 70, Winter 1968-69, p. 10-14.

2. Carver, Ronald P. "The Questionable Uniqueness of a Newly Developed Listening Test." American Educational Research Journal 5:728-30, November 1968.

Carver, Ronald P. "Use of a Recently Developed Listening Comprehension Test to Investigate the Effect of Disadvantagement upon Verbal Proficiency." American Educational Research Journal 6:623-30, March 1969.

The Effect of Reinforcement on Listening Skills of Culturally Deprived Preschool Children

Arlene Kessler Feltman

To assess specific listening skills which significantly discriminate between middle- and lower-class preschool children, five tests of auditory perception were devised for this study. The tests were administered under three conditions of reward: lights, candy, and no reward.

There were sixty children chosen for this study, all age five, attending a preschool nursery program. There were thirty children in the experimental group and thirty in the control group. All of the children had normal hearing and intelligence.

The control group, representing middle and upper socioeconomic areas, consisted of children attending three nursery schools which required tuition. The experimental subjects for this study were chosen randomly from the twenty-five schools in Columbus, Ohio, participating in "Project Headstart." Socioeconomic determinates were made on the basis of census tract data.

The experimental subjects, for the most part, came from two-parent families with an average of five people living in the home. Most of the jobs held by the fathers were in the unskilled or semi-skilled class. Many of the mothers were employed as unskilled labor, often at night, for the maintenance of office buildings. None of the parents were professional people. The broken home was common and several of the families received aid such as aid for dependent children, welfare disbursements, free medical and dental care, or free clothing from charity agencies.

Tests

Five tests were administered: two evaluated sound discrimination, A_1 and A_2; one test measured auditory memory span for nonsense words, A_3; one measured synthetic analysis of sounds into words, A_4; and one measured delayed memory and comprehension, A_5. Each test was constructed to explore a somewhat different aspect of auditory functioning in oral language.

The delayed memory for listening comprehension test, Test A_5, was adapted from the Hearing Comprehension section of the pre-primary test by Murphy and Durrell. A story was heard by each child over the recorder at the beginning of each testing session. The last subtest consisted of answering questions about the story. The answers were chosen from four sets of pictures. There were ten questions taken from the story.

Apparatus

A tape recorder, testing box, electric switch box, and candy feeder were used to present the five tests to the subjects. The correct and incorrect responses of the subjects were recorded on a prepared answer sheet.

Tests were recorded on tape recorder. For all the subtests, the words were recorded with approximately two seconds of silence between every stimulus word. The words were recorded as they would be heard in conversational speech.

An electric switch box was used to produce the light flash, which was one of the conditions of reward. When the child pushed the correct button, the picture representing the stimuli would "light up." The switch box was attached to the testing box and could be controlled by pushing the buttons on the box or by a separate hand control.

A candy feeder was adapted from a rat feeder used by the psychology department. M&M candies were placed on a turnstile. When the child responded correctly, the examiner pushed a button and the candy would slide down a chute, readily accessible to the child.

Procedure

Each child was seated before the testing box so that all pictures were at eye level. The rooms used were well lighted and as free from distractions as possible. Since one-third of the children received lights as a reward, one-third received candy, and one-third received no reward, the instructions were varied to meet the criteria.

Test A_5 was administered in two parts. At the beginning of the testing situation, the child was told to listen carefully for he would hear a story about "Mother Cat and her Five Kittens." The examiner told the child to listen carefully because later on he would be asked some questions about the story. In the second part of the test, the child was told he would see four pictures in the testing box. The voice on the tape recorder would then ask him a question based on the story. He would have to push the button under the picture that best answered the story. He would get an indication of the correct response if his picture lighted up. There were ten sets of four answers.

The administration for the other two conditions of candy reward, and no reward, were exactly the same. The instructions however, were revised accordingly. The child was told he would get an M&M candy for every correct response he made. As he made the response, the reward was immediate as it came down the chute. Under the condition of no reward, the tests were given with intervals of rest with no verbal or material reward.

Results

The first four hypotheses were concerned with the tests of listening skills:

Hypothesis One, that there is no difference between the culturally disadvantaged children and middle-class children on tests of listening skills, was rejected at the .01 level. There was a significant difference in the performance of the groups on the tests of listening skills.

Hypothesis Two, that there is no difference between the culturally deprived and middle-class children on listening skills for a comparator test of sound discrimination, a "right" or "wrong" test of sound discrimination, memory for nonsense words, word synthesis, and listening comprehension for delayed sentences, was rejected at the .01 level.

Hypothesis Three, that there is no relationship between the culturally deprived and middle-class group on the total scores of each of the five subtests, was rejected at the .01 level. The sums of the tests were ranked from highest to lowest in each of the groups tested. These scores were then correlated using the Spearman Rank Order Correlation. The relationship between the groups was $\underline{r} = .80$.

Hypothesis Four (a), that there is no difference among the five subtests used within the culturally deprived group, was rejected at the .05 level.

Further tests were administered to determine where the significance lay. Subtest A_1, a comparator test for sound discrimination, was significantly different from Subtest A_5, listening comprehension. Subtest A_1 was significantly different from Subtest A_3, memory for nonsense words.

Three Conditions of Reward

Hypothesis Five, that there is no difference between the culturally deprived and middle-class group among the three types of reward could not be rejected. There is no significant difference between the groups for each of the conditions.

Hypothesis Six (a), that there is no difference among the three types of rewards used within the culturally deprived group, was rejected at the .05 level. There was a significant difference in the means between the condition of reward (candy) and no reward. The difference of means between candy and light flashes, and light flashes and no reward, could not be rejected.

Hypothesis Six (b), that there is no difference among the three types of rewards within the middle-class group, could not be rejected. The subjects seemed to perform similarly under all three conditions.

Discussion

The relationship between a culturally disadvantaged population and middle-class population has been investigated extensively. Recent investigators have noted the difference in language skills between these two populations. The concept of a preschool enrichment program was developed to broaden the experiences of culturally deprived children and to prepare them emotionally and mentally for the school. The purpose of this study was to analyze intensively specific listening skills of those children who attended a preschool program.

It was discovered that the culturally deprived children were not as adequate as the middle-class children in all aspects of the listening skills measured. The culturally disadvantaged group did, however, improve their scores significantly when a tangible reward was used. In the middle-class group, there was no difference in the scores on the listening tests regardless of the reward. It may be concluded, therefore, that although the culturally deprived child is less adequate in his listening skills, he can be motivated to perform better with a tangible reward. The fact that the middle-class group did not perform differently under the various conditions of reward perhaps can be attributed to the novelty of the listening box as sufficiently motivating.

Educational implications were apparent since both groups had just completed a year of nursery school. The culturally deprived group appears to need more training in developing listening skills. If listening is not sufficiently developed, children will be restricted in their ability to profit from experiences and will be retarded in many learning situations. It seems essential that the preschool training program for culturally deprived children be geared to language training. This training must be tightly structured so that the child is taught how to listen and what to listen for. It has been shown that as a group, the culturally deprived come from an environment which places little emphasis on sustained listening habits. It has also been shown that the culturally deprived are inexperienced in the rewards associated with mastering a new concept; and because they are not strongly motivated to work for praise, a motivational bridge must be built. It appears that this can be accomplished through the use of tangible rewards such as candy or cookies.

Development of a Listening Comprehension Test To Identify Educational Potential Among Disadvantaged Junior High School Students

David B. Orr and Warren R. Graham

There is an important segment of the school population that is culturally and economically disadvantaged. Very often these students have grown up in situations which have inhibited their development of reading and written-language skills, with the result that their scores on traditional, printed tests of scholastic aptitude seriously underestimate their academic potential. Further, such tests often contain content which is not well suited for disadvantaged groups because of their specific subcultural interests and disinterests.

While the literature on listening comprehension tests is sparse as compared to that on reading comprehension tests and other scholastic aptitude measures, there have been indications that some children exhibit markedly better comprehension on auditory measures than on visual measures. Therefore, it was reasoned that a listening comprehension test might be developed, based on appropriate content, which would provide an important measure of educational potential beyond that measured by more traditional approaches.

Problem

The study reported here was addressed to the problem of developing a listening comprehension test based on content suitable for 8th grade disadvantaged boys, and trying it out to determine its unique variance as compared to traditional measures represented by the *School and College Ability Test* and the *Sequential Tests of Educational Progress, Reading and Listening.* (These Educational Testing Service tests are hereafter designated *SCAT*, *STEP Reading* and *STEP Listening.*)

Procedures

Aspects of listening ability to be measured were determined by reviewing the literature on listening tests and selecting the following five aspects to be incorporated into the test: memory and learning, listening comprehension, inferences, drawing conclusions, and following directions.

Content Selection

In order to develop content suitable to the interests of the proposed population, interviews were conducted with 20 boys of junior high school age (ten drawn from neighborhood youth clubs where they were interviewed by the Project Director, and ten interviewed in the street by a young male Negro, using an informal approach and a portable tape recorder). All of these boys were from disadvantaged neighborhoods in Washington, D. C., and the group was entirely of Negro ethnic background.

These interviews revealed that virtually all of the boys had television sets in their homes, and that they knew the names of and understood the contents of the adventure stories presented on television and in the movies. Sports, particularly football and basketball, were mentioned most frequently. They also expressed considerable liking for adventure stories concerning spies, detectives, cowboys, and soldiers. Similar interests were mentioned in the form of reading materials (Superman, Batman, Space Boy, Columbus, William Penn, Pocahontas, Treasure Island) as well as cartoon comics of a more humorous nature. When asked if they would like to make their own movie, the answer was always affirmative. The topics that they wanted as plots for their movies were: soldier, great Negro, comedy, detective, secret agent, football, baseball. (The general interest in sports and entertainment topics noted above was verified by questions concerning primary sources of activities after school hours.) A number of boys interviewed reported having been sent to a summer camp either by a church group or by a newspaper fund. All had a clear idea of what kind of place summer camp is, and about the kinds of activities offered there.

Television and comic book subject matter seemed to be of mutual interest to boys from both poor and middle income families. The interviews showed that interest in adventure and sports stories was not specific to boys from either class. The disadvantaged boys interviewed consistently asked for information about sports (e.g., "I want to learn how to make touchdowns."). Again, interest in these subjects apparently is shared across economic strata among 8th grade boys.

In summary, the types of topic which were indicated to be of interest to the interviewees from the disadvantaged 8th grade population are those topics which formed the basis for the contents of the test. They were primarily sports, adventure, biographies of heroes, and spy and mystery stories. The types of content used were extracted from the standard and informal interviews, and lack of apparent cultural separation of interests was a direct result of the intensive effort made to document separateness of interests. It did not appear to be possible to construct a test that would be entirely specific to disadvantaged subjects of Negro ethnic background.

Form of the Test

The preliminary test was written in the form of a script for a series of interviews. Twenty-four passages were used in the preliminary test. Most of the passages were written especially for the Listening Test. Two passages were based on books, one written by a baseball coach and the other by a football coach. Two passages were based on information obtained from an encyclopedia. A special effort was made to write several items for each passage that would require students to draw conclusions or to make inferences. Several passages were designed to measure learning, memory, and ability to follow directions. The remainder of the passages were primarily measures of listening comprehension. It was decided that the entire test including questions would be tape-recorded, with questions being repeated once and subjects directed to mark their answer sheets after the second reading.

Upon completion of the preliminary script, casting was begun with the aim of utilizing a large number of different kinds of voices for the characterizations required by the passages. The use of the subcultural vernacular was not deemed necessary since the interview procedures had revealed that students in the subject population understand English adequately. This finding is probably accounted for by their frequent exposure to standard English both in school and through radio-television. Verbatim recordings were ruled out due to the paucity of suitable material in the recorded interviews, and because the recorded interviews probably were typical of material that can be obtained this way.

In view of the fact that the experimental test was to be employed in a Negro, disadvantaged area of the District of Columbia, the announcer who narrated the script and read the questions was selected to be a native of the disadvantaged neighborhood from which subjects were drawn. He was a graduate of one of the three junior high schools sampled and spoke with a definitely identifiable Washington Negro accent. Characterizations of interviewees also included Negro male voices of local accent for approximately thirty percent of the passages used in the final test. The remaining seventy percent were voices of Caucasian males from parts of eastern, midwestern, and western United States.

Tryout

Two small groups, each consisting of approximately twenty disadvantaged junior high school boys, were employed to assist with the evaluation of the test contents. They were paid for their services, which included listening to each segment of the script (introduction, test passage, closing statement) and answering the questions. After each segment, the students were queried concerning their understanding of the passage and its questions, with respect to whether or not it was clearly spoken, and whether or not the passage was of interest to them. Each passage on the preliminary tape was reviewed in this manner by at least twenty subjects, and the more difficult passages were reviewed by forty subjects.

Most of the items that were passed by ninety percent or more of the subjects were eliminated in order to shorten the test, but a few easy items were retained for introductory passages. Whole passages that were so easy that virtually all of the questions related to them were answered by ninety percent or more of the subjects were eliminated entirely. In this manner, the 24 preliminary passages were edited, revised, and further developed into the final script of the Listening Test. As a result, 17 passages and 86 items were retained for the final 90-minute test. The distributions of item statistics for the final forms of the tests are presented in Table 1.

The final form of the test was administered on a tryout basis to a third group of 20 disadvantaged boys who took the test just as it would be taken later by a larger group. Evidence from this tryout indicated that students of a wide range of scholastic ability could take the test without difficulties, and that their attitudes toward the contents and presentation

Table 1

Frequency Distributions of Item Statistics for the Final Forms of the Listening Test (Sample L, N = 116)

Category (Percent; biserial r)	Item Difficulty frequency Form A	Item Difficulty frequency Form B	Item Difficulty frequency Form A+ B	Item-Test Correlation frequency Form A	Item-Test Correlation frequency Form B	Item-Test Correlation frequency Form A+ B
95-99	1		1			
90-94	--	5	5			
85-89	4	3	7			
80-84	4	5	9			
75-79	5	2	7			
70-74	4	5	9			
65-69	3	1	4			
60-64	1	8	9		2	2
55-59	6	3	9	3	2	5
50-54	6	4	10	3	5	8
45-49	3	3	6	4	5	9
40-44	2	2	4	7	3	10
35-39	2	--	2	10	8	18
30-34	1	1	2	3	6	9
25-29	--	--	--	3	5	8
20-24	1	--	1	2	3	5
15-19		1	1	5	1	6
10-14				--	1	1
5-9				--	2	2
0-4				3		3

were favorable.

Final Sample

The final sample consisted of disadvantaged, inner-city boys in the 8th grade of three junior high schools of the District of Columbia. The three junior high schools were previously selected by the D. C. Board of Education to be part of a special disadvantaged school district. About 99 percent were of Negro ethnic background, and a very large majority were born in the District of Columbia, as were the majority of their parents. The sample numbered 393 boys from families having an estimated income of less than

$5,000 per annum.

Final Administration

In order to minimize fatigue effects, it was decided to limit testing time to three hours per student. Consequently, three subsamples were selected from the final sample, each of which took the Listening Test and one comparison test, the order of administration of the tests being counterbalanced from class to class. The number of cases per sample was as follows:

Sample	Comparison Test	N
C	SCAT	144
R	STEP Reading	133
L	STEP Listening	116
		393

An effort was made to make the three experimental samples as comparable as possible by matching them on the basis of estimated scholastic level. The sections (classes) for each school were assigned rank orders of scholastic ability and achievement by two teachers who were familiar with the bases for assignments of the students to the sections. Since there are different numbers of sections in each school, the section ranks were numerically coded, so as to equate the ranks across the schools. In addition, the academic rating assigned by teachers to each student with respect to his class was obtained from the schools' records. The grade levels thus obtained also were coded numerically. The numerical codes were treated as arbitrary weights and combined arithmetically to produce the Scholarship Level variable.

The rank ordered classes were divided into High, Middle and Low ability groups. Each of the experimental samples was assigned about the same number of classes in each of the ability groups, and assignments of groups to samples were made across the three schools. Thus, each sample contained High, Middle, and Low ability groups from all three schools in approximately equal numbers of students. The tests were then administered to groups of 50 to 60 boys each in large classrooms.

Results

For analysis purposes, the final 90-minute Listening

Test was divided into two equivalent alternate forms (A and B), each having 43 items, with passages matched for internal consistency, difficulty, type of content, and variety of voices used to record passages. The item statistics used to match the forms were derived from an item analysis of responses of Sample L, which took the STEP Listening test. With respect to the critical correlations between the Listening Test forms and the SCAT and STEP reading tests, therefore, the Listening Test forms are derived from an independent item analysis sample. Independence is true only for the Listening test total score (Form A + B) where correlations with the STEP Listening test are concerned. The alternate forms were constructed by first matching passages on the item versus total score correlations, taking the several items of whole passages as the basis for judging similarity. Secondly, the passages were matched across the whole test, passage by passage, on similarity of item difficulty indices. Finally, the passages were matched in terms of types of test contents, types of voices, and position of passage in the full 90 minute test. The similarity of the alternate forms of the Listening Test can be seen from the distribution of item statistics in Table 1, as well as from means and standard deviations in Table 2.

Reliability

With respect to the reliability of the Listening Test, the two alternate short forms (A and B) of 43 items correlated .74. The Spearman-Brown prophecy for a test (A+ B) of 86 items was .85. The Kuder-Richardson (Formula 20) internal consistency reliability coefficient was .89 for form (A + B).

Uniqueness Analysis

The principal results of the study are the correlations between the two forms of the Listening Test and the several comparison tests (Table 3). There is a correlation .60 between the Listening Test and the SCAT (Total Score). A correlation of this magnitude indicates that many students who do well on the Listening Test may do considerably less well on the SCAT. This result is particularly apparent with respect to the Quantitative score of the SCAT, which correlates only .31 with the Listening Test total score, but it is also true for the Verbal Score (r = .61).

Table 2

Means and Standard Deviations of the Listening Test and Background Variables for Several Samples

Variable	Sample[a]			
	C	R	L	Total
Age (years)				
Mean	14.33	14.34	14.67	14.43
s.d.	0.90	0.81	0.81	0.86
Income Index[b]				
Mean	1.72	1.41	1.40	1.52
s.d.	1.18	1.17	1.05	1.15
Scholarship Index[c]				
Mean	4.69	4.98	4.83	4.83
s.d.	1.16	1.36	1.66	1.40
Form A, Listening Test				
Mean	27.22	27.56	27.48	27.41
s.d.	5.99	5.36	6.97	6.10
Form B, Listening Test				
Mean	29.22	29.77	29.16	29.39
s.d.	6.12	5.51	6.30	5.99
Form A+ B, Listening Test				
Mean	56.31	57.18	56.47	56.65
s.d.	11.57	10.19	12.76	11.51
N	144	133	116	393

[a]Sample C took SCAT, Sample R took STEP Reading Test, Sample L took STEP Listening Test

[b]0 = Public Assistance, 1 = \$2,000 to \$3,000, 2 = \$3,000 to \$4,000, 3 = \$4,000 to \$5,000

[c]Estimated 8th grade scholastic standing combining teachers' grades and achievement level of class, based on an arbitrary numerical code ranging from 2 (low) to 10 (high).

Table 3

Correlations of the Listening Test with Comparison Tests

	Listening Test			
	Form A	Form B	Form A + B	N[a]
SCAT Total	.59	.53	.60	136 (Sample C)
SCAT V	.60	.55	.61	136 (Sample C)
SCAT Q	.32	.28	.31	136 (Sample C)
STEP Reading Test	.52	.37	.49	131 (Sample R)
STEP Listening Test	.72[b]	.58[b]	.69	116 (Sample L)

[a]Ns slightly reduced by incomplete data

[b]Items and Passages for Form A and Form B were selected on the basis of the same responses used to obtain these correlations.

Correlations

The correlation between the new Listening Test (for disadvantaged students) and the STEP Listening test (for students in general) was $r = .69$. The STEP Listening test was presented by tape recorder in the same manner as the new Listening Test.

Table 4 presented correlations between the Listening Test and selected background variables. It is noteworthy that for Sample L the Listening Test (total) correlated $r = .56$ with the Scholarship Index. By contrast, the STEP Listening Test for the sample correlated .71. This result might have occurred because the STEP Listening Test requires subjects to read alternate answers, but probably also because its contents are more academic than those used for the new Listening Test.

Four multiple-choice opinion items were added to the end of the Listening Test to determine its subjective acceptance by the total sample. In general, the results show that about 81 percent of the disadvantaged 8th grade boys liked

Table 4

Correlations of the Listening Test
with Background Variables

	Sample			
	C	R	L	Total
Form A + B				
Age	-.25	-.24	-.33	-.28
Income Index	.26	-.02	.15	.13
Scholarship Index	.38	.37	.56	.45
N	144	133	116	393
Form A				
Age	-.27	-.23	-.36	-.28
Income Index	.27	.04	.10	.14
Scholarship Index	.31	.31	.57	.41
N	144	133	116	393
Form B				
Age	-.25	-.19	-.26	-.24
Income Index	.24	-.04	.16	.12
Scholarship Index	.38	.36	.47	.41
N	144	133	116	393

Note. Sample C took the SCAT, Sample R took the STEP Reading Test, and Sample L took STEP Listening Test.

the Listening Test and preferred it to a reading test covering the same contents. About 69 percent felt that at least 16 out of the 17 passages were interesting. About 71 percent found at least 16 of the passages to be clearly spoken and understandable.

The part-whole correlations between the short forms A and B of the Listening Test and the Long (A+B) form were .93 and .94 respectively for the total sample ($N = 393$). The short and long forms also were correlated to a similar degree with the three background indices (Age, Scholarship, and Income) for the total sample (Table 4). With respect to the SCAT, the short and long Listening Test forms also were correlated to about the same degree with the Verbal, Quantitative, and Total scores of SCAT, for Sample C (Table 3). There were disparities in the degree to which the Listening Test forms correlated with the STEP Reading and Listening Tests, yet both of the short tests had correlations similar in magnitude to the long test for Sample R and Sample L (Table 3). The above evidence indicates that either of the short forms can be substituted for the long form of the Listening Test with relatively little loss of information.

Discussion and Conclusions

This paper describes the development of a listening comprehension test designed particularly to aid in the identification of college potential among disadvantaged junior high school students. The test displayed acceptable statistical characteristics in terms of it reliability, its correlations with other tests and its high uniqueness as measured against standard scholastic aptitude and achievements. The two alternate forms appeared to be reliable enough for practical use if shorter testing times than required for the total form were necessary.

However, this study should not be thought of simply as a routine test development exercise. It is the contention of the authors that the research significance of the findings of this study goes well beyond that of the usual test development project. The primary hypothesis upon which the study was based was that disadvantaged children would find a listening comprehension test significantly more appropriate than the usual scholastic aptitude or achievement tests commonly used to measure their academic prospects. The high uniqueness of the test developed here, as measured against such tests, strongly supported this hypothesis. This finding suggests that the effect of disadvantagement may typically be more associated with the development of reading proficiency rather than verbal proficiency in general.

Judging from the results of the uniqueness analysis and the statistical, psychometric indices of the functioning of the Listening Test, it should be possible to identify many disadvantaged students who have greater educational potential than they have thus far demonstrated. The students so identified may then become the subjects of a program of small group and individual learning experiences and other remediation to enable them to realize their potential. Of course, further studies are planned to verify that children so identified do indeed profit from such remediation efforts.

A further research finding of apparently considerable significance was the failure of the project to identify content areas of interest to these disadvantaged groups that would set them off from middle-class groups. On the contrary, the content areas identified as most interesting by the boys interviewed (sports, adventure, biography, TV and movies) would certainly be among those expected from a group of middle-class boys. While it is highly likely that middle-class boys would have a number of additional interest areas not common with those of disadvantaged boys, this finding suggests that there does exist a core of common interests which will support efforts to measure comprehension across these subcultural levels, using listening techniques. One can only speculate at the source of this common core of interest areas, but it appears likely that the mass media, particularly television, have been influential.

Finally, as has been noted in many current studies, one of the most important educational deficits of many disadvantaged students is low reading achievement. It is presumed that reading training will be one of the important remedial efforts if poor readers are to be brought to a suitable level of proficiency to enable them to complete high school and to enter college. But not all disadvantaged students have a reading problem; consequently, it will probably be found necessary to treat other motivational, emotional, and educational limitations if college entry potentials are to be realized in practice.

Chapter VIII

Listening in Business and Industry

The sector of American life which has shown the greatest realization of the importance of effective listening has been business and industry. While other sectors have shown an increasing awareness of the damaging effects of poor listening, business sees it as being expensive in dollars and cents, as was pointed out by Dover.[1]

Unfortunately, business has not been equally alert in devising ways of creating effective listening. Too often, one lecture or some type of quickie course or other form of lip service to the concept of teaching listening has been accepted in place of a sound program of instruction.

The first item in this chapter is written by Laird and Hayes. Dugan Laird writes a monthly column for Training in Business and Industry, and the material used here from one of these columns bears out the comments made in the preceding paragraph.

The first substantial survey of the extent to which provisions for the teaching of listening existed in American business and industry was made by Carter.[2] While the surveys by Patterson and Johnson which make up the remainder of this chapter are not as extensive as Carter's, they are more recent and tend to give a good picture of the present situation with reference to training in listening in business today.

A number of courses especially designed to be used in business training courses have appeared recently and are described in a recent article which I wrote.[3]

Notes

Abbreviated references refer to the entry number in Sam Duker's Listening Bibliography 2nd Ed. (Scarecrow, 1968) where the full citation may be found.

1. Dover, 301.

2. Carter, 187.

3. Sam Duker. "Teaching Listening: Recently Developed Programs and Materials." Training and Development Journal 24(5):11-15, 1970.

Communications Skills or Pink Pills

Dugan Laird and Joseph R. Hayes

Should industry teach courses in reading skills, listening, better writing? A great many training administrators have honestly ambivalent feelings about that question. Their viewpoints range all the way from dismissing such courses as "kindergarten at the executive level" to praising them as industry's "eventual recognition of some genuine training needs."

Attackers of such basic communications courses say that these subjects merely teach adults what they should have learned in grammar school. In rebuttal comes the comment, "Maybe our men should have learned these things in the first grade, but they still can't read or listen or write with very much skill. But these things are important to them on the job, so they should have an important place in our training activity."

Being "in" doesn't help much

For the pro's and con's behind these viewpoints, go to any ASTD or NSPI convention. Gather at the non-conference tables (these are the afterhours tables where people say what they really think!) and you will hear both of the extreme attitudes just quoted. You will also hear a third position, one which is growing increasingly prevalent. This viewpoint supports basic communications training, but hastily adds that such courses are useless if they are just status symbols. It deplores the tendency of some training directors who merely want to hang a sign on their door saying, "Yes, I have a listening program," or, "Of course I have a writing program." By doing this, such men can prove that they're included in the Communications Syndrome; what they cannot prove is that being "in" has helped their company very much.

One point of agreement at these informal cocktail-klatsches is that reading, writing and listening are fundamental, real-life behaviors demanded of both the white-collar and blue-collar worker. Only occasionally do you hear anyone question the rather random studies on which this assumption is based. (The Rankin survey, quoted by Ralph Nichols and Leonard Stevens in Are You Listening? covered only 68 people, and Nichols himself mentions that, in themselves, these statistics "may mean little.") Nevertheless, a lot of industrial communications programs quote Rankin's findings that 70 percent of the businessman's working day is devoted to verbal communication, that nine percent of this time goes to writing, 16 percent to reading and 30 percent to talking. We would be unfair to omit Nichols' favorite data: that 45 percent of this waking time is spent in listening.

At about this point in those after-session conversations at the convention, someone usually asks, "Just how far should any corporation go in paying for these basic skills courses? Can't we expect our employees to bring a few qualifications with them when they sign on?"

Despite the logic (?) of this question, most companies sponsor these programs on company time and in company meeting rooms. To be sure, there are always those zealots who voluntarily enroll in the courses at a local night school. Whether or not they are subsidized for their zeal seems to depend on how promotable they are considered by their company, not on any uniform company policy. Those companies which pick up the tab seem to reason that if they had installed a new lathe, they would show the operators how to run the machine. At least a few training directors feel that there is equal reason to show people how to read and listen and write if those people must read and listen and write in doing their jobs.

In support of this rationale, someone is sure to add that the state of the art has changed considerably since today's executives went to school. For example, most of them probably learned to read by using techniques which haven't been taught for decades. They probably learned first to pronounce words out loud. Then they graduated to the place where they read silently, but moved only their lips. Then there was the third step: no lip movement but just "subvocalizing" in which one pronounced the word in his mind. Younger crowds learned to read by looking at a word in its entirety, then understanding it much as one looks at a picture and understands.

Just as there is a new mathematics there is a new reading. In late 1965 Time magazine explained the new structural linguistics approach developed by Maurice William Sullivan. Yes, there is a lot of evidence that employees at all levels perform daily routines in obsolete ways. Thus the convention conversations indicate quite clearly that industrial trainers believe that there are more reasons why companies should offer basic communications training than there are reasons why they should not.

Yet why do the courses sometimes fail? (Quite a few would insist that the word is "often" or "usually" rather than sometimes.) Advocates of such training quickly point out that programs which fail are only "pink pills," three-hour quickies which pretend to destroy habits people have been building up all their lives. Do you recall that "in" training director with all the right signs hanging on his door?

Learn from boasters and Bolsheviks

One finds few failures in those firms which have validated a legitimate need, established a precise objective, and implemented a tested program. Usually the bull sessionists agree on this, and then their conversation becomes a series of soap boxes for each to extoll the glories of the last program they designed or conducted. The press releases they would have written for themselves are, naturally enough, interrupted by frequent hecklers who exclaim, "Oh, that doesn't work at all!" Yet if you listen carefully to both the boaster and the Bolshevik, you can pick up a good many ideas about what to do and what to avoid on that apparently inevitable day when you will start some basic communications training in your own company.

First of all, take reading-improvement courses. The average adult doesn't read very fast or very well. He's probably about as skillful as he was when he was in the eighth grade. Unfortunately, there has been great emphasis on speedreading, but actually there is a great deal more in effective reading than mere speed. One does not read better just because he reads faster. What all training men need to remember is this: the good reader has flexible speed. If industry can teach its men when to read fast and when to go slowly, then it has a good chance of offering a productive reading-skills program. Furthermore, some pretty well-established authorities indicate that people in general don't need to read faster. True, retention and comprehension may suffer if you clutter your mind with the many details that slow reading might deposit there. But well-directed slow reading can produce better results for some purposes. For example, perhaps engineers, chemists or lawyers should never be taught speedreading. Maybe they should underline and write questions in the margins in their business reading. They may profit a great deal from doing this whenever they find a gap in their own understanding, or in the writer's thinking, or when they want to use the writer's ideas to stimulate their own creative thinking.

The mere suggestion of such painstaking reading on the job usually produces a flurry of protest, like, "But I thought that speedreading was so all-fired important!" Soberer people will nod sagely and remind everyone that speedreading was just another fad, "like all this stuff is just a fad."

Conclusions? A practical, productive reading course will of necessity have varying goals for varying men. It might conceivably even teach one man to skim-read on one bulletin, another to underline while he reads the same material. It could very likely teach the same man to skim on one report and to underline on another. Such varied-skills objectives are consistent with the doctrine of schools like New York University, which has always decried the blind use of hardware like tachistoscopes.

Nowadays, most training administrators seem to feel that most companies can effectively support a resident program in discriminative reading. Such programs must help each trainee decide when he needs speed and when he needs care, and must give him a workable method for accomplishing both these goals.

Fewer disagreements among listening trainers

In the field of listening training, there is somewhat more agreement. One reason is the relative newness of the subject. There hasn't been time for sharply divergent schools of thought about method to crystallize, mobilize and meet in smoky combat at conventions! There have been very few studies, so there are also few authorities and few materials on the market. By far the best-known name is Ralph

Nichols of the University of Minnesota. Here's a comment from a man who once taught for him: "Before I got into industrial training, I went to St. Paul and met Nick, just after the end of World War II, and thought he was inanely insane to be telling college freshmen how to listen to lectures, and to grant them college credit for learning how! Now it's twenty years later, and I'm one of the many who regularly administer the Basic Systems [Editor's note: Now known as the Xerox course] taped programmed instruction course in listening."

The Basic Systems item is easily the best-known single package in listening training. The data any firm collects in the pre- and post-tests will invariably prove impressive, although some scoffers argue that the tests are so contrived that only impressive data can be generated. These impressive test comparisons ("contrasts" would be a more accurate word) have been likened to the output of some creative-thinking workshops: all your managers may be able to connect seventeen dots with four straight lines, yet have no impact whatsoever on your corporate profit picture. The more vocal skeptics ask for concrete results of the listening-skills programs. They say, "Name one sale that can be directly traced to a salesman's doing a better job of listening after he finished the program, or show me one management decision that was better because the parties to the decision were good listeners." Of course nobody can do just what they demand, yet you hear large numbers of trainers say, "I've administered these programs to lots of people, and I've never talked to a trainee who didn't think it was great." (This is especially true of the Basic Systems tapes, which are invariably applauded.)

Users of the Basic Systems program also say that it teaches one not only to listen for facts, but also to listen for structure. Unless you can summarize successfully, you cannot make correct responses to their frames. For this reason the program may have more value than is at first apparent. Nonetheless, it does concentrate on the intellectual rather than the emotional (or "feelings") message of the sender. Neither the programers nor its vendors have ever pretended that the program is anything but a "listen-for-facts" discipline. They do, however, point out that regional and racial dialects, plus background noises, are introduced as barriers to the listening process. Idealistic trainers argue that industrial listeners not only miss the facts when they listen, but that they miss the facts because of their own feelings. This in turn causes them not to hear the feelings of the speaker at all. "Thoroughgoing listening training," say the behaviorists at the bull sessions, "simply must improve listening for feelings as well as listening for facts!"

It's quite true that graduates of "pink pill" listening programs frequently feed back comments like, "I keep forgetting to practice what I learned in training." There is an urgent message for program designers here; they must do their utmost to see that the training is "generalized." Without drills which strongly simulate on-the-job listening conditions, trainers may have trouble proving on-the-job behavorial change. Top management has every right to demand such change. To insure such results, many trainers yearn for an as yet nonexistent program which would teach a listener to do everything even a Carl Rogers might desire. In other words, the real enthusiasts are saying, "Give us a validated program that trains every student to be able to repeat to the speaker's total satisfaction the message the speaker has just sent. Give us just that capacity, and we'll change the whole nature of industrial relations!"

This desire implies that in genuinely effective listening, the feelings are perceived and shared, not necessarily agreed upon, but necessarily understood. That's a total listening which implies subtle reflection, probably asking questions to make sure you understood. Trainers who are overworked (and who isn't?) will detect this as an all-or-nothing-at-all school of thought. But the enthusiasts who want this high quality in their listening training believe that any program will be impotent to the degree that it ignores feelings, indeed that the failure to listen for feelings is the reason some graduates have not successfully generalized their own training to accomplish a genuine on-the-job behaviorial change. Only the discipline of genuinely empathic listening, they argue, will permit the trainee to divorce his mind from his own problems, both personal and professional, so he fully concentrates on the speaker. They insist that a training program which settles for a lesser objective is only an academic exercise.

Even if we admit the almost divine level of interpersonal relationships Rogerian listening requires, we still must admire the ambition of men who seek (and hope someday to produce) listening training which will accomplish all this. In the meantime, few training directors and fewer instructors who work for them have the knowledge or skill to develop so profound a program. If such a package does emerge, some firm must someday find the deep need, then find the psychologist who has the time, discipline and creativity to validate an action-oriented training program. In other words, some profit-making firm will need to strike the creative fire in the right university professor.

It takes an expert to teach listening

At those ASTD bull sessions, just mention university professors and you will strike some conversational fire of your own! The cry of "ivory tower" and "egghead" is sure to follow, loud and clear and with considerable justification. Much academic effort in basic communications training has been just that, academic. Yet in a few fields, The Training Director has managed to find The Professor who was able to speak directly and meaningfully to our industrial population. Such a combination may yet appear to develop a Carl Rogers-level listening package just as a well-known drug firm linked with Basic Systems to produce the present taped PI package. In the meantime, the more thoughtful training directors grow increasingly certain that they must go to an expert in listening skills, or that they must use a tested program. Amateur programs seem to jeopardize not only the reputation of the training package; they endanger the reputation of the whole department and the entire concept of basic communication-skills training.

Incidentally, line managers may not be too sorry to hear of attacks against training in reading, listening or writing. If so, they are exercising an entirely understandable defense mechanism. To attend a basic communications skills-training session may be a man's admission that he is a high-level functional illiterate. If he cannot manage to read all the 6000 pages that will cross his desk each year, accurately hear both the thoughts and feelings of his associates, or effectively put his own ideas down on paper--well, is he really any more qualified to function than the stock clerk who cannot read or write at all? The stock clerk knows he is in trouble, so he welcomes training; but the executive, even when he knows his needs, may ill afford to admit it.

Communication is never easy

Well, did this bull session on which we eavesdropped settle anything at all? Surely the comments prove that communications problems are painfully real to the individual, the department, the corporation, and for that matter to society. Easily the most difficult skill industry has tried to teach is the Carl Rogers goal of perfectly reflecting a speaker's ideas and feelings. Many regard this as just plain superhuman. If this is true, we are in trouble. The bull session usually ends when some Scotch-on-the-rocks Socrates moodily mutters, "We've just got to understand everyone in the organization, even those nauseating new college grads. And brother, they aren't like us! Our generation came up through a discipline which says that older people and people in authority were probably right. New hires don't buy that." He shakes his head sadly. "These kids challenge all our proven philosophies, and too often they're right! I guess they just know more than we did when we graduated. At least that's the way our chairman of the board put it the other day."

Our Socrates and his chairman make an important point: the knowledge explosion makes communication all the more difficult. So if the debate we overheard seemed inconclusive, it at least reflected our times. The training director must still decide whether to sponsor or ignore basic communications skills training. If he decides to sponsor, then he must answer another vital question: will he use a program that changes people, or buy another pink pill?

When these postconvention conversations break up, the talkers walk away and you can see their clothing. The ones who seem to wear the most expensive suits are those who have decided to sponsor on going programs. You hear them saying, "Sure our managers at the office are studying the same things their grandchildren are studying in the public schools. Well, the kids are learning what they'll use in later life, and our men are learning what they've needed all along."

A Survey of the Teaching of Listening in the United States Air Force and Business Management Schools

Kenneth M. Patterson

QUESTIONNAIRE
(Business Management Course)

1. Do you teach listening as a unit of instruction or as part of some other unit of instruction in your executive development and employee training programs?

_____Yes _____No

Part I - Curriculum Scope

2. As a part of your training programs, do you teach
   a. Appreciative listening? _____Yes _____No
   b. Comprehensive listening? _____Yes _____No
   c. Critical listening? _____Yes _____No

3. What proportion of your training program is devoted to teaching listening skills?

___Less than 10% ___10% to 25% ___25% and above.

4. Do you teach note-taking as an aid to listening?

_____Yes _____No

5. What is your purpose for teaching listening? Answer all that apply.
   a. _____As an aid to student learning.
   b. _____As a managerial skill.
   c. _____To increase comprehension and retention.
   d. _____As an aid to identifying key ideas.
   e. _____As an aid to identifying transitions in oral presentations.
   f. _____As an aid in making mental outlines of oral presentations.
   g. _____(Other)

Part II - Curricular Methods

6. Which of the following methods do you use to teach listening?

____Lectures ____Programmed learning courses

____Laboratories ____Films

____Tape Recorders ____(Other)__________

Part III - Curricular Mechanics

7. How much time do you devote to teaching listening?

_____1 hour _____5-10 hours

_____2-5 hours _____over 10 hours

8. Are the instructional periods taught as a block of instructions?

______Yes ______No

9. If not taught as a block, how are the periods distributed throughout the course?

_____Equally

_____More in the first half of the course

_____More in the last half of the course

10. To whom is listening taught?

____Top management

____Middle management

____First-line supervisors

____Volunteers

____(Other)__________

11. What is the experience level of the instructor who teaches listening?

____Master's degree or higher?

____Baccalaureate degree

____(Other)__________

12. What materials do you use in teaching listening?

____Textbooks ____Articles

____Outlines, syllabi ____(Other)__________

____Periodicals

Part IV

Please note below any other information of particular or unusual importance relating to listening instruction in your management training program.

United States Air Force

Questionnaires were sent to 84 USAF bases with 60 responding. Nine of the reporting bases did not teach a management course.

Business

The number of businesses surveyed was 42, 30 of which returned the questionnaire. Of those reporting, only 10 taught listening in management courses while three stated that they had listening programs under development but they did not have information available at this time.

Summary

A brief summary of the data is presented in the following chart.

Summary of Survey Results

	United States Air Force Management Schools (In percentages)	Business Management Schools (In percentages)
1. Per cent teaching listening	64	33
2. Type of listening taught		
(a) appreciative	30	30
(b) comprehensive	60	80
(c) critical	57	100

	United States Air Force Management Schools (In percentages)	Business Management Schools (In percentages)
3. Proportion of course devoted to listening instruction		
(a) less than 10%	66	80
(b) 10% to 25%	28	20
(c) 25% and above	6	0
4. Per cent teaching note taking	60	30
5. Purpose of Instruction		
(a) aid to student learning	48	40
(b) managerial skill	82	100
(c) to improve comprehension and retention	45	60
(d) aid to identifying key ideas	45	70
(e) identifying traditions in oral presentations	30	10
(f) making mental outlines of oral presentations	42	20
6. Teaching Methods		
(a) lectures	66	80
(b) laboratories	75	20
(c) tape recorders	15	50
(d) programmed learning courses	9	30
(e) films	54	60
(f) demonstrations	24	20
7. Length of Course		
(a) 1 hour	19	10
(b) 2-5 hours	61	60
(c) 5-10 hours	14	0
(d) over 10 hours	6	30
8. Distribution of Instruction		
(a) block instruction	24	60
(b) equally throughout course	40	30

	United States Air Force Management Schools (In percentages)	Business Management Schools (In percentages)
(c) more in first half	6	10
(d) more in last half	30	0
9. Students taught		
(a) all enrollees	93	N/A
(b) military	0	N/A
(c) civilian	3	N/A
(d) volunteers	3	N/A
(e) top management	N/A	30
(f) middle management	N/A	100
(g) first line supervisors	N/A	90
10. Experience Level		
(a) Master's degree or higher	16	50
(b) Baccalaureate degree	35	50
(c) other	54	0
11. Materials Used		
(a) textbooks	42	30
(b) outline, syllabi	42	50
(c) periodicals	36	50
(d) articles	45	40

From Theory to Practice: Does Management Listen?

Stuart Condon

The second hypothesis of this study stated that:

> There is disagreement between management and labor regarding the degree of listening which management believes it offers.

To prove or disprove this hypothesis, a series of questions was incorporated in the general questionnaire used in the case study.

We contend that reception of meaning can be by the eye as well as the ear. We also believe that a reaction results from the reception of a message. For example, labor requests the ear of management to ask for a specific object. Management can listen, but if no action is evident labor will assume that listening has not occurred. We do not infer that management must act favorably to labor's request. What is meant is that management must respond in one way or the other. Labor must know that a reaction has taken place, so that it will realize that management listened and understood. The author believes that if there was no reaction, then listening did not occur. It is equally important that management signal its reception to labor by some response.

Five questions were designed to determine the degree of listening which (1) management indicated it gave and (2) labor indicated it received. From the answers to these questions the second hypothesis will be accepted or rejected. The following data was used to make that determination:

Management	Labor
Question 1: Constructive criticism is welcomed by management.	
strongly agree..........42%	strongly agree.......... 0%
agree..................41%	agree..................14%

Management		Labor	
disagree	7%	disagree	51%
strongly disagree	0%	strongly disagree	35%

Question 2: Management thoroughly understands the problems their men face everyday.

strongly agree	34%	strongly agree	0%
agree	59%	agree	21%
disagree	7%	disagree	61%
strongly disagree	0%	strongly disagree	12%

Question 3: Management encourages discussion of working procedure prior to the start of a new job.

strongly agree	4%	Strongly agree	0%
agree	86%	agree	12%
disagree	10%	disagree	62%
strongly disagree	0%	strongly disagree	26%

Question 4: Labor is encouraged to discuss any problem with management.

strongly agree	42%	strongly agree	0%
agree	57%	agree	16%
disagree	1%	disagree	67%
strongly disagree	0%	strongly disagree	17%

Question 5: In general, management is too busy to thoroughly discuss job related problems.

strongly agree	0%	strongly agree	47%
agree	2%	agree	40%
disagree	64%	disagree	13%
strongly disagree	34%	strongly disagree	0%

The following questions were asked of labor alone. Replies to the questions are also recorded.

Question: What are the results of the suggestions you make?

-I don't know - I never see any results.

-Several of my suggestions have been used. I have been told of their use and am proud to have been of help.

-I don't make any suggestions. It don't do no good.

-What I've suggested has later been done but it's someone else's idea then.

-My supervisor doesn't want to know what I think. Just do the job exactly like he tells me to.

-In some cases we talk about different ways to do a good job and that is good.

Question: Can you talk freely with your supervisor?

-I can talk freely with the top man but not to my immediate supervisor.

-Yes, he is interested in how I would do the job.

-My supervisor is too busy to really listen.

-When I come up with what I think is a better way to do a job, it makes my foreman look bad. I don't do it anymore.

-My foreman is paid to talk - not to listen.

-Yes, my foreman and I talk together real good.

Data Comparison

	Management	Labor
Question 1	+ 93% - 7%	+ 14% -86%
Question 2	+ 93% - 7%	+ 21% -73%
Question 3	+ 90% -10%	+ 12% -88%
Question 4	+ 99% - 1%	+ 16% -84%
Question 5	+ 2% -98%	+ 87% -13%

Data recorded in answer to this section resulted in a much deeper area of disagreement than was anticipated. Individual interviews with both management and labor personnel substantiated this disagreement. Management acknowledged many cases in which it was unable to fulfill a particular request. This inability on management's part was not, however, communicated to labor, which resulted in labor's assuming that no listening had occurred. Management perceived itself to be a good listener, but labor did not appear to agree. Questionnaire responses, interview and observation validated this finding.

This study, on the basis of the recorded data, accepts the hypothesis that there is disagreement between management and labor regarding the degree of listening management offers.

A Survey of Listening Programs of
a Hundred Major Industries

Janice D. Johnson

LISTENING SURVEY

I. Does your organization offer a course in oral communication? Yes___No___

A. If not, does your organization recognize a need for a communication course? Yes___No___

B. Is there any provision for the initiation of a communication course in any of your training programs? Yes___No___

II. Does "listening" play a part in the communications program you now have or in the program you are planning? Yes___No___

A. If your answer is yes, what part of the entire communications program is devoted to the teaching of listening?

One-fourth of the course time ___

Less than one-fourth of the course time ___

It is a separate course ___

B. What time factor is involved in the training program? ___Hours

___Days

___Months

III. Why was the listening program established?

Breakdown in upward/downward communication ______

Poor plant morale ______

Drop off in sales ______

Other, please explain ______________________________

____

IV. What are the aims and objectives of your listening course? ______________________________

____

V. Has any counseling service been used in preparation of this listening course? Yes___No___

VI. If yes, what type of service was used?

College or university speech department ______

College or university public/industrial relations department ______

Private concern dealing in public relations ______

Educational-training department of another industry ______

VII. What problems, if any, did you encounter as this program was being developed?

____

____

VIII. When was your "listening" course established?

In the last year ______

Within the last five years ______

Within the last ten years ______

IX. Who participates in this program?

Managers ______

Salesmen ______

Receptionists ______

Foremen ______

All personnel are eligible ______

Other, please explain: ______________________________

X. Do you use supplementary material in your listening program? Yes___ No___

XI. If yes, what type? Tape___ Visiting speakers___
Text___ Charts___
Film___ Other___

XII. Who is the person in charge of your listening program?___________________________

Please give his title ___________________________

XIII. If you have used any measurement of the success or failure of your listening program, how has the program's effectiveness been tested?

Follow up survey ___
Retesting of candidates' listening ability ___
Improvement of morale within plant ___
Other, please explain ___________________________

____

XIV. Is there any club or organization of employees which focuses on oral communications? ___

A. If your answer is yes, does listening play a part in the program of such an organization? Yes___ No___

B. Does this organization invite guest speakers and authorities on listening to the meetings? Yes___ No___

C. Do representatives from this organization participate in oral communications in the community? Yes___ No___

XV. Comments___________________________

____

____

Thank you for your assistance in completing this survey,

(Mrs.) Janice D. Johnson
1715 West Willow-Wood Drive
Peoria, Illinois 61614

Sixty-three of the one-hundred one surveys were returned. Of these respondents thirty-seven said that they did have some provision for listening training.

The first question asked whether a course in oral communications was offered. Twenty-eight said "yes," twenty-three said "no." If the answer was "no," the survey then asked whether a need for such a course was recognized. Of those who responded to this question, 18 replied "yes" while 13 said "no." Upon being asked whether such a communication course was being considered, 17 replied "yes" and 16 said "no." (These numbers and those to follow will not always sum to the total number of respondents because certain questions were inappropriate for each organization, and therefore not answered.)

Although a few indicated that they had used Ralph Nichols' recording, "Listening Is Good Business," films, and Xerox listening tapes, they did not interpret this as a listening course per se, or as listening training.

Thirty-one responded that "listening" did play a part in their communication course, while 11 said "no." Twenty-one noted that the listening course was set up as a separate course but 8 said that listening took less than one-fourth of the course time, while 6 reported that it took one-fourth or more of the allotted course time. The overlap here seems to have arisen from the ambiguity of the term "separate course" to some of the responders.

The amount of time involved in listening varied greatly. The most frequent answer was three hours.

The third question dealt with the reason for the establishment of a listening program. The alternatives offered were (1) a break-down in upward/downward communication; (2) poor plant morale; (3) drop off of sales; (4) other, please explain.

Eleven admitted a breakdown in upward/downward

communications, while one attributed the establishment of a course to poor plant morale. Eight attributed the move simply to "need." Fifteen others attributed the move to a need also, but they were more definite and attributed it to general needs, need to define/refine listening habits and need to teach advantages/techniques.

Other reasons given for establishing such listening courses included:

1. Better human relations
2. Basic factor in selling
3. Requested by personnel
4. General needs
5. Ineffective listening
6. Sales training
7. Deemed advisable
8. Without listening, there can be no communication

The fourth question asked what the aims and objectives of the listening course were. Typical answers included:

1. To develop and refine listening habits.
2. To train managers to listen to subordinates.
3. To make management conscious of the benefits and values of good listening.
4. To teach the advantages of good listening.
5. To improve communication and understanding.
6. To penetrate emotional factors.
7. To eliminate errors.
8. To train employees to hear and retain facts.

When asked whether any counseling service had been used in preparation of the listening course, 17 responded "yes," 14 said "no," and 5 gave no answer.

The next question was aimed at those who had a counseling service and asked what kind of service had been used. The alternative included a college or university speech department, a college or industrial public relations, or educational-training department of another industry.

The University of Chicago and Bradley University are two such universities which have worked with industries in analyzing needs in upward/downward communication. Xerox is an example of a private concern dealing in improvement of communication.

Eleven of the polled industries indicated that they had used the education-training department of another industry. Four said that they had had the services of a university speech department, while four others said they had dealt with a private concern and only two had used the services of a public relations department of a university. Some, like Caterpillar, had used a combination of these services.

Caterpillar, recognizing a need for improvement in various areas of communications, contacted Dr. Robert Burns in the Industrial Relations department of the University of Chicago and asked him to survey their situation and make suggestions which would lead to improvement. The program which developed was set up to cover eight topics (e.g., Questioning and Listening). All the materials for the established courses were developed by the University of Chicago.

The next question asked what problems had been encountered as the listening program was being developed. Seven replied that no problems had developed. Fifteen did not even answer the question. Time seemed to be a problem. Sometimes the course had to be scheduled into the employee's work day. Another problem was that of condensing the subject matter into the time allowed.

One person pointed out that the commercially prepared courses did not fit nor satisfy the needs of a specific plant and often the training programs had to be revised to "fit" the interests of the company.

Others told of the problem of selecting appropriate exercises for the maximum development of the skill desired.

Another problem seemed to be the lack of understanding as to why training in listening was necessary at all. The attitude, very difficult to overcome, seemed to be that "I can hear, so why should I go through a training program?"

Judging from some of the answers on the questionnaire, this attitude is not limited to blue collar workers, but is shared by some training directors as well.

The next question was asked to determine whether or not listening training was on the increase. Six had developed their programs within the last ten years. Twelve responded that their program had developed within the last five years and eight had started their programs within the last year. Eleven did not answer.

The ninth question dealt with who could take the listening/communication course. In at least sixteen plants all individuals were eligible.

The survey list included:

Managers	19
Salesmen	12
Foremen	11
All personnel are eligible	16
Other, please explain:	2

General sales department members, management trainers and supervisors.

Supplementary materials are used in most training courses. Tapes are the most popular type of supplementary material, and texts are a close second choice. Other materials used in order of their popularity are films, charts, visiting speakers, and programmed instruction.

Question thirteen asked whether a follow-up had been done to measure the success or failure of the listening program and if so, how had the program's effectiveness been treated? Six reported that they had used a follow-up survey; six more responded that they had retested the candidate's listening ability. Four measured the success/effectiveness of such a program by the improvement of morale within the plant. Others responded that a follow-up survey is being planned for the near future. Others reported that the success of their program was measured by the improvement of communications within the organization and by the good reactions of participants.

The final question asked whether there was any club or organization of employees which focused on oral communications. Of those respondents who had some listening training, 14 said "yes," 16 said "no." Listening played a part in three-fourths of these organizations' speech program. At least two-thirds of the organizations invited guest speakers and authorities on listening to meetings. Five-sixths of these organizations participate in oral communications in their communities.

The following table lists those industries and businesses

which answered the survey and indicates whether or not they have implemented a listening program.

Summary of Survey Responses

Name of Industry	Answered Survey	Has Program
Alcoa Aluminum	No	---
Union Carbide	Yes	No
American Cyanamid	Yes	Yes
Formica Corp.	No	---
Ingersoll-Rand	Yes	Yes
Flintkote Co.	Yes	No
Rand McNally and Co.	No	---
Monsanto Co.	No	---
Pittsburgh Plate Glass Co.	No	Yes
Presolite	No	---
General Tire and Ruber Co.	Yes	No
Zenith Radio Corp.	No	---
Xerox Corp.	Yes	Yes
LeTourneau, R. G. Inc.	No	---
Bell and Howell	No	---
Bemis Bag Co.	Yes	Yes
Bendix Corp.	Yes	Yes
Bethlehem Steel Corp.	Yes	Yes
Caterpillar	Yes	Yes
Howe Richardson Scale Co.	No	---
Howe Sound	No	---
Hondaille Industrial Corp.	No.	---
Honeywell	Yes	Yes
Chrysler Corp.	Yes	Yes
C. F. and I. Steel	Yes	Yes
Clevite Corp.	Yes	No
Ford Motor Corp.	Yes	Yes
Coca Cola Co.	Yes	No
I. T. T.	Yes	Yes
Johnson and Johnson	Yes	Yes
Gerber Products	Yes	Yes
Vic Maitland and Associates	Yes	No
MacManus and Adam, Inc.	No	---
Friend Reiss Advertising, Inc.	No	---
Courtenay Jamison Advertising	Yes	Yes
Bayard Advertising Service	No	---
Roberts and Reimers	No	---
Newmark Posner and Mitchell	No	---
Don Kemper Co.	Yes	No

Name of Industry	Answered Survey	Has Program
Powell Schnenbrod and Hall Advertising, Inc.	Yes	No
Western Electric Co.	No	Yes
Abbott Laboratories	Yes	Yes
Baxter Laboratories	No	---
Aetna Life Insurance Co.	Yes	No
Equitable Life Assurance Co.	Yes	Yes
New York Life Insurance Co.	Yes	Yes
Nationwide Life Insurance Co.	Yes	Yes
Prudential Insurance Co.	Yes	Yes
Atlas Assurance Co.	Yes	No
A. B. C.	Yes	No
C. B. S.	No	---
N. B. C.	No	---
Pepsi Cola General Bottlers	Yes	No
General Motors	Yes	Yes
Keystone Steel and Wire Co.	Yes	Yes
Celanese Chemical Co.	Yes	No
Masonite Corp.	No	---
Youngstown Steel	Yes	Yes
Blaw Knox	Yes	No
ASARCO	Yes	No
American Radiator and Standard Sanitary Corp.	Yes	No
Minn. Mining and Mfg. Co.	No	---
American Machinery and Foundry Co.	No	---
Mirro Aluminum Co.	No	---
Eaton Mfg. Co.	Yes	Yes
Firestone Tire and Rubber Co.	No	---
General Mills Inc.	Yes	Yes
Case, J. I. Co.	Yes	No
General Electric Co.	No	Yes
Casting Eng.	No	---
Ace Paper Box Corp.	No	---
F. M. C. Corp.	Yes	No
Link Belt Co.	No	---
Admiral Corp.	Yes	No
Hoover Electric Co.	No	---
ITT General Controls, Inc.	Yes	No
Hewitt-Robins, Inc.	Yes	Yes
Bellows-Valvair	No	---
Anchor Hocking Glass Corp.	Yes	Yes
Goodrich, B. F.	No	---

Name of Industry	Answered Survey	Has Program
General Foods Corp.	Yes	Yes
Borg Warner, Corp.	Yes	No
Glidden Co.	Yes	No
Allis Chalmers Mfg. Co.	Yes	No
Armstrong Cork Co.	No	---
Allied Chemical	No	---
Swift and Co.	Yes	No
Cratex Mfg.	Yes	No
Polaroid Optical Goods	Yes	Yes
Westinghouse Electric Corp.	No	---
Whitney-Blake Co.	No	---
Whiting Corp.	No	---
Wicker Corp.	Yes	Yes
Singer Co.	Yes	Yes
Sunbeam Equipment Corp.	Yes	No
Standard Oil Co. (Ind.)	Yes	No
U. S. Steel Corp.	Yes	No
Uni Royal U. S. Rubber Co.	Yes	Yes
Stauffer Chemical Co.	Yes	No
R.C.A. Victor	Yes	Yes
Caterpillar Tractor Co.	Yes	Yes

Summary and Conclusions

The purposes of this study were: (1) to survey one hundred one representative major industries to determine whether or not they had some kind of communications course; (2) to determine whether or not listening played a part in such a course; (3) to ascertain whether said industries were contemplating the formulation of a listening program if one did not already exist; (4) to evaluate the apparent trends implied by the survey and compare them with an industry currently using a listening-training program; (5) to ascertain whether or not the trend toward increased listening-training does indeed exist.

I. Summary

Significance of listening. Industry relies heavily upon listening as an element of communication. Listening affects the understanding of a problem, the retention and attention of an individual and the morale of a group.

Good communication is dependent upon good listening. Further, good listening affects the efficient use of time. Finally, many dollars are tied up in the training of individuals. During the training period a large percentage of time is spent listening. The effectiveness of this training relies upon efficient listening and thus directly affects the expense of operation.

Tests given by Xerox following listening training programs have shown tremendous improvement in listening ability.

Survey results. One hundred one surveys were sent to businesses and industries representing:

1. Heavy industry
2. Insurance companies
3. Communication companies
4. Advertising agencies
5. Transportation industries
6. Electronics industries
7. Chemical--drug industries
8. Food industries
9. Building supplies industries

Of 63 who responded, 36 had some provision for listening training. Three industries who are known to have a program did not answer the survey.

II. Conclusions

One thing became eminently apparent as the survey results were tabulated. There is a lack of universality of terms in the business world. This was evidenced by the multiplicity of titles given to the personnel-trainer. It was further evidenced by a lack of understanding of the term "listening program."

The ambiguity of the term "listening program," or complete lack of understanding or ignorance of the subject led to inaccurate answers to questions about listening training.

The amount of time spent in listening training varied immensely from industry to industry. Judging from some comments on individual surveys it seemed as though the amount of time spent in training was a major criteria in considering whether or not "training" was being offered in listening. Some respondents told of using film, tapes and speakers on the subject of listening, but they did not interpret this as a listening program to any degree.

A majority of the industries polled recognized a need for some form of oral communications program within the plant.

While only 36 out of 63 respondents replied that they had listening training of some sort provided in their course of instruction, it should be pointed out that six reported they were contemplating the addition of a listening course to their program, or would make listening a part of a communications course were they to offer one.

At least five of the responding industries had provisions for sending individuals who needed training in oral communications to outside sources (e.g. Dale Carnegie Courses) for training but did not provide any training within the plant.

It was noted earlier, but it should be pointed out again, that at least three businesses and industries known to have a listening program did not answer the survey.

The results seem to indicate a growing awareness of a need.

Like Caterpillar, industries having listening training programs offer the course for almost all employees--the obvious exception being the receptionist. For the most part, the courses have been established within the last five years and incorporate supplementary materials such as tapes, texts, visiting speakers, charts and film.

While Caterpillar used the services of university--public--industrial relations department, the majority of respondents had used the counsel of an educational-training department of another industry.

Six respondents reported that a follow-up survey was used to measure the program's effectiveness. Six more reported that retesting of the candidates listening ability took place. This would seem to indicate that little, if any, measurement of the success or retention of training has taken place. As pointed out earlier, the programmed listening tapes are not inexpensive. Industries must be satisfied with the results and improvements must be self-evident or they would not continue to invest in such a project.

A problem encountered by many training personnel seemed to be a lack of awareness of the need for listening skill. This lack of awareness seems to be a problem because the training manager himself is not aware of the need, or he has trouble convincing others of the need. It becomes a problem of educating the employees to the need. The need must be realized by those concerned, and the place to start seems to be with informed, trained personnel managers.

Another thing became evident from the responses of the survey. A listening program is relatively expensive and would not be practical for small concerns regardless of their net profit.

It was interesting to note that, as suspected, certain categories of industry and business seem to stress listening programs more than others. The following table points out the number of industries in each category which were included in the survey sample. Insurance, transportation, food, electronic and communication industries seem to have the greatest percentage of listening programs. This might tend to indicate that those industries which must sell themselves and which do not satisfy any immediate need of the public are very much aware of the need for adequate communication. As a result, these industries spend time and money on various aspects of oral communications.

The trend toward more increased listening-training seems evident from the survey results.

Categorical Results of Survey

Categories	Total Representation*	Listening Program	Percentage
Heavy Industry	42	11	26.6%
Insurance Co.	6	4	66.6%
Communications	9	4	44.4%
Advertising	9	1	11. %
Transportation	6	4	66.6%
Electronics	5	1	20. %
Chemical--Drugs	8	3	37.5%
Food	5	3	60. %
Building Supplies	9	3	33.3%

*Two businesses could not be categorized.

Bibliography

Abbreviated references refer to the entry number in Sam Duker's Listening Bibliography 2nd Ed. (Scarecrow, 1968) where the full citation may be found.

Dover, C. J. 301.

Harwood, Kenneth A., 525.

Hildebrandt, Herbert, 564.

Nichols, Ralph G. and Leonard A. Stevens, 895.

"Now Hear This," 909.

"Training--Xerox U.," Time, 91:73, January 5, 1968.

Chapter IX

Research on Listening, I

In this chapter two relatively lengthy passages from research studies in the field of listening are presented. Both are excellent examples of superior research and both are taken from unpublished doctoral dissertations. Dr. Fry, now associated with the Psychology Department at the University of Virginia, obtained his doctorate at the University of Rochester. Dr. Wood did his doctoral work at Indiana University and is now associated with the schools of Sonoma County, California.

It must be apparent to the reader of this collection that it is my viewpoint that relationships between listening and various psychometric variables are of the utmost importance to the student of listening. Fry's study is a well-designed experiment having to do with two communication modes: speaking and listening. The ingenuity of the plan of research cannot help but intrigue the reader but it should not distract him from the interesting questions Fry seeks to answer: Will specific training in listening improve not only listening but speaking as well? Is there a difference in the effects of training subjects for listening alone, for speaking alone, or for speaking and listening? A careful study of the results obtained in this study, as well as of the research techniques employed, should prove profitable to the reader.

In the introduction to the fifth chapter the point was made that an article dealing with an experiment having to do with rate controlled speech was nevertheless highly relevant insofar as listening was concerned. In that introduction references were also given to enable any interested reader to investigate the nature of compressed speech.

The excerpt from C. David Wood's thesis again presents this problem. The thesis was about compressed speech but the method of testing comprehension seems to possibly be equally suitable for ordinary listening. In fact, it is very likely that Wood's experiment may point the way to effective measurement of listening ability at the elementary school level. It is equally possible that Fry's study may present clues for the consideration of adequate measures of listening at the college level.

The Effects of Training in Communication and Role Perception on the Communicative Abilities of Children

Charles Luther Fry, Jr.

Sixty-four fifth grade girls participated in the experiment. All of these were pretested on several types of communication tests to permit the later examination of both improvement with training and degree of generalization stemming from the communication training involved. Of the 64, 16 were assigned to the control group which received no training at all, and 48 were assigned to various training groups. There were three such training groups of 16 members each which were known as the integration, listening, and speaking groups. The control and the three experimental or training groups were all equated as to the I.Q. of their members. Training group members were then assigned to sets consisting of four members each in which the actual training occurred. The set membership was determined as shown in Figure 1. Each member of the integration group was assigned to one of the sets marked 1, 2, 3, and 4. During the training received in these sets the subjects took turns taking the role of speaker and listener in the various communications involved. Each member of the listening and speaking groups was assigned to one of the sets marked 5 to 12 in Figure 1. Each of these sets contained two members from the listening group and two members from the speaking group. The listening group members of these sets received training in the role of the listener only, while the speaking group members received training only in the role of the speaker. All sets met on five occasions for an hour each time yielding a total training time of five hours each, and the amount of material covered during training was the same for each set. Training consisted of delivering or listening to communications designed to permit a listener to discriminate a single picture from a group of pictures in an array. The listeners then attempted to make the discrimination called for in the communication. In attempting to make this discrimination the listeners demonstrated to others in the set the success or failure of the communication. In part dependent upon their success in picking the correct

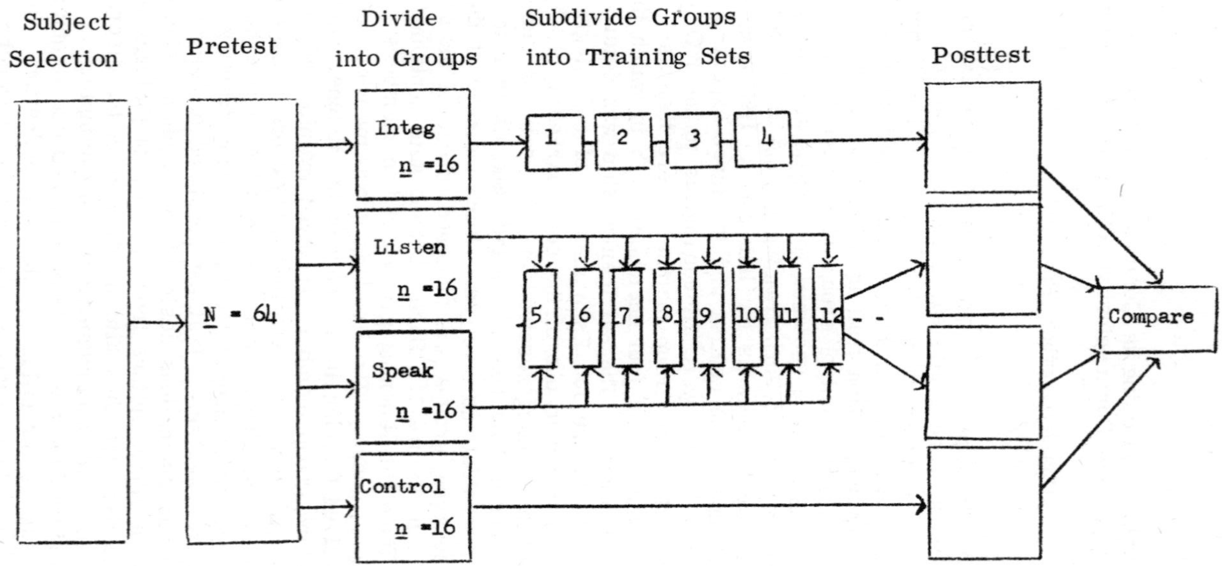

Figure 1. Flow chart representing the disposition of subjects used. Sixty-four subjects were selected and pretested and broken down into four experimental and control groups equated for I. Q. The experimental groups' subjects were assigned to training sets as indicated. There were four sets of integration subjects and eight made up of two listeners and two speakers each. The subjects were then posttested and the pretest to posttest improvement scores were compared for each group.

picture, a discussion ensued regarding the adequacy of the communication made. Posttests were then administered to all subjects. With minor exceptions the posttests were identical to the pretests and the pretest to posttest improvements were compared in each of the experimental and control groups.

Subjects

The subjects used in this experiment consisted of 64 fifth grade girls. Subjects were restricted to those whose I.Q.s ranged between 100 and 146 as measured on the California Mental Maturity Test. The mean I.Q. of the subjects used was 117.3 and the standard deviation was 11.1.

It seemed wise to maintain a reasonable homogeneity of interests and abilities in the subjects used in the various groups and sets. It was hoped that this similarity would facilitate communication among the members. Thus two limitations were placed upon the subject population: (1) only female subjects were used, and (2) the subjects used had a restricted I.Q. range. Females were used rather than males as the available literature seemed to indicate a tendency for girls to have both a superior empathic ability, and to demonstrate greater improvement of empathic skills with practice.

Interaction Within the Training Sets

Each experimental training set consisted of four members who met with the experimenter. The author served as experimenter for all the training sessions in all the sets.

At any given moment during training for all training sets regardless of their experimental condition, the subjects were engaged in the following activities or roles: (1) two subjects, designated as listeners, were engaged in listening to a communication, identifying what they in fact understood by the communication, and suggesting possible improvements in the communication; (2) one subject, or speaker, was actually engaged in tasks related to delivering the communication and getting feedback from the listeners as to the adequacy of the communication; and (3) one subject, also called a speaker, was preparing the next communication to be delivered by examining the next set of pictures to be used, determining which picture was to be identified, and planning what would have to be said in order for listeners to make the proper discrimination.

The material used as the basis of the communications consisted of 68 series of pictures which increased both in general level of complexity and in degree of similarity of the pictures within a series. On the lower right hand corner, each picture had a letter designation (A, B, C...N), and on the back of one of the pictures in each series (therefore not observable when the pictures were placed face up) an "X" designation had been made. This "X" indicated which of the pictures was to be differentiated out of the series of pictures. The information as to which of the pictures had the "X" on the back was available only to the speaker. Presumably, she was aware of which picture was to be specified, while the listeners were not.

The speaker about to perform the actual act of communicating returned from the adjoining room carrying a series of pictures which she had just examined. While in the adjoining room she had determined which picture in the series had the "X" designation on the back and prepared her communication with an eye to communicating just enough about the picture series so that someone listening to the communication could correctly identify the picture containing the "X" on the back from the rest of the series. When this speaker returned from the adjoining room, the second speaker got a different picture series from the experimenter and took them into the adjoining room to prepare the next successive communication. Thus it was, except in passing, only one of the two speakers was in the training room at a given time. The speaker about to deliver her communication proceeded into the training room with her series of pictures which she spread out face up on the table in the middle of the room. The two listeners were seated facing this table, and the speaker placed the pictures in front of the listeners in an upright position (the A, B, C,...N letters were placed so that they would appear in the lower right hand corner of each picture from the listeners' point of view). Then the speaker stepped back to a position just behind the two listeners. From this position behind the two listeners she was able to view the array of pictures spread out on the table, but the listeners, having their backs toward the speaker, were unable to observe the speaker's eye movements, body orientation, and other gestures which might have given additional nonverbal clues to the correct picture. Standing in this position the speaker delivered her communication so as to inform the two seated listeners as to which of the pictures in front of them contained the "X" mark on the back (without referring to the letter designations, of course). The communication was heard by the two listeners and recorded by the experimenter on a small stenographic tape recorder. The tape recorded communication was then played back. Thus, the listeners heard the communication twice which, hopefully, helped to insure that they took account of all aspects of the communication. Also, the speaker was placed in a position of having to listen to her own communication, and to this extent, all speakers took the role of the listener. Like the listeners she heard her own tape recorded voice delivering the communication while standing in a position immediately behind the listeners which was not very different from the position of the listeners. It is not known to what extent the speaker actually tried to take the role of the listener during this phase of the communication training. During the playback of the tape recorded communication the listeners started attempting to decide which picture the speaker had intended to identify. Each listener was permitted to come to her own independent conclusion when agreement between listeners was not possible. In attempting to come to some solution, the listeners often gestured and talked with one another both while the tape was being played and afterward. This demonstrated to the speaker what many of the statements meant to the listeners. The listeners were permitted and sometimes did actually request that part or all of a communication be played over again. This request was always complied with, although, as it turned out, no requests were made to have a communication repeated more than twice past the initial playback. Requests for replay occurred, for the most part, when the meaning intended by part or all of a communication was vague or completely uninforming. The listeners were not permitted to ask further questions of the speaker, and were asked to try to come to decisions as to which picture the speaker had intended to specify on the basis of the communication they had already heard. If the listener(s) felt that no firm conclusion was possible she (they) would say so and add what their best guess would be. On a number of occasions listeners felt that they had no basis for even a speculative conclusion and were unwilling to commit themselves to any choice. On these occasions the experimenter asked the listener(s) at least to indicate which pictures had been eliminated from the listener's consideration in attempting to come to a conclusion. All this gesturing, discussing, eliminating, etc. was observed and served as feedback to inform the speaker as to the adequacy of her own communication in terms of the meanings which it had conveyed to the listeners.

Following the listeners' decisions (or lack thereof) the listeners were informed as to which picture had been intended (i.e. had the "X" on the back). Then the listeners and the speaker entered into a discussion about the communication and the pictures. The experimenter sometimes entered into these discussions in order to insure that in the course of discussion the following three points were covered: (1) whether enough information was communicated to clearly enable the listeners to come to the correct conclusion, (2) whether the speaker gave redundant or nondiscriminating information which was of no value to the listeners in discriminating the correct picture, and (3) whether the listeners could suggest other, and perhaps better, ways of communicating the same information or the correct picture. Of course, at each point the speaker was allowed to defend her position by indicating why the listener(s) should have understood the communication; thus, on rare occasions, the listeners were placed on the defensive as it appeared that they had not adequately taken account of some point which was actually covered adequately in the speaker's communication.

Treatment Groups

Control Group. With respect to the pretests and posttests, the 16 subjects in the control group were treated in exactly the same manner as subjects in the three experimental groups. However, this group did not meet between the pretesting and posttesting situations, and was subjected to no experimental training at all. As this group attended a different school from the rest of the subjects used, these subjects were not aware that others were being treated in a somewhat different manner.

Integration Group. The 16 subjects composing the integration group were assigned to the four integration sets consisting of four members each. In the interaction which took place within these sets the various roles involved in the training procedure rotated from set member to set member. After a speaker had examined a series of pictures, prepared a communication, delivered the communication, and discussed this communication with the listeners, she then replaced one of the listeners sitting at the table for the next two series of pictures to be communicated. During this period she performed the functions associated with listening. She first listened to the communication, selected the pictures from the series on the basis of her understanding of the information communicated, and suggested improvements or alternative methods of communicating the information required. In turn, of course, the listener whose job had been usurped by the speaker, became a speaker. She got another series of pictures from the experimenter and proceeded into the adjacent room to prepare her communication. Thus a round robin rotation system was established which insured that each integration group member performed all the interaction tasks. For each integration group member approximately one quarter of the training time was spent delivering and getting feedback from her communication, one quarter of the time spent preparing the communication, and one half was spent listening to communications of others and giving feedback to the speaker. Members of the integration group actually had occasion to practice each others' roles during the course of the communication training. It would be for this reason that one might expect an integration group subject to learn more adequately what the role of the other person was like, and, therefore expect an integration group subject to improve more in her ability to communicate than other training group subjects who had not had training so well geared to seeing another person's role.

Listening Group. The 16 members of the listening group were assigned to the eight remaining training sets such that each of these sets had two members of the listening group. Unlike the four integration sets, members of these sets did not take turns or reverse their roles in the training situation. Thus these eight sets can be referred to as segregated sets because the roles involved were segregated: a given segregation set member was restricted to playing only one of the two roles in the training situation, either that of speaker, or listener. Listening group members spent their entire five hours of training time performing tasks related to listening. They listened to the speakers delivering communications, attempted to pick the correct picture out of the series from the information received in the speaker's communication, and then attempted to give feedback to the speaker about the adequacy of that communication. As these 16 subjects spent the same total amount of time in training as the integration subjects, they covered approximately twice as much material while fulfilling the role of the listener as integration subjects in that same role. This was simply because the integration subjects had to divide their time and, therefore, spent half their training time and covered half their training material while serving in the role of speaker. For this reason it might have been expected that these listening group subjects would improve more than other groups in their listening skill as a function of the training.

Speaking Group. Like the listening group, the speaking group also contributed two members to each of the eight segregation sets. In the training situation these speaking group subjects performed only roles related to preparing and delivering communications. A member of the speaking group having completed the tasks related to the actual delivering of a communication and receiving feedback from the listeners, in the set, got another series of pictures from the experimenter and went to the adjoining room to prepare her next communication delivery, while the other speaking group member returned from the adjoining room to make her delivery.

Pretests and Posttests

All experimental and control subjects were tested both in groups and individually prior to and following the training period (or in the case of the control group the three week time lapse). The same tests were used on both occasions although a few additional tests were added in the posttest.

The changes recorded from the pretests to the posttests served as the dependent variables. Pretest scores were not used in order to match or equate the various experimental and control groups, but were used as additional evidence that the groups were equal at first testing.

Group administered tests were administered between 10 and 13 days prior to the beginning of training, and one to three days after the end of training. The administration of individual tests preceded the beginning of training by three to 12 days, and followed the end of training by one to nine days.

The training period lasted two and one half weeks, during which time no testing took place. Roughly, the average lapse of time between the first and second administration of the group tests was 30 to 31 days, and between the first and second individual test was 29 to 30 days.

Group Administered Tests

The Educational Testing Service Sequential Test of Educational Progress: Listening, form 4a, part two, was administered both pretest and posttest as a measure of listening ability. Because of the length of the administration time required for the whole test only half (part two) of the test was used. It was anticipated that the listening group, having spent the entire training period at the listening task, would improve the most on this test in the pretest to posttest comparison.

The second group-administered test was constructed specifically for this experiment by the author. The test was divided into three parts. The first part presented the subject with a simple configuration of geometric figures. A space was provided below the picture and the subject was instructed to describe the picture in words so that someone reading her description would be able to draw the picture just as it appeared in the test booklet without having seen the picture simply from the description. This was an entirely descriptive task in which the more information the subject gave about the picture the more adequate was that response.

The second part of this test presented the subject with a series of four pictures one of which was identical to the picture in the first part. The other three pictures resembled this picture in some ways, but were different in certain specific respects. This time the subject was asked to write enough in the space provided below the four pictures so that someone reading what she had written and looking at the pictures would be able to pick one particular picture out of the group. The picture to be identified was the one which was identical to the picture described in the first part. This was essentially a discriminative task. Unlike the first part it was not necessarily true that the more information a subject gave about the picture the better the response (although this was true within limits), but the best possible response included a maximally parsimonious combination of facts or bits of information so as to eliminate the other three pictures and leave only the correct picture.

The third part of this test attempted to discover to what extent a subject was aware of differences between parts one and two. Here subjects were simply asked to tell what the differences between these two tasks were. This information could then be compared to the actual changes which the subjects manifested in the responses to parts one and two.

The particular usefulness of this test stems from the fact that the subject must deal with the same picture on two separate occasions which require the subject to adopt two different frames of reference with respect to the purpose to which the communications should be addressed. Like other tests, each of the communications were analyzed separately, but this was the only test which kept the picture constant and asked the subject to change the communication about it in order to conform to a different purpose.

Individual Tests

The first few moments of the testing session consisted primarily of meeting and putting the child at ease. The experimenter tried to engage the child in conversation and told the child about the tape recorder. The child was not allowed to hear herself over the tape recorder for fear that this would constitute possible training for the subject in listening to herself speak. Throughout the interview the child was aware that the tape recorder was recording her communications.

If the child was to communicate it was evident that she would have to communicate to someone. It might have been possible to have brought a second adult into the testing session for the purpose of giving the child someone toward whom the various communications might have been directed. It would have been difficult to have found such a person. It was felt that such a person would have had difficulty reacting in the same manner to all subjects, and also that different subjects might be better able to relate to such a person than other subjects. Another person was not, therefore, introduced into the test situation. To avoid allowing the child completely free rein to imagine any sort of listener she wished, and to give the imagined listener some of the characteristics of a real person, photographs were introduced of a person who was to be imagined as the listener in the test situation. The person was introduced as "Mr. Munson," and it was suggested that in the near future "Mr. Munson" would take the test materials and the tape recorder and attempt to arrive at a conclusion from listening to the communication. The not blindfolded picture was used for all tests except the Pig game. As the Pig game involves a blindfolded listener, the blindfolded picture of "Mr. Munson" was introduced in addition to the other not blindfolded picture in order to show the subject what the blindfolded listener would look like with the Pig game materials spread out in front of him.

The first task for the subject was to tell "Mr. Munson" how to put five pieces of a puzzle together so as to form a perfect square. The child was given a moment with the disassembled pieces to see whether she could solve the puzzle herself. No child succeeded unassisted in the pretest situation, although a number were able to recall enough of the solution in the posttest situation to succeed unassisted. Failing to solve the puzzle alone, the experimenter either helped the subject along to the proper solution or showed the subject a diagram of the proper solution. In any event, the subject assembled the puzzle in front of her. The experimenter then disassembled the puzzle again, and the subject was asked to tell "Mr. Munson" how to assemble it. Having just seen the correct solution she was in a position to perceive correctly and easily what the proper relationships of puzzle pieces should be. To perform the task adequately the subject had to extricate herself from her own familiarity with the puzzle and see what the effect of her communication would be from a completely naive point of view or position, a position in which she had been until but a moment before. The puzzle task was used first because it was felt that the few minutes involved in trying to solve the puzzle would ease the child's anxiety about the test situation and defer the trial of the first tape recorded communication.

The next test introduced used the materials labeled Test Picture Series A. The task involved in this test was highly similar to the ones used in the training sets, but the particular series of pictures were spread out in front of the child and it was suggested that although the pictures had many things in common, no two of them were identical. The child was asked to acknowledge that she saw that no two pictures were identical. If she could not, she was asked to look again and compare pictures she might initially have thought identical. This procedure was continued until the child recognized that all the pictures were different. Next the tester pointed to one of the pictures. The child's job then became one of imagining "Mr. Munson" sitting with the pictures spread out in front of him listening to her communication about the pictures and trying to select the correct picture from the series. The subject was told to indicate all the information "Mr. Munson" would need to know without indicating anything superfluous. Test Picture Series A involved the eight possible combinations of three dichotomous discriminanda. Adequate communication required that the subject specify all three variables in the picture. In this particular Test Picture Series there were few irrelevant constants which could be specified; however, a statement which indicated simply the presence of either the circle or rectangle could be considered such a constant.

Test Picture Series B was presented next. The procedure for doing so was exactly the same as the one described for Test Picture Series A. The only conceptual difference between the two series was that Series B contained a relatively large number of nondiscriminating constants (e.g. statements about the triangle, the half circle, the degree of tilt of the half circle, the horizontal line, etc.), and only a single critical or discriminating feature (the orientation of the rectangle). Thus, while the task involved in performing on Test Picture Series A was mainly one of finding and communicating the several discriminating feactures, here in Test Picture Series B the task was mainly one of seeing which aspects of the picture series were not discriminating when communicated.

Next, the last for the pretest, the Pig Game materials were introduced. This was a simple child's game the rules of which were taught to the subject by testers actually playing the game with the subject. The tester, by using only gestures, avoided giving the child descriptive labels for communicating the information about this game. Having played the game through once, the child was asked whether she understood how the game was played. To this question all children agreed. The task then became one of communicating information as to how to play the game over the tape recorder to the "naive" "Mr. Munson." In addition it was pointed out that "Mr. Munson" would be blindfolded when trying to learn how to play the game. Sometime in the near future he would put on his blindfold, listen to her communication, and try to figure out how to play the game. In this task the child not only had to recognize what the naive position of a listener would be like, but also had to perceive what the effect of the blindfold would be on "Mr. Munson's" receipt of the communication. To facilitate this, the picture of the blindfolded "Mr. Munson" was introduced. This was a highly complex test, for although the game was a simple one it involved a number of pieces and several rules and exceptions to rules, all of which required communicating.

The criterion measures were selected with several factors in mind. The first question which the criterion measures had to answer was this: did the training bring about improvement in subject's ability to communicate in situations similar to the training task itself?

> Hypothesis I. Subjects receiving such training should show greater improvement than control subjects in their ability to communicate in situations similar to the training situation.

The evidence seems to point quite convincingly toward the fact that the training experience did affect the behavior of subjects performing tasks similar to the training situation itself. With few exceptions the experimental groups showed consistent and significant changes which were not demonstrated by the Control Group. The form and direction of these changes were generally as follows: (1) there was a curtailing of the number of words in a communication, (2) there was a decrease in the number of different words used in a communication, (3) there was a diminishing of the amount of useless or misleading information in a communication, and (4) there was an increase in the overall quality of a communication as evaluated, in part subjectively, by independent judges. One would expect that increases in the amount of useful information in communications would have accompanied these other changes. This expectation is consistent with the results for the amount of useful information measure in Test Picture Series C (see Table 1) and for the logical analysis measure in the Group Administered Communication Test Part 2 (see Table 2). It should be remembered, however, that the former test was not as carefully controlled as most, and the latter's logical analysis measure included other considerations than simply a count of the statements containing information about discriminanda (this was because the test was particularly complex in that it required a communicator to adopt only one of several available communicative strategies). The remaining three tests lend no support to this expectation. Although an increase in the amount of useful information was demonstrated, and significant Fs obtained, the change was equally reflected by the Control Group.

A possible, but perhaps oversimplified, interpretation of the changes would suggest that trained subjects simply learned to eliminate or at least abbreviate useless or mis-

Table 1

Mean Scores and Significance of the Overall F Tests Performed on Measures Taken of the Individually Administered Test Picture Series C

Measure		Group			
	F	Integ	Listen	Speak	Control
Number of words.....	N.S.	36.1	38.4	39.7	59.9
Number of different words....	N.S.	22.3	23.4	24.2	28.2
Overall goodness[a] ...	.005	3.6	2.9	2.9	4.4
Useful information...	.025	1.1	1.19	0.9	0.6
Useless information..	.01	3.1	2.9	3.2	5.9

[a]The lower the overall goodness score the better the response.

leading information in their communications. At least the results obtained are consistent with the results one would expect if this were the case. Clearly one would expect the amount of useless information to decrease. This decrease would have the effect of shortening the total length of the communication and consequently decrease the number of words and number of different words. Also, because useless information is likely to confuse or mislead a listener, one would expect communications to be judged "better" without useless information. Finally, also consistent with the results obtained, one would not anticipate an increase in the amount of useful information.

One variable used in selecting the various test picture series was the degree of similarity or number of common features between the various pictures within the series. Pictures Series A contained three picture dimensions which had to be specified and little else. Picture Series B and D con-

Table 2

Mean Pretest to Posttest Changes and Significance of Changes on Measures Taken of the Group Administered Communication Test Part 2

Measure	Pretest to post-test F	GROUP: Integration Change	t	Listening Change	t	Speaking Change	t	Control Change	t
Number of words	.001	-12.3	.01	-14.4	.01	-10.4	.02	+0.9	N.S.
Number of different words	.001	-6.7	.01	-7.3	.01	-4.8	.02	-0.4	N.S.
Overall Goodness	.001	+2.6	.01	+2.4	.01	+2.0	.01	+0.1	N.S.
Logical analysis	.001	+1.2	.01	+1.0	.05	+1.1	.02	+0.3	N.S.
Useless information	.001	-1.5	N.S.	-3.1	.01	-1.5	N.S.	-0.2	N.S.

tained only one variable which needed specifying in each series, and both contained considerable amounts of nondiscriminating common features. Thus there was considerable variation in the amount of useless information for picture discrimination in these tests. If training taught communicators to eliminate useless information from communications, and if this was what the increase in "goodness" and decrease in length of communications was dependent upon, then one would expect no changes to have taken place where useless information did not exist and pronounced changes where useless information was abundant. The magnitude of changes, particularly of the number of words and number of different words, was considerably greater for picture series containing much useless information than for picture series with little. Nevertheless, sizable changes also took place on the measures relating to Picture Series A, and it appears that there was a tendency toward brevity beyond the simple elimination of useless information. This point cannot be taken as firmly established, however, as the amount of useless information in Picture Series A also decreased in spite of the nature of the series.

In terms of the theoretical implications for this research it is reasonable to ask whether the changes demonstrated toward eliminating useless information from communications and making them briefer can meaningfully be related to the ability to perceive the role of a second person in a communication situation. Although this ability is usually framed in a positive way involving the ability to see what the second person <u>does</u> need to know, there is no reason to restrict it to this and one should include the ability to see what a second person <u>does not</u> need to know. In terms of this research this ability to see what another person does not need to know would be the ability to see what information is useless to a listener and this would lead to the consequent elimination of such useless information from communications. This ability to see what is not necessary to communicate is as deeply involved in seeing the role of the other as the ability to see what is necessary to communicate.

If the ability to see and account for the role of the other person in communicative interaction can be thought to be involved, it is difficult to understand why or how this ability would become subdivided into these two aspects: (1) the information a listener would find necessary in order to understand a particular concept, and (2) the information a listener would find unnecessary if it were communicated.

Presumably the ability to see the role of the other would be a unitary one because a speaker who becomes aware of what another person needs to know can do so only by simultaneously seeing what that other person knows already. It is the boundary between the "he needs to know this" and the "he does not need to know that" which is being established, and each logically defines the limits of the other. Thus to know one is to know the other and the discovery that a person can take into account what a listener does not need to know without also being able to see and account for the information which a listener does need to know becomes logically absurd. This argument would clearly suggest that an alternate ability was involved and some other interpretation should be sought to explain the obtained results.

In the first place, the argument just given assumes that the individuals in communication behave in a particularly logical manner while in communication. Especially for children, this does not seem likely to be the case. Secondly, the argument does not account for the situation in which the individual learns the role of the other person. In everyday communicative interaction as well as in the training situation, the recognition that another person has a different perspective from one's own evolves out of communication failures and the recognition that the failures have occurred. The child assumes and in some situations, such as the training situation, may get some positive feedback indicating successful communication, but such feedback is only positive as long as the listener understands a communication in the way in which the speaker intended. It becomes essentially negative when the speaker observes the listener misunderstanding his intended message. The training situation attempted to overcome this problem during the discussion by insuring that listeners corrected speakers by indicating what the listeners thought the speaker should have said. In spite of that, the speaker's initial feedback was negative while the positive feedback may have seemed to be something of an afterthought. Clearly in everyday interaction when communication failure occurs, positive feedback almost never ensues, and speakers may be ill prepared to accept it when it does. In any event, the situation that motivates a person to alter his conception of another's point of view can only be communication failure, and in this situation of communication failure the individual may not learn what to say, but only what not to say. From this point of view it does not seem so surprising to find that what not to say would be learned at least prior to if not to the exclusion of what to say.

One final point concerning this hypothesis. The results discussed so far can be framed in such a way as to make them seem singularly unimpressive. It does not seem very momentous to suggest that subjects trained to perform a task, be it communicative or otherwise, would outperform untrained subjects in the performance of that task. However, the reader should be reminded that the task was one of communication which is a field in which everyone receives considerable practice every day. This fact should minimize any simple practice effect. Further, the training involved was of a more or less nondirective sort in which the subjects gave each other feedback about communications in much the fashion one would expect individuals to do in normal daily interaction. If communicative improvement resulted, as it apparently did, there is good reason for saying that the subjects taught each other and evolved a better system between themselves. This is quite a different sort of learning than might be found with five correct repetitions on a memory drum.

In summary, the results support Hypothesis I indicating that practice in the training situation did, in fact, lead to improved performance on tasks similar to the training task. The nature of this improvement seemed to be that subjects had learned to eliminate unnecessary noninforming information from their communications and had abbreviated communications in a fashion which, rather than adversely affecting the overall quality, actually improved the judged quality of the communications.

> Hypothesis II. Improvement in the ability to communicate should not be restricted to improvement in tasks identical to the training situation, but should generalize to other, less similar tasks of communication due to the subject's improved ability to perceive the role of the other person. Improvement in this ability should facilitate all communicative skills.

The results applicable to Hypothesis II were not as pronounced as had been hoped. In general it appears that some generalization did take place, but the changes were not nearly as clear cut as they were for Hypothesis I. There seems to have been a shortening of communications particularly as measured by the number of words, but also as measured by the number of different words measures. In the Pig Game this trend was also demonstrated by the Control

Group. It was not entirely clear from the test situations to just what extent this abbreviation was adaptive or indicative of a higher level of performance. As tasks become more descriptive and less discriminative the statement that the more said the better becomes increasingly true. However, at least as measured by the overall goodness measures, there was no tendency for the decrease in length to effect adversely the overall quality of the communications. Therefore, at least in abbreviating communications the trained subjects discriminated useful from useless words from the listeners' point of view and deleted only the latter. If it can be said of two equally informative statements that the shorter one is better, than the obtained shortening represented an improvement. The amount of useful information measure gave no indication of significant or consistent changes at all. On the amount of useless information or inadequate information there was a consistent but never significant trend for the experimental groups to decrease their scores. Useless information here had not the same significance as it had for training-task-specific types of tests. Rather than referring to the content of the communication, the useless information measure here referred more to formal problems which lead to actual communication failure. Nonetheless the experimental groups tended to decrease these failures more than the Control Group. Finally, experimental groups demonstrated improvement on the Listening Test which the Control Group did not show.

> Hypothesis III. Some subjects received training in only one or the other of the roles of speaker or listener, while other subjects had the experience of actually taking the position of the other person in the communicative situation. Hypothesis III suggests that subjects trained to adopt both roles would improve more than those trained in only one role of the communicative interaction because of the more varied role taking experience.

Hypothesis III concerned the relative merits of the three types of training employed in this research. The results give absolutely no suggestion in this direction. Although quite a few of the interaction *F* tests which examined the differences in changes of communicative behavior in the various groups were found to be significant, this significance could be almost entirely attributed to the difference between the Control and experimental groups rather than differences between the various experimental groups themselves.

A few of the differences between the individual experimental groups did prove significant. If these meager results could be considered a trend, the Speaking Group would have to be said to have demonstrated the greatest change from training, next the Listening Group, and finally, the Ingegration. The evidence was so flimsy as to make even this tentative statement too strong.

Young Children's Comprehension of Compressed Speech

C. David Wood

The purpose of this study was to determine the ability of elementary school children to comprehend compressed speech. The effects of four independent variables on comprehension were investigated. These were rate of presentation, grade level, intelligence classification, and amount of practice.

One measure of listening efficiency is the amount of verbal material that can be comprehended in a given time. As speech compression allows more material to be presented in a given time, the effects on comprehension of different words-per-minute rates of presentation has been an important consideration in previous research. The determination of such effects in young children was the primary objective of the present study.

Children's efficiency in reading, computation, and other learning skills usually increases as they progress through elementary school. It was not known whether this growth pattern also applied to their ability to comprehend compressed speech. Thus, an objective of the present study was to find and compare differences in comprehension, if any, by children at the first, third, and fifth grade levels.

In verbal learning situations it is a well-established finding that intelligence is a factor that affects the degree of success. Prior research has shown that the amount of comprehension of compressed speech by adults is positively related to level of intelligence. In the present study, this relationship was investigated in young children.

Although students may initially have difficulty in comprehending compressed speech, they may nevertheless have less difficulty after they have had some training. The design of the present study was such as to allow a determination of whether the subjects' comprehension improved during the course of an experimental session.

In addition to the main effects of the four variables described above, the two-, three-, and four-way interactions among them were examined. Only four of these interactions were considered of primary interest, and these correspond to the following questions: (a) Does the variation in comprehension as a function of rate of presentation differ from one grade level to another? (b) Does the variation in comprehension as a function of intelligence classification differ from one grade level to another? (c) Does the variation in comprehension as a function of rate of presentation differ from one intelligence classification to another? (d) Does the difference from one intelligence classification to another in the variation in comprehension as a function of rate of presentation differ from one grade level to another?

Method

Subjects for this experiment were public school pupils selected with respect to grade level and intelligence quotient. Tape-recorded, imperative sentences, time-compressed at rates from 175-400 words per minute were used as stimuli.

The experimental task was for the subject to listen to a stimulus sentence and then respond to it. If the subject performed as directed in the stimulus sentence, he was judged to have comprehended.

Subjects

Ninety subjects participated in the experiments. They were boys and girls from the first, third, and fifth grades. Prior to selection of subjects, the California Test of Mental Maturity, Form 57-S, was administered. This gave an intelligence quotient for each child.

Three pre-experimental groups of 16 children each were formed at each grade level. Selection of these 48 children at each grade level was such that the three groups were maximally separated in terms of group I.Q. means within each grade, but such that the mean I.Q. for a given group at each grade level was approximately equal to the mean I.Q. for corresponding groups at the other two grade levels.

Stimuli

At the time of the study, apparently no standardized listening test had been designed to be used at all of the grade levels involved in this experiment. Therefore, it was necessary to develop special material to measure listening comprehension. Tests dependent upon reading and/or writing ability to indicate listening comprehension were deemed inappropriate because of the wide range in these abilities to be expected among children in grades one, three, and five. Hence, a testing method reported by Schlanger[1] that did not require reading or writing skills was adapted for this study. This method involved presenting a subject with a number of sentences, each of which directed him to perform a specific task. If he performed the task he was judged to have comprehended the sentence.

Fifty-seven simple, imperative sentences requiring a variety of overt responses were developed. They were then recorded at approximately 175 words per minute. These sentences were tested on two five-year-old children, three seven-year-old children, and one ten-year-old child. Fifty-four of the original sentences were judged by the experimenter to elicit correct, readily discriminable responses.

The words-per-minute rates to be used in the study were selected with respect to those used in previous studies of compressed speech, and with respect to the compression capability of the equipment to be used. From a base rate of 175 wpm, rates were chosen in increments of twenty-five words per minute up to a maximum of 400 wpm--a total of ten different rates. The extent of compression is defined as the percentage of the original listening time that is eliminated, e. g., 0 per cent for 175 wpm, 30 per cent for 250 wpm, and 56 per cent for 400 wpm.

It was assumed that any difference in the inherent comprehensibility of the various imperative sentences would be of negligible consequence, and that random assignment of sentences to compression rates would negate any minor differences. Accordingly, the fifty sentences were randomly assigned to the ten rates of presentation with the restriction that five sentences be assigned to each rate. Upon completion of the recording of the fifty-four sentences at approximately 175 wpm, each one was time-compressed to its assigned rate.

Following time-compression, the sentences were cut from the recording tape and assembled in stimulus-response units composed of the following three parts: (a) pre-stimulus interval--a one-second tape segment of a pre-recorded 500 cps tone followed by a one-second segment of non-recorded, silent leader tape, (b) stimulus--a time-compressed sentence, and (c) response interval--a seven-second segment of non-recorded, silent leader tape. These parts were spliced together as a unit.

When all the stimulus-response units were completed, they were spliced together in the predetermined order for rates and practice blocks and a master tape copy was made of these assembled units. This master copy included the sentences to be used as a part of the instructions to subjects as well as the sentences to be used during the experiment proper.

Procedure

The experiment was conducted during the regular elementary school hours in an unoccupied classroom at the University Elementary School, Bloomington, Indiana.

The subject and the experimenter were facing each other about six feet apart. The experimenter had available a tape recorder, pre-recorded tape, two headphones, individual data recording forms and pencils.

Subjects took part in the experiment individually, with approximately fifteen minutes being required for each session.

After each subject was seated he was instructed in the task and during this time was presented examples of compressed speech by means of the tape recorder speaker, and through headphones.

At all times that the subject was using headphones, the experimenter monitored the tape recorder output through similar headphones.

During the experiment, the subject listened by means of headphones to a tape recording of fifty imperative sentences compressed at rates from 175-400 wpm.

The subject's task was to respond to each sentence he understood by performing as commanded in the sentence. The experimenter observed each response and recorded it on the data form as either correct or incorrect (a lack of response was considered to be an incorrect one). A correct response was considered an indication that comprehension of the stimulus had taken place.

Results and Discussion

Results were based upon responses made by subjects to the presentation of 4, 500 samples of compressed speech. An analysis of variance was applied to the results and is summarized in Table 1:

Table 1. Summary of Analysis of Variance

Source of variation	SS	df	MS	Required .05 value	F
Between subjects					
A (grade level)	8.08	2	4.04	3.11	28.86*
B (intelligence)	.82	2	.41	3.11	2.93
AB	1.21	4	.30	2.48	2.14
Subjects within groups [error (between)]	11.26	81			
Within subjects					
C (practice block)	6.53	4	1.63	2.40	27.16*
AC	.28	8	.04	1.97	.67
BC	.48	8	.06	1.97	1.00
ABC	.80	16	.05	1.68	.83
C x Ss within groups [error (within)]	18.43	324	.06		
D (rate)	33.07	9	3.67	1.90	73.40*
AD	7.33	18	.41	1.61	8.20*
BD	1.05	18	.06	1.61	1.20
ABD	1.85	36	.05	1.44	1.00
D x Ss within groups [error (within)]	39.12	729	.05		
CD	101.07	36	2.80	1.43	56.00*
ACD	9.53	72	.13	1.29	2.60*
BCD	3.07	72	.04	1.29	.80
ABCD	8.72	144	.06	1.21	1.20
CD x Ss within groups [error (within)]	148.29	2916	.05		

*Significant at .05 level of confidence.

Results

Rate of presentation effect. The total number of errors at each of the ten words-per-minute rates of presentation was: 175 wpm--3; 200 wpm--5; 225 wpm--16; 250 wpm--1; 275 wpm--69; 300 wpm--60; 325 wpm--36; 350 wpm--40; 375 wpm--111; and 400 wpm--104.

The difference between rates with respect to mean number of errors over all subjects was statistically significant. Thus, it may be stated that comprehension varied significantly as a function of rate of presentation.

Grade level effect. The total numbers of errors made by the first, third, and fifth grade children were, respectively, 237, 117, and 91. The differences between grade levels with respect to mean number of errors was statistically significant.

Intelligence classification effect. The total numbers of errors made by the average, superior, and very superior intelligence classifications were, respectively, 177, 135, and 133. The differences between these classifications with respect to mean number of errors was not statistically significant. Thus, there was no evidence that performance varied significantly among the three levels of intelligence.

Grade level by rate of presentation interaction effect. The interaction between grade level and rate of presentation was statistically significant. Thus, the differences between the mean number of errors as a function of rate of presentation varied significantly from one grade level to another.

Grade level by intelligence classification interaction effect. The F for the interaction between grade level and intelligence classification was not significant. Thus, differences between the mean number of errors as a function of grade level did not vary significantly from one intelligence classification to another. This also indicates, of course, that differences between the mean number of errors as a function of intelligence classification did not vary significantly from one grade level to another.

Intelligence classification by rate of presentation interaction effect. The F for the interaction between intelligence classification and rate of presentation was not significant. Thus, differences between the mean number of errors as a function of intelligence classifications did not vary significantly from one rate of presentation to another. This also indicates, of course, that differences between the mean number of errors as a function of rate of presentation did not vary significantly from one intelligence classification to another.

Grade level by intelligence classification by rate of presentation interaction effect. The F for the three-way interaction of grade level by intelligence classification by rate of presentation was not significant. Thus, differences between the grade level by intelligence classification interactions did not differ significantly from one rate of presentation to another. Also, of course, the differences between the grade level by rate of presentation interactions did not vary significantly from one intelligence classification to another. And, finally, the differences between the rate of presentation by intelligence classification interactions did not vary significantly from one grade level to another.

Summary of primary effects. Of the eight primary research effects studied, those significant at the .05 level were as follows: rate of presentation, grade level, practice, and the two-way interaction of grade level and rate of presentation. Those effects which were not significant were intelligence classification, the interaction of intelligence classification and rate of presentation, and the three-way interaction of grade level, intelligence classification, and rate of presentation.

Summary of significant effects. The results show the following six primary and secondary research effects to be significant at the .05 level of significance: (a) rate of presentation; (b) grade level; (c) practice; (d) grade level by rate of presentation interaction; (e) rate of presentation by practice interaction; and (f) grade level by rate of presentation by practice interaction.

Discussion

Previous studies of the comprehension of compressed speech have suggested that an inverse relationship exists between comprehension and the words-per-minute rate of presentation. These studies have involved adults and older children as subjects. The results of the present study would seem to indicate that a similar inverse relationship exists in the comprehension of compressed speech by elementary school children.

Any more detailed discussion of the results should be prefaced by some qualifying remarks. First, the difference in stimulus material and test procedures between the present study and previous ones make direct comparisons of questionable validity. The comparability of the imperative sentences to which subjects made immediate overt responses, with the narrative readings and objective tests used in previous studies is very doubtful. However, it was felt that a comparison of some of the previous and present findings might contribute to a better understanding of the present results. Thus, an attempt is made to relate the findings of this study to previous ones.

Secondly, it appears possible that one of the major assumptions of the study may be questioned; namely, that all of the imperative sentences would be equal in inherent comprehensibility at any one of the rates used. Despite the lack of any evidence in the pilot studies that this assumption was not justifiable, it seems that some sentences may have varied considerably in inherent comprehensibility because of phonetic or other differences.

Although it is evident that some sentences varied considerably in inherent comprehensibility, nevertheless, the sentences as a group were comprehended quite well. Of the 4,500 responses to the sentences, 90.1 per cent were made correctly.

The present study did not result in a very orderly inverse relationship between comprehension and words-per-minute rate, but the change in comprehension as a function of rate was statistically significant. The general direction of the results was toward a decrease in comprehension with an increase in rate.

A significant relationship was demonstrated in this study between grade level and the extent of comprehension. The fifth and third grade children with 93.9 per cent and 92.2 per cent comprehension, respectively, were more than ten percentage points above the first graders with 84.2 per cent comprehension. Apparently, the important point to note here is that the extent of first graders' errors rose much more steeply than the other two grades at rates above 250 wpm.

There was no evidence in the present study that comprehension of compressed speech was related to intelligence classification. In part, this lack of relationship may have been due to the subjects' being composed only of students with I.Q. ratings of average and above, i.e., more competent students. In the broad sense of listening ability, less competent students are supposed to be less capable listeners than those who are more intelligent. There was no opportunity in this study, however, to assess the comprehension of compressed speech by less competent students. Realizing that the restricted I.Q. range characteristic of the present study seriously limits comparability of results with other studies, it might be noted, however, that the results of this study would seem to be in conflict with Fairbanks and Kodmans'[2] conclusion that listener "aptitude" contributes to comprehension of compressed speech. On the other hand, the results would seem to support Fergen's[3] finding that intelligence was not a significant comprehension variable when children listened to verbal material that was spoken (not compressed) at a faster rate.

Notes

Abbreviated references refer to the entry number in Sam Duker's Listening Bibliography 2nd Ed. (Scarecrow, 1968) where the full citation may be found.

1. Schlanger, Bernard B., The Effects of Listening Training on the Auditory Thresholds of Mentally Retarded Children, Cooperative Research Project No. 973, U.S.O.E., West Virginia University, Morgantown, 1961.

2. Fairbanks and Kodman, 387.

3. Fergen, 395.

Chapter X

Research on Listening II

This chapter, like the previous one, contains two rather lengthy excerpts from research studies, together with a shorter report. There is no claim that the five research activities represented by the excerpts in these two chapters are the "best" or the "most significant" on the subject of listening. It can safely be said, however, that they are examples of superior studies insofar as design, integrity of procedure, and analysis are concerned.

The first study is by Ralph W. Kellogg, presently Assistant Superintendent of Schools in Palm Springs, California. It is an excellent example of the ways in which a study which intends to make use of classroom teachers is organized, and it is included here primarily for this reason.

This study was done at a time when Dr. Kellogg was Director of Curriculum for the San Diego County School System, which has long been in the forefront of curriculum research. Results from the research on reading carried on there have been of great value to students of this mode of communication. The light thrown on ways to teach listening to young children in the Kellogg study constituted a giant step forward in the knowledge available about teaching listening in the early school years. A study of the entire thesis, which may be obtained from University Microfilm, is highly recommended to any reader seriously concerned with this problem.

The second study by Dr. Belle Ruth Witkin of Alameda County, California is an excellent review and analysis of existing research as well as of needed research in the area of listening. True scholarship is required first to locate, then to read and digest the research studies cited, and then to organize one's analysis in the skillful manner exhibited here. If prospective writers of doctoral disserations about a phase of listening would use an article like this as a model for their background reading and research, much duplicative research and much that is concerned with trivialities would be eliminated.

Loren D. Crane, an Ohio State University Ph.D., Richard J. Dieker, who earned his doctorate at Michigan State, and Charles T. Brown, who has been identified in a previous introduction, are all at Western Michigan University where among many other activities they engage in research on listening. A matter that has not often been looked into has caught their attention: the question of physiological reactions to listening and to other communication modes. The study reported here is a relatively modest one but may well be the entering wedge to further investigation in this area.

Development of the Experimental Literature Listening Program

Ralph W. Kellogg

Guidelines for the development of the listening program were identified as was a pattern of instructional strategy for each listening lesson. Implicit within these guidelines were assumptions about each of the seven determiners of the curriculum indicated by MacKenzie[1] as related to this program. These determiners were: students, content or subject matter, materials, methodology, teachers, facilities, and time.

The listening program was formulated at the listening comprehension level for use with students in typical heterogeneous first-grade classrooms. Children's literature was utilized as the content vehicle of listening in order to cast the instructional program with the content of the English language arts curriculum area. The program was developed for inclusion with a minimum of disruption in existing language arts curriculums in which teachers might be employing different language arts methodologies. An easily transported set of paperback books for children's stories with specified lesson plans constituted the materials of instruction. Relative to methodology, the teacher's role was that of direct teaching to a total class group rather than as a co-ordinator of pupil self-instructional strategies. Direct instruction in listening skills as opposed to incidental or indirect instruction was the focus of classroom strategy. A progression of lessons from simple to complex was formulated with the assumption that rather explicit instructions to teachers would be necessary due to their limited professional training in listening instruction. Within each lesson a listen-think-respond strategy relating to the ideas of the story was utilized throughout. Games for motivation, skill development in the classroom, and reinforcement in the home were employed wherever possible. Considerable attention to student oral reconstruction about each particular skill and his development of it through the various games were included as a further means of reinforcement. It was assumed that teachers would be predominately female with a wide range of age and experience background, and that instructional facilities in which the program would be taught would be typical self-contained first-grade classrooms in San Diego County. A series of forty literature listening lessons was designed, each lesson approximately twenty minutes in length. This structured the time factor. This program designed with these guidelines and assumptions relating to the determiners of the curriculum became the experimental structured literature listening program.

A second experimental literature listening program against which to test the first was devised. It consisted of a minimum of instructions to teachers giving directions to read stories from the same children's read-aloud set of books for a series of forty lessons of approximately twenty minutes each. In this program teachers were told to use whatever procedures in reading the stories they normally used. This second program was designed to duplicate as nearly as possible classroom procedures normally used by teachers without an experimental program. Called the unstructured literature listening program, it provided a legitimate control group against which to measure the structured literature listening instructional program.

The following listening skills were incorporated in the forty lessons:

1. Maintaining attention through oral presentation
2. Vocabulary study
3. Discovering the main ideas
4. Making use of context clues
5. Recognizing illustrative examples
6. Discerning between fact and opinion
7. Recognizing that which is relevant and/or important
8. Making logical inferences from what is heard

Lesson plans were supplied for a series of lessons involving the same skill or skills, rather than a different lesson plan for each individual lesson. The pattern of lesson plans designed for particular skills was:

Lesson Number	Listening Skills to be Practiced
1.	Introduction of the Program - The Importance of Good Listening

Lesson Number	Listening Skills to be Practiced
2.	Maintaining Attention Through Oral Presentation
3-10.	a. Vocabulary Study b. Discovering Main Ideas
11-13.	Making Use of Context Clues
14-19.	a. Recognizing that which is Important and/or Relevant b. Vocabulary Study
20-24.	a. Recognizing that which is Important and Relevant b. Vocabulary Study
25-27.	Differentiating Between Fact and Opinion
28-30.	a. Making Use of Context Clues b. Vocabulary Study
31-35.	a. Recognizing Illustrative Examples b. Vocabulary Study
36-40.	Making Logical Inferences

In each lesson plan the stories which were to be used to teach the skills were identified. Where necessary, portions of particular sentences or paragraphs in each story which were important to the skill development were identified in the lesson plan for the teacher.

A brief description of the skill and what was involved in teaching it was presented as background for the teacher. Teachers were asked to read each of the stories, which they were to use in a lesson, in advance of teaching the lesson. They also were encouraged to think about the particular listening skill and how they would proceed to teach it based upon the ideas in the lesson plan.

Literature Listening Program

Initial Instructions to Experimental Teachers

Thank you for your commitment to participate in the

Literature Listening Program experiment. You have been randomly assigned to follow Experimental Approach S. Remember that you should indicate nothing about this approach to any other teacher until after the experiment is completed at the end of the year. By not mentioning anything about it to any other teacher, you will avoid questions and, thereby, will be keeping the approach as intended in the experiment. At the end of the experiment you will be asked to verify that you have not discussed the experimental program with other teachers.

Experimental Approach S consists of following the lesson plans which will be sent to you by mail. These lessons have been designed to help you teach a specific listening skill while reading to the children literature stories from the enclosed Read-Aloud Literature Listening paperback books. The major purpose of the program is to help children improve their listening skills. You will be asked to administer a listening achievement test at the end of the experiment. An additional purpose of the program is to help children in their reading achievement. Therefore, reading achievement tests will also be administered. Over three-fourths of the studies reported thus far show that a specific listening skills program also improves students' reading achievement. There is only one other listening skills program at the first grade reported in the professional literature and this did not use children's literature for content. Therefore, you are the first teachers to be involved in such a program. Many of the listening skills in this program are similar to reading skills. The lesson plans sent to you will focus on the teaching of listening skills, not of reading skills. You are encouraged to show the children the relationships between these listening skills and those in reading whenever possible, however. For example, the listening skill of "Making Use of Context Clues" is very much like the similar skill in reading.

Overview of the Literature Listening Skills Program

An overview of some of the design factors included in the listening skills program may help in your understanding of it, thereby assisting you in your teaching of the program. The skills which will be emphasized first are these:

Listening Skills

1. Maintaining attention through oral presentation.
2. Vocabulary study

3. Discovering the main ideas
4. Making use of context clues
5. Recognizing illustrative examples
6. Discerning between fact and opinion
7. Recognizing that which is relevant and/or important
8. Making logical inferences from what is heard

Each lesson plan will include the following kinds of instruction for your consideration.

Lesson Plan Format

a. Lesson number
b. Listening skills to be practiced
c. Story or stories to be used
d. Teacher preparation
e. Student readiness activity
f. Teaching procedures
g. Student reconstruction
h. Student follow-up activity

Each lesson will have a specific design, however, certain recurring teaching procedures will continue throughout the experiment.

Recurring Teaching Procedures

(1) Concentrated attention is important in all listening regardless of skill or level, therefore, setting the proper attentive mood at the beginning of each lesson will be emphasized. (2) Good listening cannot be separated from good thinking. In fact, you have undoubtedly already recognized that if this program is successful it will improve students' thinking processes. Therefore, a Listen-Think-Respond sequence of instruction will be incorporated throughout. (3) Finally, any skill becomes useful to the learner when he habitually applies it himself outside the classroom without the teacher's direction. Therefore, a student follow-up activity in which students are encouraged to practice specific listening skills in their homes will be built into every lesson. Feedback of such practice in the home back to the class in the form of sharing will help reinforce this independent application of the skills.

Directions for Teaching the Literature Listening Program

1. Look through the Read-Aloud Literature books sent

to you.

2. Read each lesson plan before each Literature Listening Lesson to familiarize yourself with the lesson and in order to make any preparations which are indicated. (All lessons will be sent by mail.)

3. Teach each lesson utilizing approximately 20 minutes per lesson during the time when you normally hold your reading and language arts instruction. Follow the enclosed schedule of lesson times. (Morning hours are preferred.)

4. Use your regular methodology in the language arts whether it be the traditional method or language experience approach. Integrate the Literature Listening Program into that methodology.

5. Fill out your evaluation of each lesson. You will be given specific instructions on when to mail these in so that we might have the data to improve the lessons at a later time.

A Point of View

As teachers of Experimental Approach S you should be informed of the basic philosophy or point of view from which it has been developed.

Instructional materials provided for teachers and students reflect certain assumptions about the subject and about learning. A brief statement of the point of view embodied in the development of this Literature Listening Program may help you utilize the program more effectively.

1. Language is the tool or vehicle through which much if not most of our thinking takes place and is communicated.

2. Language is the symbolized form of experience which all persons have had within their environment.

3. For the normal child, the development of comprehension in speaking, writing, and reading rests upon prior comprehension of language through listening.

4. The development of listening skills is important in itself because of the tremendous amount of time we spend gaining information through the listening process. Listening

skills are also important for their positive effect upon reading, speaking, and writing.

5. Since comprehension in listening is related to thinking, the teaching of thinking processes is inevitably involved in the teaching of listening skills.

6. The elementary teacher has a responsibility for the development of a tremendous amount of information and skill in an already crowded curriculum. Listening skills taught through the use of children's literature will save instructional time by avoiding having to teach them separately from other parts of the curriculum.

7. The child comes to school an active listening and speaking individual. There is great individuality in his language development. Individuality is to be encouraged; however, many listening skills can be taught collectively in group situations with individuality development provided through applications of these skills during other parts of the school day and at home.

8. The teacher will not be able to teach listening skills if she does not know what the listening skills are. In similar fashion the child will not efficiently learn to use good listening skills if he does not know what they are and understand how to apply them. A child may develop some of the listening skills incidentally without either the teacher or student knowing what they are or focusing directly upon them. Incidental learning is not to be depreciated. However, it does not provide the foundation for teaching and efficient learning. Therefore, direct teaching of listening skills should be done by the teacher.

9. Listening as one of the input communication processes has significance only as it stimulates thinking which can be communicated in the output process of speaking or writing. Therefore, a Listen-Think-Respond sequence on the part of children should be encouraged by a Literature Listening Program.

10. It is hoped that these Literature Listening lessons will:

a. Provide easily followed lessons for the teacher involving a minimum amount of teacher preparation.

b. Be easily integrated into the teacher's current

methodology in the language arts.

c. Be interesting and stimulating to the children and teacher.

11. It is hoped that these Literature Listening lessons will accomplish the following objectives:

a. Significant measured improvement in selected listening skills.

b. Significant measured improvement in reading achievement.

Literature Listening Program: Sample Lessons

Lesson Number 11 to 13

Skills to be Practiced

Making Use of Context Clues

Stories to be Used

Stories to be used are listed on the last page of the lesson plan.

Teacher Preparation

Read through this lesson plan. Read each of the stories which will be used, marking the vocabulary words which are to be learned through context and clue words. These are listed for your convenience on the last page of this lesson plan. Think about this skill and how it is related to the similar skill in reading. Making use of context clues simply involves listening for clue words which will help the listener guess or learn the meaning of a word which he does not already know. This skill may be thought of as a form of vocabulary study by the children themselves without using a dictionary or learning all of the meanings of an unknown word. As you think about teaching this skill to children, remember that you are probably only helping them become a bit more systematic with what they already do. Probably most of the new words a child or adult learns in his listening vocabulary are learned through context within a sentence or paragraph in which they are first heard.

Student Readiness Activities

The set of the class in getting ready for the literature listening lesson should be fairly well established by now. Getting ready, sitting quietly, concentrating on listening with their eyes, ears, and minds should be encouraged at each lesson, however. The sharing time in which individual children bring back to the class things which they have done at home in practicing listening for the main idea should have encouraged many of them to begin practicing their listening skills at home. Your encouragement as the teacher for them to practice at other times during the day in the classroom when they listen and at home will help greatly in reinforcing their behavior. Again, remember that if a child can tell in his own words what the listening skill is that he is or has been using and how he can use it, the chances for his understanding and practice of that skill will be much greater. The sharing time should provide time for and reinforce this.

Teaching Procedures

1. Always start with the readiness activity including sharing.

2. Talk with the children about the fact that they have been hearing some new words in the stories which they have been reading these past two weeks.

Now rather than having you, the teacher, always tell them what a new words means, they can learn to play a game which will help them learn the meaning of some of the new words they hear all by themselves.

The name of the game is Detective Listening Game. At this point you might have a discussion about what a detective does. You can lead them to the understanding that a detective is very alert. He concentrates, he listens with his eyes, ears, and mind, and he searches for clues to help him find answers.

In this detective listening game each child is to listen for clue words which will help him learn the meaning of a new word which they might not know.

3. Give them an example of the game. Use "The Ugly Duckling," Read-Aloud Nursery Tales, p. 36. Use the first paragraph. Read the paragraph to them. The word, man-

sion, is the new word. The clue words are house and moat, specifically house. If moat is a new word for most of them, see if they can find the clue word for it: water.

The children will probably not respond to this at first reading, so read it again having them listen carefully for the clue words to help them understand the meaning of mansion and/or moat.

4. After clarification as to how to play the game, proceed on with this same story. On page 27 is a new word, monstrous. The clue word is big. In the next paragraph is the word gloriously. The clue word is fine. Later the word plumped appears. The clue words are sprang, in and water.

5. At this point you should probably discuss with the children that not all new words can be learned in the game of detective by just listening for clues. Sometimes there are no easy clue words to help. Show an example at the bottom of page 38 with the word, splendor. There are no good clue words here. Winter and sun and setting tell that splendor has something to do with a setting winter sun but does not tell what splendor is.

When this happens, the detective should do what good detectives do--that is, ask questions. They should listen carefully for clue words. If there are none, then they should ask questions of the teacher, parent, or whoever is speaking to them.

6. Normally you, as the teacher, should be helping them with new words in the stories for which there are no clue words. In the development of listening vocabulary it is important only that they have an explanation of the unknown word. At this point in the listening lessons it is not important that they be able to spell or read the new word. You are trying only to help the children get the new word in their listening comprehension vocabulary. The appropriate spelling and reading vocabulary of children is already in their present listening vocabulary. You are attempting to extend their listening vocabulary as a basis for spelling and reading at a later stage.

7. Continue to play the game of detective with other stories listed in this lesson plan for three 20-minute lessons which are scheduled. Encourage students to stop you and

ask questions about the meaning of new words which have no clue words. This should be done in the lesson and at any other time during the school day. If they will consciously begin to do this, it will help you, as the teacher, know when they are not understanding. This questioning on the part of the students will also help reinforce their development of comprehension in their listening vocabulary.

(Students who ask about the meaning of words they hear you use, their parents use, or other persons use have to be listening and thinking in order to recognize the words they don't understand. Therefore, this kind of questioning should be encouraged to stimulate listening and thinking.)

Sometimes children may ask you rather than listen for clue words. If there are clue words, you should always encourage them to think about these before they ask for the meaning of a word.

Student Reconstruction

Have the students tell in their own words how they have learned to play the Detective Listening Game.

Student Follow-up Activity

The follow-up activities for Lessons 11 and 13 are to have the children tell their parents about the game and to practice it at home, reporting back to the class at sharing time how they have played the game with someone else outside of the classroom. The degree to which children can be encouraged to play this game within the class throughout the school day and at home will affect their independence in listening vocabulary study.

Stories to be Used

	New Words	Clue Words
Read-Aloud Nursery Tales		
The Blind Men and the Elephant, p. 80	approached, p. 81	came close
The Three Wishes, p. 83	uttered, p. 84	said aloud
	mansion palace, p. 84	fine house

Stories to be Used	New Words	Clue Words
Animal Stories to Read-Aloud		
A Gossiping Fly, p. 24	nibbling, p. 24	teeth
	queer, p. 24	three-cornered head
	position, p. 25	head down - feet up
Favorite Poems to Read-Aloud		
Good Night and Good Morning, p. 10	rooks, p. 10	flew, flight, bird
There Was a Little Girl, p.23	horrid, p. 23	bad
	squalled, p. 23	screamed, yelled bawled
Waiting for Something to Turn Up, p. 50	shirk, p. 20	didn't work
	nonsense, p. 53	head
When Mother Reads Aloud, p. 63	fray, p. 63	armies
	lances, p. 63	spear
	prowling bands, p. 63	jungle
The Shoemaker, p. 65	feeble, p. 65	old, bent
	awl, p. 65	makes hole
Hans Christian Andersen's Fairy Tales		
The Emperor's New Clothes, p. 53	Costume, p. 53	clothes
	tailors, p. 54	weave, fabrics
	peculiar quality, p. 54	becoming invisible
	distinguish, p. 54	discover
	courtiers, p. 58	selected faithful men
	chamberlains p. 62	carry train

Conclusions

The purpose of the study was reasonably well fulfilled. Each of the four assumptions underlying the development and field testing of the listening skills program at the beginning of the study have been corroborated in some fashion through evidence collected: (1) A listening skills program suitable for the first grade level language arts curriculum was constructed and evaluated. (2) Achievement in listening of boys was significantly improved in five of a total of six tabulations made. Achievement in listening was significantly improved for girls in three of a total of six tabulations made. (3) Achievement for boys in reading was significantly improved in seven of a total of ten tabulations made. Reading achievement was significantly improved for girls in one of a total of ten tabulations made. In all cases the listening program produced either positive effect or none at all. In no case did the program negatively affect the achievement of children. (4) Procedures for classroom field testing of the listening skills program were devised which yielded reasonably reliable information regarding the effect of the listening skills program.

The literature listening program, as developed by the author, was judged to be a readily usable program in its present form; one which would positively affect listening, achievement of boys and girls and reading achievement of boys in typical first grade classrooms.

On the basis of the evidence gathered in the study, the investigator concludes that the literature listening skills program in its present form would significantly affect achievement in listening of first-grade class groups taught by most language arts methodologies used in the public schools. This prediction relates only to gross achievement gains of total classes, not to the achievement of individual children. The greatest possible achievement gains from use of the program undoubtedly would result from its selective use with boys being taught by the traditional method in reading and language arts. This is the predominant methodology currently in use across the nation.

The third and final conclusion of the study is that a great potential exists to stimulate and refine the thinking processes of young children through a well-designed listening program. Listening comprehension through the effective use of listening skills is inextricably linked with thinking. The refinement of thinking processes through the development of listening comprehension is, without question, the dominant reason for teaching listening skills. That the listening program had some measurable effect upon achievement in listening and reading is evidence that refinement of

Auditory Perception - Implications for Language Development

Belle Ruth Witkin

The purpose of this paper is to present an overview of some of the most significant research in auditory perception, to describe new measures which have been developed, and to indicate some implications for language development.

Definition

Perception should be distinguished from sensation and cognition. Gould defines perception as "sensory experience which has gained meaning or significance. When, as the result of learning experiences, one understands the relationships of objects which were previously merely raw, undifferentiated sensory experiences, he is said to perceive these objects" [10:491]. And again, "...almost without exception the word is used to indicate those relations of man and his environment which lie midway between the sensations of classical psychophysics and the cognitive processes which are usually subsumed under the heading of concepts. Perception occupies an intermediate position between simple and complex behavior" [10:492].

English and English define perception as "An event in the person or organism, primarily controlled by the excitation of sensory receptors, yet also influenced by other factors of a kind that can be shown to have originated in the life history of the organism .... It is an organized complex, though its separate components can sometimes be separately recognized" [5:378].

Allport states, "A phenomenological experience of an object, that is to say, the way some object or situation appears to the subject as dependent upon his own organism, as observer-involved, non-denotive, and 'private', is called a percept" (1:23).

Regarding sensory reception in listening, the primary concern is with the hearing acuity of the individual and his ability to receive the sensation of sound without distortion. In cognition, the concern is with the ability to comprehend and retain spoken language and to perform such tasks as recognizing main ideas, analyzing, recalling details, and associating ideas.

Auditory perception involves focus, attention, tracking, sorting, scanning, comparing, retrieving, and sequencing of spoken messages at the moment of utterance. The parameters to be dealt with in this paper are: (1) focus on and attention to the message, (2) tracking of the message through time, (3) discrimination of speech sounds and syllables, (4) auditory memory span, and (5) auditory sequencing.

1. Attention -- Competing Messages

Attention plays a crucial role in learning, and in recent years both psychologists and speech scientists have investigated some of its characteristics. No listening can take place without there first being focus on and attention to the speech signal. Exactly what the mechanism of attention and of the neurophysiology involved are is not known.

Research relevant to attention has been largely concerned with the ability of the individual to pay attention to and comprehend two messages presented simultaneously; and alternatively, to listen to two competing messages but pay attention to only one.

Interest in this problem arose in recent years because of the necessity for efficiency of control systems, such as those for regulating air traffic at airports. Broadbent points out, "A major cause of failure in these systems is that the human operator has too much information to handle simultaneously, or that he reacts to an unimportant signal when he should be dealing with an important one." The capacity for transmitting information is defined as "the number of equally probably messages of which one can be sent in a specified time." In education, competing messages are often an integral part of the learning situation, with the involved spoken message being subject to distraction from noise, music, and other speech. Broadbent notes:

> One of the earliest findings, and one that agrees with everyday experience, is that it is harder to understand two messages arriving simultaneously than two messages arriving one after the other. One might be tempted to explain this as a purely physical interference between the two stimuli; for example, the louder passages of one message might drown out the softer passages of the other and vice versa, rendering them both unintelligible. Actually the matter is not so simple. By recording the messages on tape and playing them for different subjects instructed to respond in different ways, the intelligibility is shown to depend on psychological factors. Specifically, either message becomes understandable if the listener is instructed to ignore the other. But the two messages together cannot both be understood, even though the necessary information is available to the ear [3:143].

A number of experiments have demonstrated conditions which make comprehension easier. Some of these conditions are: (1) having the two voices very different in physical characteristics, as in a man's and a woman's voice; (2) spatial separation of the two voices; (3) if one message has no importance for the listener and does not have to be answered; and (4) if each message is drawn from a small range of possibilities. "When the listener is thoroughly familiar with a situation, so that he knows to within a small number of alternatives what each message will be, he can comprehend two simultaneous messages. But when one or both messages are drawn from a large number of possibilities, the filter in the brain lets only one message come through" [Broadbent, 3:146].

Cherry [4] performed a number of experiments on the recognition of speech with one and two ears. In one group of tests, two different spoken messages were presented to the subject simultaneously, using both ears. The subjects were presented with two mixed speeches recorded on tape and asked to repeat one of them word by word or phrase by phrase. Subjects reported great difficulty in accomplishing the task but were able to separate the messages with almost no errors. When the same experiment was performed using messages constructed from 150 clichés strung together, however, the task of separating the two messages became almost impossible.

In the second group of tests, one spoken message was fed to the right ear of the subjects and a different message to the left ear. The subjects were able to repeat without error one of the messages concurrently while listening. It was found, however, that they often had little idea of what the message was all about and were often unable to tell whether the "rejected" message was in English or in some other language. They were aware of changes of voice from male to female but could not recall detailed aspects of the "rejected" message.

Maccoby and Konrad [13] conducted a series of studies of selective listening, considered as one aspect of skill in focusing attention. In 1966, they reported a study comparing age levels--kindergarten through fourth grade--with respect to the effects of three variables on the accuracy of selective listening: practice, binaural versus dichotic presentation of stimulus words, and number of syllables in stimulus words. Their interest was in whether there are age trends in the ability to select one auditory message when two are simultaneously present [12].

The subjects listened to 23 pairs of words spoken simultaneously by two speakers, with monosyllables and multisyllables alternated in the list. All subjects listened twice; in one run, they were instructed to repeat the words spoken by the male voice and in the other, the words spoken by the female voice. In the binaural condition, the voices of both speakers came to both ears. In the dichotic condition, the voices were separated, the male voice coming to one ear and the female voice to the other. Within each pair of words, the words were matched for number of syllables, and the two voices were equated for loudness on the basis of judgments by adult judges.

The study showed that skill in selective listening, under the conditions of the experiment, does increase with age from kindergarten through fourth grade. Performance on monosyllabic words tended to level off between grades two and four, while performance on multisyllabic words continued to increase through grade four. The authors suggest that "older children's superior performance in selective listening arises at least in part from their greater familiarity with the redundancies in the material to be selected" [12:121].

Their later studies confirmed the fact that selective listening improves with age, from kindergarten through grade six, when the task is to give an accurate report of one of two simultaneous verbal messages. The performance of the sixth-graders was between 40 and 50 percent better than that of the kindergartners, the magnitude of the improvement being determined partly by the difficulty of the stimulus materials.

In this set of studies, the messages consisted either of single words varying in familiarity or of two-word phrases varying in sequential probability. The authors found, "The improvement with age is greater for high sequentially probable phrases than it is for low-probability phrases. We interpret this to mean that one factor underlying the improvement in selective listening between ages 5 and 11 is an increasing familiarity with the probabilities of the language, permitting older children to fill in partially heard material more easily on the basis of their knowledge of what words would be likely to occur in a given linguistic setting" [Maccoby & Konrad, 13:26].

Hedrick conducted a developmental study of the ability of children from pre-school through third grade to respond to competing messages varied in intensity and content. The mean chronological ages ranged from approximately five years to nine years. Male and female voices provided contrast for the signal (the wanted message) and the distraction (unwanted message). Messages were varied systematically in two ways - in intensity and in content. Three signal/distraction relationships were used: + 5, 0, and -5. Responses were made by pointing to pictures on a card. The content of the unwanted messages also varied in three ways: (1) both the signal word and the distraction word were found on the response card; (2) the distraction word was not on the response card, and (3) the distraction was a nonsense syllable.

Hedrick drew the following conclusions:

1. The accuracy of children's performance increases with age.

2. The relative intensity of the unwanted message was the variable most affecting the accuracy of the younger children's listening abilities.

3. The content of the distraction message was the variable most affecting the accuracy of the third grade children's listening abilities.

4. There were no significant differences in selective listening abilities between boys and girls [22].

Hedrick's findings compare with those of Maccoby and Konrad regarding the increase in ability to select from competing messages, from kindergarten through grade three. Some important differences in procedure should be noted. Whereas Maccoby and Konrad presented both the wanted and unwanted messages at the same intensity level, Hedrick systematically varied the intensity relationships. Maccoby had found that in order to make the task difficult enough, it was necessary to "blur" the messages. Hedrick achieved the necessary range of difficulty with intensity and content variation.

Implications. There are many implications for both regular and special education in the research on competing messages. For example, hard-of-hearing children have difficulty in the classroom not only with the sound level of the information that is presented but also with any distracting noises, either speech or non-speech, that are present at the same time. Furthermore, there is some evidence that children with an apparent minimal type of brain damage have difficulty with a competing message task. Further research is needed to determine whether a tape-recorded competing message test might be developed for use by the classroom teacher or the language specialist as a diagnostic tool for auditory perceptual problems with children who have reading problems or with those who are easily distractible and have difficulty attending to what is being said in class.

On the basis of their research, Manning and Hedrick developed a tape-recorded auditory perceptual training program for normal classroom use. The use of competing messages for training to improve attention is new, and the lessons need considerable refinement before they can be confidently used in the classroom. Nevertheless, the program shows some of the possibilities for the application of basic research to instruction. There are three questions that need to be answered: (1) Can attention and vigilant behavior be improved with practice, or are there built-in constraints in the perceptual process in normal individuals? (2) If there are constraints, can they be compensated for in any way? (3) If attention through listening to competing messages can be improved with practice, will the improved perception lead to improved listening comprehension?

2. Tracking--Compressed Speech

Another area of increasing interest is that of rate-controlled speech, also known as compressed speech. The research question is: How fast can individuals track and process information presented orally? Is there a built-in limitation to the amount of information per unit of time that can be comprehended and retrieved?

Until recently, it was impossible to vary the rate of recorded speech without also profoundly altering the pitch and thus the intelligibility of the speech. For example, if speech that has been tape-recorded at a slow speed is played back at a higher speed, the result is a very rapid, high-pitched, unintelligible "Donald Duck" effect. Conversely, if the message has been recorded at a faster rate and is played back at a slower rate, the result is a low-pitched, slow growl.

Spoken discourse usually ranges from 125 to 175 words per minute (wpm). Speech compressors can retard the speech to half its rate or can accelerate it to about three times its rate.

There have been two major thrusts in the research on the educational implications of rapid listening. Foulke [7] has been a leader in investigating the possibilities of faster information retrieval for blind students. Orr, Friedman and Williams [17] published a landmark study on the trainability of listening comprehension of speeded discourse for adults with normal vision. They found that practice resulted in considerable improvement in the ability to comprehend speeded speech, and that up to a certain amount of compression, the group given practice showed improvement in both speed and comprehension.

Foulke and Sticht [9] showed that a moderate compression (250-275 wpm) seemed to be practical for blind students, although mean intelligibility scores as high as 84 percent were found for speech compressed at 425 wpm. They also found a high correlation between reading rate and ability to comprehend compressed speech.

Zemlin, Daniloff and Shriner found that normal listeners prefer speech at about 30 percent time compression. Blind students, however, prefer 35 to 40 percent time compression. They state, "If the generalization is made that both the normal-sighted and the blind have an initially similar conception of the difficulty of speech, then it is clear that the blind tolerate speech at conditions rated three to four times higher in difficulty relative to normal in exchange for increased rate of flow of information" [21:879].

Flowers investigated what he called the central auditory abilities of normal and lower group readers of early elementary school age. He used four perceptual tests: low-pass filtered speech, accelerated (compressed) speech, accelerated and filtered speech combined, and competing messages. The competing messages were word lists and a children's story, presented at 0 db signal/distraction ratio; the accelerated speech was processed at 280 wpm. He found significant differences between the two reading groups on filtered speech, accelerated speech, and competing messages.

Implications. Some implications of the research areas of tracking and compressed speech are suggested, for example, by Flowers who concludes that the measures "may have prognostic and limited diagnostic value with respect to reading achievement and/or disability" [6:20]. The measures could be used to provide early identification of children who may encounter difficulties in learning phonics in the reading readiness program and would be useful for group type predictions.

To sum up: (1) Both children and adults find some degree of accelerated speech both intelligible and comprehensible, with the compression at about 275-300 wpm apparently the right range. After initially brief negative reactions in some cases, subjects do not dislike listening to compressed speech.

(2) Subjects can learn to comprehend material presented at faster speeds through simple practice listening routines. Maintaining a high level of motivation through the practice sessions is a key factor. No particular training method apparently is better than any other, although spaced practice is more efficient than massed practice [Orr and Friedman, 16].

(3) Retention of the material presented under accelerated conditions is not adversely affected as compared to normal rates.

(4) There is substantial variability among people in their ability to comprehend compressed speech. Language factors and related abilities to discern and match language interrelationships are important, as are listening arrangements and stimulus parameters.

Aside from the possibilities for rapid retrieval of information presented orally, there is the question of whether training in listening to compressed speech might be used to inculcate habits of attention and tracking which could be transferred to listening in real time. This question has not yet been subjected to experimentation.

3. Auditory Discrimination

The most thoroughly investigated aspect of auditory perception has been that of auditory discrimination, the capacity to distinguish between phonemes. The Phonetic Inventory, a test of speech sound discrimination, is the most basic diagnostic tool of the speech therapist, and much remedial speech work centers on discrimination of various kinds. There is a corresponding need for training in discrimination in the pre-school and primary years.

Kronvall and Diehl [11] define auditory discrimination as "a judgment calling for a distinction or comparison among sounds." The judgment most commonly used in tests reported in the speech literature has been the discrimination of allophones of two different phonemes, using stimuli consisting of "minimal pairs" of words or nonsense syllables. For example, the subject is asked to tell whether the syllables /ot/ and /od/ are the same or are different. This discrimination of phonemic differences is essentially an acquired skill in recognizing the sound structure of one's native language.

Adequate auditory discrimination is essential for the acquisition of language and for learning to read. Wepman summarizes what speech clinicians have learned over the years about auditory discrimination.

> 1. There is evidence that the more nearly alike two phonemes are in phonetic structure, the more likely they are to be misinterpreted.
>
> 2. Individuals differ in their ability to discriminate among sounds.

3. The ability to discriminate frequently matures as late as the end of the child's eighth year. A few individuals never develop the capacity to any great degree.

4. There is a strong positive relation between slow development of auditory discrimination and inaccurate pronunciation.

5. There is a positive relation between poor discrimination and poor reading.

6. While poor discrimination may be at the root of both speech and reading difficulties, it often affects only one of the two.

7. There is little if any relation between the development of auditory discrimination and intelligence as measured by most intelligence tests [19:326].

Children should be studied as they reach school age to determine whether their auditory abilities have reached the level of maturation where they can benefit from phonic instruction in reading or from auditory training in speech. Unless this is done, we will continue to make the error of approaching all children as though they can learn equally well through the same modality. Children who are poor in discrimination will be given the same instruction as others with good discrimination, etc. The need to individualize instruction, at least to the point of grouping visual learners and auditory learners separately at the onset of reading instruction, seems an obvious way to minimize the problem [19: 332].

Implications. Knowledge of the importance of auditory discrimination in language development and in learning a second language or a variant dialect of a first language is particularly crucial for teachers of the disadvantaged and the culturally different. For racial and ethnic minorities who speak a non-standard dialect of English or for whom English is a second language, the acquisition of speech sounds for any given dialect is learned very early and is usually well established by the time a child starts school. Omissions, additions, substitutions, or distortions of the speech sounds of the standard dialect may be due either to problems of auditory discrimination per se or to the phonology and morphology of the child's native dialect. Teachers are often confused as to whether deviant speech patterns are due to faulty articulation, non-standard usage or the basic linguistic structure of the speaker. There is a need for a multi-disciplinary approach to research in language development and reading improvement, to utilize the knowledge from speech science, linguistics, and psychology.

4. Auditory Memory Span

In order for an individual to judge whether two or more speech sounds are alike or different or to make more difficult judgments, the sounds must be kept in memory and retrieved for comparison. No simultaneous comparisons are possible, as in visual discrimination. Thus, auditory discrimination is partially dependent upon auditory memory span, which Anderson defines as "the number of discrete elements grasped in a given amount of attention and organized into a unity for purposes of immediate reproduction or immediate use" [2:95].

Little experimentation has been done with memory for individual speech sounds, as contrasted with memory for digits. Anderson devised two tests, one using eight vowels and diphthongs, the other using six voiceless consonants.

A more sophisticated type of phonetic memory task is the auditory synthesis test developed by Mange. He tape-recorded a number of individual continuant sounds and spliced them together to form several series of three sounds, which contained the sounds and sequence required to produce a familiar word. He states, "It was assumed that the ability to perform well on this test required an auditory-cortical function of a higher level than that required for auditory-peripheral reception" [14:69-70].

Witkin [20] devised a battery of 10 tests to analyze the dimensions of phonetic ability in young adults. The study grew out of the recognition that there was a wide range of ability among college students in mastering the techniques of phonetic transcription, which depends largely on auditory perception. There is considerable variability in the capacities of both children and adults to imitate speech sounds, to learn new ones (as in a foreign language), to change dialectal habits, and in general to demonstrate skill in the reception, storing, or transmission of speech sounds or in what one might call "speech-sound mindedness."

Witkin postulated the existence of some specialized aptitude, perhaps analogous to musical or artistic talent, which might be designated "phonetic ability." This was defined as skill in dealing with tasks of sound discrimination, imitation, analysis and synthesis, divorcing speech sounds from orthography, and in learning new sounds.

Witkin's auditory synthesis test consisted of 24 series of sounds uttered by the speaker "in isolation" in the order in which they would occur in a word, such as /b-e-k-t/ for "baked." Subjects were to recall the sounds and write the correct word. Sounds in each series were tape-recorded and separated by one-second intervals, with pitch and intensity kept constant. The test was similar to that of Mange [14], except that the words increased in length from 3 to 8 phonemes, and there were usually fewer sounds than letters. The task was thus difficult enough for adults.

Other tests in the battery which pertained to auditory memory and synthesis were the "reversed sounds" test and "phonetic anagrams." In the former, the subject heard a word spoken, such as "some," and was asked to write a new word made up of the same sounds in the stimulus word but in the exact reverse order--in this case, "muss." No words were used of such a nature that a new word could be made by simply reversing the letters, as in "mat-tam." Thus, the subject had to be able to analyze the stimulus word mentally into its component sounds, remember the order, and reverse the sounds to form another word. The task thus involved auditory memory, sorting, comparing, auditory synthesis, and the ability to deal with sounds independently of orthography.

In the phonetic anagrams task, the experimenter recorded a series of "isolated" vowels and consonants, ranging from three to five, which could be rearranged to form the sounds of a familiar word, such as one might do with letters in the game of anagrams. The task was to write any word that could be formed from the sounds, using all the sounds uttered. For example, if the series was /s-t-i/, the words might be "seat," "eats," or "east." Again, the subject had to be able to remember and manipulate sounds mentally without regard for orthography.

Another test which utilized auditory memory span was one for the recognition of the number of syllables in spoken discourse. Subjects listened to a series of sentences, some of them spoken with slurred and careless articulation, and were asked to determine the number of syllables actually uttered, without regard for the number in the written text.

The ten perceptual tests were correlated with measures of intelligence, verbal facility, age, sex, speech experience, academic achievement, and success in learning phonetic transcription. The 29 variables were subjected to a principal axes factor analysis, and nine factors were extracted.

The most striking result of the analysis was the finding that the perceptual tests apparently defined at least three separate factors of phonetic ability--a general factor containing most of the tests, a segmentation factor, and a pitch or intonation factor. The general phonetic factor appeared to require auditory discrimination, auditory memory, vocal control, flexibility in adapting to new speech-sound tasks, and ability to deal with speech sounds independently of orthography. The reversed sounds and phonetic anagrams tests were good predictors of success in learning phonetic transcription. The auditory perception measures were independent of the measures of intelligence, age, sex, articulation ability, and school achievement.

Implications. The significant correlation of spelling ability with several of the perceptual tests and the high loading of this variable on the general phonetic factor suggest that there may be some mode of perception common to spelling and speech-sound-mindedness. This is particularly interesting in view of the fact that the perceptual tests required the subjects to analyze, remember, and synthesize speech sounds which had little relation to the conventional spelling of the words. Most of the words used had more letters than sounds, with "silent" letters, blends, and diphthongs making the task more difficult. Since none of the subjects knew the International Phonetic Alphabet, this added further to the difficulty of remembering and manipulating sounds silently, with no visual memory aids.

Witkin's study showed that there is considerable intercorrelation among auditory perceptual abilities, such as discrimination, synthesis, and memory span. Because speech production is rapid, the auditory perceptual tasks of attention, focussing, tracing, discrimination, sorting, scanning, and sequencing need to be accomplished in such a brief time span that for all practical purposes they occur instantaneously. It should, therefore, be kept in mind that tasks used in studies which attempt to isolate one or another aspect of auditory perception may really be testing two or more abilities.

5. Auditory Sequencing

Closely related to auditory memory span is auditory sequencing, the recall of sounds in proper temporal sequence. Sequential behavior is necessary for the acquisition of language skills. Words and sentences are made up of series of sounds presented in a temporal order, and this order is a major dimension of language. Although the importance of auditory sequencing has been recognized, it has received little attention experimentally, especially with children who hear normally.

The Illinois Test of Psycholinguistic Abilities is in wide use for the purpose of identifying psycholinguistic abilities and disabilities in children between the ages of two and one-half and nine [McCarthy & Kirk, 15]. The nine tests used in the battery were generated from a communication model which includes channels of communication, levels of organization, and processes. The test most dependent upon auditory memory is the auditory-vocal sequencing test, which resembles the standard digit repetition test except for differences in rate of utterance, intonation, and repetition of the same digit. This increases the discrimination of the test over others in use. Considerable research has been done with this test, particularly in reference to the reading and language abilities of neurologically impaired and retarded children. Although there is some indication that impairments in auditory sequential memory are related to reading disabilities, the research is not conclusive on this point.

Smith [18] studied the short-term storage capabilities of children with non-organic articulation problems. He used recall of single digit sets, of sequential-digit sets, and of digits under a competing message condition. The children with non-organic articulation problems recalled significantly fewer digits, both in immediate and delayed recall, for all three types of digit-sets than did the children with normal speech. However, these children were not inferior on a strictly visual task.

Summary

Investigation of the parameters of auditory perception,

with the exception of speech-sound discrimination, is still in its early stages. There is no generally accepted model of auditory perception; and the exact components, their temporal order of occurrence, and their inter-relationships are not completely known.

In the acquisition of language, in listening comprehension and speech, and in the development of reading abilities, the individual must focus on and attend to complex auditory stimuli, distinguish figure from ground, track through time, sort, compare, discriminate, remember phonemic elements, and recall temporal sequences. Although it is difficult to determine the boundaries of the perceptual and cognitive processes, there is no doubt that the tasks of listening comprehension, such as recall of main ideas and making critical judgments, cannot be adequately accomplished if there is impairment or dysfunction in any of the perceptual parameters.

Recent research in selective listening, using competing messages, has added to knowledge of the attention factor. Studies of auditory discrimination have shown the relationship of faulty discrimination to speech and reading problems. It has also been found that deficits in memory span and in auditory sequencing affect discrimination.

The application of new technology such as compressed speech to educational problems holds considerable promise for the development of new teaching procedures. Most of the educational use of compressed speech has been with the blind, as a means for quicker retrieval of information, and the research has focused primarily on the intelligibility, comprehension, and retention of rate-controlled speech. There are implications, however, for using this technology to investigate the time-gap between thought and speech, with the possibility of devising training programs which will increase the listener's ability to follow spoken discourse without mind-wandering. The question of whether such gains made under compressed speech conditions will transfer to listening in real time still needs to be studied.

In the applied realm, there are important questions to be answered for educators. Because some children learn better auditorially than visually, auditory educational methods are assuming a larger role in the educational process. Further, the use of audio-visuals is growing, as is the use of new technologies such as tele-lectures, dial-access tape lectures, computer assisted instruction, and other types of auditory presentation.

The field presents difficult methodological and conceptual problems. Collaboration of effort among speech scientists and pathologists, psychologists, linguists, specialists in language development, and curriculum planners would yield valuable information for education.

Notes

Abbreviated references refer to the entry number in Sam Duker's Listening Bibliography 2nd Ed. (Scarecrow, 1968) where the full citation may be found.

1. Allport, Floyd R. Theories of Perception and the Concept of Structure. New York: Wiley, 1955.

2. Anderson, Virgil A. "Auditory Memory Span as Tested by Speech Sounds." American Journal of Psychology, 52:95-99, 1939.

3. Broadbent, Donald E., 114.

4. Cherry, E. Colin. "Some Experiments on the Recognition of Speech, with One and Two Ears." Journal of the Acoustical Society of America, 25:975-79, 1953.

5. English, Horace B. and Ava Champney English. A Comprehensive Dictionary of Psychological and Psychoanalytical Terms. New York: Longmans, Green, 1958.

6. Flowers, Arthur. Central Auditory Abilities of Normal and Lower Group Readers. U. S. Office of Education Cooperative Research Project S-076. State University of New York, Albany, 1964.

7. Foulke, Emerson, 417.

8. Foulke, Emerson, 417.

9. Foulke, Emerson and Thomas G. Sticht, 423.

10. Gould, Julius and William L. Kolb (Eds.) A Dictionary of the Social Sciences. Glencoe, Ill.: Free Press, 1964.

11. Kronvall, Ernest L. and Charles F. Diehl. "The Relationship of Auditory Discrimination to Articulatory Defects of Children with No Known Organic Impairment." Journal of Speech and Hearing Disorders, 19:335-38, 1954.

12. Maccoby, Eleanor E. and Karl W. Konrad. "Age Trends in Selective Listening." Journal of Experimental Child Psychology, 3:113-22, 1966.

13. Maccoby, Eleanor E. and Karl W. Konrad. The Effect of Preparatory Set on Selective Listening: Developmental Trends. Monographs of the Society for Research in Child Development. Serial No. 112, 1967, Vol. 32, No. 4., 29 p.

14. Mange, Charles V. "Relationships Between Selected Auditory Perceptual Factors and Articulation Ability." Journal of Speech and Hearing Research, 3:67-74, 1960.

15. McCarthy, James J. and Samuel A. Kirk. The Construction, Standardization and Statistical Characteristics of the Illinois Test of Psycholinguistic Abilities. Urbana: Institute for Research on Exceptional Children, University of Illinois, 1963.

16. Orr, David B. and H. L. Friedman. "Effect of Massed Practice on the Comprehension of Time-Compressed Speech. Journal of Educational Psychology, 59:6-11, 1968.

17. Orr, David B., Herbert L. Friedman, and C. Williams. "Trainability of Listening Comprehension of Speeded Discourse." Journal of Educational Psychology, 56: 148-56, 1965.

18. Smith, Curtis R. "Articulation Problems and Ability to Store and Process Stimuli. Journal of Speech and Hearing Research, 10:348-53, 1967.

19. Wepman, Joseph M. "Auditory Discrimination, Speech, and Reading." Elementary School Journal, 60:325-33, 1960.

20. Witkin, Belle Ruth. An Analysis of Some Dimensions of Phonetic Ability. Doctoral dissertation. Seattle: University of Washington, 1962.

21. Zemlin, Willard R., Raymond G. Daniloff and Thomas H. Shriner. "The Difficulty of Listening to Time-Compressed Speech." Journal of Speech and Hearing Research, 11:869-74, 1968.

22. Hedrick, Dona Lea. A Developmental Investigation of Children's Abilities to Respond to Competing Messages Varied in Intensity and Content. Doctoral dissertation. Seattle, University of Washington, 1967.

Physiological Responses to Communication

Loren D. Crane, Richard J. Dieker, and
Charles T. Brown

In the 1960's one of the most significant discoveries in the field of education since the work of Pavlov occurred. A direct relationship was established between memory and physiological arousal. Briefly summarized the relationship is: (1) Low arousal (as measured by Galvanic Skin Response) results in good short-term memory and poor long-term memory; (2) High arousal results in good long-term memory and poor short-term memory; (3) This relationship holds whether the arousal occurs slightly before or slightly after the presentation of information [7] and whether the information is meaningful [2] or meaningless [3]. Some studies have presented discrete items of information to subjects[2]; others have presented continuous flow of data by means of movie projection [7]. Some studies have been made under the condition of natural arousal [3, 4]; others have experimentally induced arousal [2]. In all instances the results support the above conclusions.

The purpose of this experiment was to explore the psycholinguistic variables inherent in various channels of communication, and to discover the parameters of each channel in producing emotional response in subjects. The particular communication media chosen for this study were: reading, listening, writing, speaking, and evaluating (speaking judgmentally). An analysis of the problem led us to believe that a test of "emotional impact" of media would have to include not only a measure of the degree of arousal but also a measure of its positive or negative valence. One of the best available measures of overall arousal of the organism to stimuli is the Dermohmeter which measures galvanic skin response (GSR). One of the best tools for measuring pleasant vs. aversive responses of subjects at the physiological level is the cardiotachometer, which records heart rate. Research has demonstrated that pleasant stimuli produce heart deceleration and unpleasant stimuli produce heart acceleration [1]. Lacey, in addition, has posited that deceleration of the heart rate indicates "openness" to the environment and acceleration reflects a closing off of distracting stimuli in order to facilitate internal coding or "thinking [5]." Therefore, the relative power of media of communication to produce "openness" or "closedness" may be examined by a study of heart rate. The study reported here asked two questions of each channel of communication under investigation: 1) Is there channel differential in stimulating emotions? 2) Is there a channel bias for the arousal of pleasant or unpleasant responses?

Procedures

The subjects, volunteers for the study, consisted of a range of students from freshman through graduate ranks, and extended across most of the curricula of the university. The data are based on 30 males and 33 females. Stimuli consisted of a list of 21 words selected by a panel of 11 graduate students in communication. Seven words which were classified as pleasant by this panel of judges were 1) beauty; 2) love; 3) Heaven; 4) kiss; 5) friend; 6) happy; and 7) success. The seven words classified as aversive were 1) cancer; 2) hate; 3) liar; 4) evil; 5) coward; 6) pain; and 7) death. Seven words classified as personal were for each subject 1) his first name; 2) his last name; 3) his father's first name; 4) his mother's first name; 5) his major in school; 6) his year in school; and 7) Western Michigan University. The personal category was included for comparison purposes because in earlier experimentation personal references produced strong GSR responses.

The students were assigned sequentially to one of five orders of presentation of the stimuli. These orders varied such that each treatment appears in each of the five serial positions to eliminate any order effect. The orders were as follows:

I.	Evaluating	Reading	Writing	Speaking	Listening
II.	Listening	Speaking	Reading	Writing	Evaluating
III.	Writing	Listening	Evaluating	Reading	Speaking
IV.	Reading	Evaluating	Speaking	Listening	Writing
V.	Speaking	Writing	Listening	Evaluating	Reading

Further, the 21 words were printed on slide transparencies permitting a random drawing of each word for each of the five treatments.

When a subject arrived at the temperature controlled, acoustically treated experimental room he was seated comfortably in a large leather chair with his head against an attached headrest. His palms were cleaned of body oils with rubbing alcohol and the electrodes from the Dermohmeter were attached to the palm of each hand. The photoelectric pickup of the cardiotachometer was placed on an ear or a little finger, whichever gave the stronger signal. The subject was handed a clipboard and asked to read the following directions:

> During this session you will see or hear a list of words. None of the words will be objectionable. You will feel no discomfort. If you have any questions ask the experimenter in the experimental room with you. Try to relax and concentrate on the words. Any movement will effect the measurements we are taking, so while the words are being presented, please try not to move. Place your feet flat on the floor, lean back and get comfortable. The session will last approximately 20 minutes.

The subject was asked if he had any questions. Questions about the experiment were answered in a friendly way and an offer was made to show the subject his recordings on the graph after the experimental session. Questions about the study were given only general answers. During this period of easy conversation designed to allay anxiety, the graduate assistant in an adjoining room was recording with a tape recorder the 21 stimulus words he had previously randomized. He timed himself with a sweep second hand to maintain the proper time interval and pronounced the words so that there were no significant differences in inflection, volume, or stress as judged by the principal investigator. This time lapse for the purpose of making the recording was approximately 10 minutes and allowed the subject's hands to hydrate where the electrodes were in contact with the skin. It also permitted the subject to relax and adapt to the physical surroundings. The subject could hear some clicks from the automatic range finder of the Dermohmeter as the instrument located the subject's base line. The reason for these noises was explained to him. He became used to the feel of the electrodes and ear clip. This time also allowed the experimenter to find the best sensitivity setting necessary to obtain a stable heart rate reading on the cardiotachometer. The sensitivity setting for the GSR was set at X10 for all individuals.

When the assistant returned, the lights in the room were dimmed and the experiment began. The assistant, having randomized the slides, placed them in the projector, and read the appropriate instructions preceding each of the five treatments. For the listening treatment, the instructions were, "You will hear words played on a tape recorder. Listen to the words." For the reading mode, the subject heard, "You will see words projected on the wall. Read these words silently." For writing, the subject was told, "You will see words projected on the wall. Write the words you see and try not to move your head by looking up and down." (This instruction was to prevent head movements affecting the ear clip.) The subject was given a pencil and a clipboard with a piece of paper attached for the writing treatment. In the speaking treatment, the subject was told, "You will see words projected on the wall. Say these words out loud as you see them." For the evaluating treatment a pasteboard showing a diagram of a seven point bipolar scale labeled "good" at one extreme and "bad" at the opposite was hung on the wall so that the projected words would appear directly below the scale. The subject received the directions, "You will see words projected on the wall. Say the word out loud and say the number also that indicates your evaluation of the word."

The procedure provided for a one-second exposure-to-stimulus time, and one-second reaction time leaving eight seconds for responses to be recorded on the graph before the next stimulus word was presented.

Results

The data were punched on cards and a two factor repeated measurement design with repeated measures on both factors was programmed and run by Computer Center. The first factor consisted of the three stimuli conditions, and the second factor was the five treatment conditions. This was run once for males and one for females. The Newman-Keuls test was then used to compare the means of the treatments and stimuli conditions.

GSR Measurements: The five treatment conditions under investigation fell into an increasing order of arousal as follows: Reading, Listening, Writing, Speaking, Evaluating. Both Speaking and Evaluating were significantly different from *Reading*, *Listening*, and *Writing* at the .01 level. *Speaking* and *Evaluating* were also significantly different from each other at the .01 level. The above was true for both males and females, as shown in Table 1. The data for males and females were then combined.

Table 1

Male and Female GSR Mean Changes For Reading, Listening, Writing, Speaking and Evaluating

Males	.5	.9	1.2	2.3	3.1
(F=22.31)	Reading	Listening	Writing*	Speaking**	Evaluating**
Females	.12	.74	.95	2.80	4.29
(F=36.88)	Reading	Listening	Writing*	Speaking**	Evaluating**
Combined	.31	.83	1.05	2.54	3.72
Males-Females	Reading	Listening	Writing*	Speaking**	Evaluating**

Newman-Keuls Procedure
*p = .01
**p = .05

With the increased sample, a difference at the .05 level was found between the arousal of *Reading* and *Listening*, and between the arousal of *Reading* and *Writing*. No significant difference was found between *Listening* and *Writing*. These findings are shown in Table 1.

Turning to the stimulus words which were grouped into *Pleasant*, *Aversive*, and *Personal* categories, significant differences were again found. *Personal* words produced greater arousal than the other two groups at the .01 level of significance. The Newman-Keuls procedure was applied for these findings and the data is shown in Table 2.

Table 2

Analysis of Variance of Male and Female
GSR Mean Changes for Stimulus Words

Male	1.32	1.43	2.03
(F = 16.54)	Aversive	Pleasant	Personal*
Female	1.45	1.45	2.45
(F = 18.11)	Pleasant	Aversive	Personal*

Newman-Keuls Procedure
*p = .01

Heart Rate Measurements: In comparing the five treatments for heart rate, no significant differences were found by the analysis of variance. In addition, no significant differences were found among the three groups of stimulus words. However, when individual words rather than categories were studied, specific differences appeared for each sex. The Cochran Q statistic was used to reveal significant patterns. The data on males showed significane at the .01 level for the word "success" and significant at the .05 level for the name of the students' major, W.M.U., and death. For females the subjects' first name, and the words evil and pain were found to be significant at the .05 level. No consistent pattern among the treatments was found.

Further, the oral evaluations of words given by the subjects were correlated with the heart rate increases and very low relationships were found. For males, the range was from -.417 to .416. The female data had a range from -.270 to .231.

Conclusions

The first question under investigation, that of differences between channels in stimulating emotional response, was very clearly answered in the affirmative. The data show:

The significant differences established at .01 level are seen to be approaching a geometric progression. The Speaking mode produces wave forms which are approximately twice the magnitude of the wave forms for Reading, Listening, and Writing. And the wave pattern for Evaluating is approximately twice the magnitude of the pattern for the Speaking mode.

The study also confirms prior findings that personal words evoke more response than non-personal words, pleasant or unpleasant. The study does not suggest any difference in degree of arousal, however, between pleasant and unpleasant words.

In trying to answer the second experimental question, concerning channel bias for pleasant or aversive words the study suggests there is no difference.

Implications for further Research

At this point we do not know, for instance, whether the mode of reading tends to filter out aversive connotations more than the channel of listening does, or any of the other three channels used in this study. There is a suggestion of sex differences and individual word differences in various channels, but these are near chance expectancies and need further investigation. Therefore, the concept of channel bias in positive or negative directions was not established nor disproved by this research and remains a "live" question.

The implication of the primary finding of this study is that words said in judgment will be remembered longer than words said without evaluation, and words said will be remembered longer than words written, heard or read. The data suggest that words read will fade in memory faster than words experienced in any of the other four modes.

Notes

1. Darrow, C. W. 'Differences in the Physiological Reactions to Sensory and Ideational Stimuli." Psychological Bulletin 26: 185-201, 1929.

2. Kleinsmith, Lewis J. and Kaplan, Stephen. "Paired-Associate Learning as a Function of Arousal and Interpolated Activity." Journal of Experimental Psychology 65: 190-93, 1963.

3. Kleinsmith, Lewis J. and Kaplan, Stephen. "The Interaction of Arousal and Recall Interval in Nonsense Syllable Paired-Associate Learning." Journal of Experimental Psychology 67: 124-26, 1964.

4. Kleinsmith, Lewis J., Stephen Kaplan and Robert O. Tarte. "The Relationship of Arousal to Short-and Long-Term Verbal Recall." Canadian Journal of Psychology 17: 393-97, 1963.

5. Lacey, John I. "Somatic Response Patterning and Stress: Some Revisions of Activation Theory." Psychological Stress. Mortimer H. Appley and Richard Trumbull (eds.) New York: Appleton, 1967, p. 34-35.

6. Lacey, John I. "The Evaluation of Autonomic Responses: Toward a General Solution." Annals of the New York Academy of Sciences 67: 123-64, 1956.

7. Levonian, Edward. "Retention of Information in Relation to Arousal During Continuously-Presented Material." American Educational Research Journal 4:2, 1967.

Index of Names

Subject Index